THE U.S. ARMY IN TRANSITION II

Also by Lt. Gen. Frederic J. Brown

Chemical Warfare: A Study in Restraints (1968)
The United States Army in Transition, coauthor (1973)

An AUSA Book

The U.S. Army in Transition II

Landpower in the Information Age

Lt. Gen. Frederic J. Brown, Ph.D.
USA (Ret.)

BRASSEY'S (US), Inc.

A Division of Maxwell Macmillan, Inc.
Washington • New York • London

U.S.A. (Editorial)	Brassey's (US), Inc. 8000 Westpark Drive, 1st Floor, McLean, Virginia 22102, U.S.A.
(Orders)	Attn: Brassey's Order Dept., Macmillan Publishing Co., 100 Front Street, Box 500, Riverside, New Jersey 08075
U.K. (Editorial)	Brassey's (UK) Ltd. 165 Great Dover Street, London SE1 4YA, England
(Orders)	Brassey's (UK) Ltd. Orders, Purnell Distribution Ctr. Paulton, Bristol BS18 5LQQ, United Kingdom
ASIA/PACIFIC	Maxwell Macmillan Publishing, Singapore Pte., Ltd., 72 Hillview Ave., 03-00 Tacam House, Singapore 2366, Singapore
AUSTRALIA/ NEW ZEALAND	Maxwell Macmillan Pergamon Publishing, Australia Pty., Ltd., Lakes Business Park, Bldg. A1, 2 Lord St., Botany, New S. Wales, 2019 Australia
JAPAN	Maxwell Macmillan Japan, Misuzu S. Bldg. 2F, 2-42-14 Matsubara, Setagaya-ku, Tokyo 156, Japan
CANADA	Maxwell Macmillan Canada, Inc., 1200 Eglington Ave. E., Ste. 200, Don Mills, Ontario M3C 3N1, Canada
LATIN AMERICA/ EXPORT	Maxwell Macmillan International Publishing Group, 28100 U.S. Hwy 19 North, Ste. 200, Clearwater, FL 34621
EUROPE	Maxwell Macmillan International Publishing Group, Ferievagen 15, S-161 51 Bromma, Sweden
UNITED KINGDOM/ EUROPE/MIDDLE EAST/AFRICA	Maxwell Macmillan International Publishing Group, c/o Nuffield Press, Hollow Way, Cowley Oxford OX4 2PH, United Kingdom

---

Copyright © 1993 Brassey's (US), Inc.

Brassey's (US), Inc., books are available at special discounts for bulk purchases for sales promotions, premiums, fund-raising, or educational use through the Special Sales Director, Macmillan Publishing Company, 866 Third Avenue, New York, NY 10022.

Library of Congress Cataloging-in-Publication Data
Brown, Frederic Joseph.
    The U.S. Army in transition II : landpower in the information age
/ Frederic J. Brown.
        p.   cm. — (An AUSA book)
    Includes bibliographical references (p.   ) and index.
    ISBN 0-02-881034-1 (cloth)
        1. United States. Army—Organization.   2. United States. Army—
Recruiting, enlistment, etc.   3. United States. Army—Data
processing.   I. Title.   II. Title: United States Army in transition
II.   III. Title: US Army in transition II.   IV. Series: AUSA
Institute of Land Warfare book.
    UA25.B76   1993
    355.3'0973—dc20   92-12999
                                                              CIP

Printed in the United States of America
10 9 8 7 6 5 4 3 2 1

To Kathryn, Hatsy and Judy
For the security of your generation

THE ASSOCIATION OF THE UNITED STATES ARMY, OR AUSA, was founded in 1950 as a not-for-profit organization dedicated to education concerning the role of the U.S. Army, to providing material for military professional development, and to the promotion of proper recognition and appreciation of the profession of arms. Its constituencies include those who serve in the Army today, including Army National Guard, Army Reserve, and Army civilians, and the retirees and veterans who have served in the past, and all their families. A large number of public-minded citizens and business leaders are also an important constituency. The Association seeks to educate the public, elected and appointed officials, and leaders of defense industry on crucial issues involving the adequacy of our national defense, particularly those issues affecting land warfare.

In 1988 AUSA established within its existing organization a new entity known as the Institute of Land Warfare. Its purpose is to extend the educational work of AUSA by sponsoring scholarly publications, to include books, monographs, and essays on key defense issues, as well as workshops and symposia. Among the volumes chosen for designation as "An AUSA Institute of Land Warfare Book" are both new texts and reprints of titles of enduring value that are no longer in print. Topics include history, policy issues, strategy, and tactics. Publication as an AUSA Book does not indicate that the Association of the United States Army and the publisher agree with everything in the book, but does suggest that the AUSA and the publisher believe this book will stimulate the thinking of AUSA members and others concerned about important issues.

CONTENTS

Contents

Foreword

As president of the Association of the U.S. Army, although retired from active service, I feel privileged to be able to continue to observe closely major trends in America's defense posture and within the U.S. Army. I agree with the current leadership of the Army that we again face a major watershed; decisions made now will profoundly affect American landpower and secutity into the next century.

Gen. Frederic Brown again has offered a perceptive analysis for the Army's future. Twenty years ago he and Zeb Bradford laid out their proposals for the post-Vietnam Army in the thoughtful volume, *The U.S. Army in Transition*. *The U. S. Army in Transition II* proposes nothing less than a new way of thinking about future conflict and landpower, not just some novel thoughts in old analytical frameworks. This provocative book has already caused much discussion inside the Army; its ideas have stimulated new approaches—many consistent with the future plans and policies of our current Chief of Staff, U.S. Army, Gen. Gordon R. Sullivan. I do not speak for the chief of staff, or the U.S. Army, or the sometimes diverse views of Army leaders. I do know, however, that our chief thinks this book suggests the sort of creative thinking that is necessary now at the end of the cold war. I am reasonably comfortable that General Sullivan would agree with much of my foreword.

The United States won the cold war with the U.S. Army playing a central role through the sound application of the principles of what one might call "industrial warfare." Our doctrine, technology, organization, and leadership concepts were based on experience as an industrial power going

back to the Civil War. As Rick Brown points out so well, Operation Desert Storm was a graphic transition to a new era of warfare, one beyond the industrial era.

Consequently, Americans—citizens, politicians, and soldiers—need to free their thinking to achieve principled, innovative solutions to today's security challenges. We could ignore the future shown to us during Operations Just Cause in Panama and Desert Storm in the Gulf. We could continue to prepare for an industrially based, mass production, mobilization conflict—a war that is highly unlikely. But it would be far more sensible to inaugurate the next phase of history, which has been divided into two distinct periods.

The first period stretched from the Revolution to World War II. That period saw America secure itself with a small force of regulars, backed by a large, mobilizable, yet relatively untrained militia and emergency conscripts. After WWII, intercontinental flight and the division of the world into two armed camps forced America to a second system of ground force preparedness and security. For the first time, a large standing force, well trained and equipped with the latest technology, was reinforced by a big reserve component—the Army Reserve and the National Guard. Both components were organized, equipped, trained, and manned for a mobilization war on the plains of central Europe and a potential global conflict that never came.

Today, the events beckoning to a third organizational phase coincide with the revolution in technology so evident in the world. We are invited to seize the opportunity to forge a new army to secure America's enduring global interests into the next century. This volume's strength is that it recognizes the connection between U.S. traditions, the institution of the Army, and the requirements of the emerging world.

Rick Brown notes the three areas of change that have critical impact. The strategic environment offers uncertainty and instability; bipolarity *will not* be replaced by American hegemony—it is unsuited to our national character and ill-advised given our relative capabilities. The domestic environment will continue fractious and constraining as the nation addresses deferred or ignored social, economic, and fiscal problems. Finally, the intellectual environment has moved to what General Brown calls the information age.

The dissolution of the Soviet Union released worldwide long-subordinated ethnic, socio-economic, religious, and irredentist strife. These changes require the following for our Army: reorientation from a focus on European-mobilization mass war to a global capability for crisis intervention; change from response to a Soviet-based communist threat to a set of regional, diffuse, and ambiguous threats; a smaller forward presence to protect interests instead of large forward deployments to constrain a single adversary; non-nuclear forces based in the United States for rapid response; tailored force packages ready or deployed to counter threats to U.S. interests.

Army budgets will continue the decline in real terms that began in 1985. The basic decision adjusting to these resource constraints has been made; the Army of the future will be trained and ready. Force structure reductions are part of a coherent plan that restructures the Army in light of the evaporating Soviet threat and releases resources to keep the contingency-oriented Army trained and ready. We are investing in a prudent research and development program to maintain the current relative and dynamic technology lead over any potential adversaries.

The third area of change—the advent of the microprocessor (computer) in warfare—is a main focus of this book. This advance in the sophisticated equipment of modern armies can also revolutionize the way armies, and countries, think about, prepare for, and engage in conflict. Brown's perceptive analysis confirms that the microchip, harnessed in new ways, affects *all* aspects of the Army—from quality people and training through leader development, doctrine, and force structure.

The microprocessor provides the capability to achieve decisive victory by using information to multiply the effects of maneuver and firepower. The Army assaulted 27 objectives simultaneously at night in Panama; seven Army divisions maneuvered across trackless wastes in Iraq with the purpose of paralyzing the opposing force. The sure knowledge of where the enemy is and the ability to operate day and night in all weather and terrain mark an Army capable of decisive victory. Marshaling and employing information through the microchip—whether in a single precision munition, in a direct fire control system, or in the fusion capability of aerial reconnaissance systems such as the Joint-Surveillance Target Attack Radar System (J-STARS)—marks the transition to a new way of war. The Army can operate and sustain with precision; select the critical point on the battlefield; apply paralyzing, overwhelming force without massive expenditure; and reduce the need for the "mountain of iron" required in industrial warfare.

Microchip capabilities provide opportunity for rapid, violent, conclusive victory with a minimum of casualties but little likelihood of the grinding offensives of industrial-age warfare. Brown correctly perceives the military parallel with the global economy. The "niche market" and the ability to determine and exploit opportunities, rather than overwhelm on a broad front, are keys to business success. In military conflict, the ability to discern and exploit critical strengths and weaknesses, rather than massing overwhelming capability on all fronts, is the path to decisive victory.

This pervasive, revolutionary change results from the microchip's relation to the traditional technology hierarchy, where technology improved performance by applying resources and esoteric materials at the top end. But the microchip adds value at all levels of the technology pyramid and can affect every step—design and analysis, functional capability, manufacturing, end use, and training. The microprocessor is like a major, new raw material. To take advantage of this revolution requires open and innovative

thinking that will project across some twenty years since the Army, a human system, requires a generation for total change.

Brown's concept of "gold-collar" leadership has tremendous implications for the commissioned and noncommissioned officer, because developing leaders requires the longest lead time. Battalion and division commanders, first sergeants and sergeants major, and competent staff officers and noncommissioned officers take twenty years to train and develop. Enhancing their capabilities through the use of computers and information processing will place new demands on their organizational, leadership, and conceptual skills.

Combat training centers already use some high technology to provide instant feedback for assessments, corrections, and improvements. Still, we have only scratched the surface. Stimulators, simulations, and training devices embedded in equipment all offer training to fit the anticipated mission and save resources. Imagine "virtual reality" networks for developing and testing operational plans or for refighting controlled battles, after changing parameters to determine the best mix of hardware, tactics, information dissemination, and command and control.

In another area where principle and tradition can benefit from the new technology, America's Army will continue to rely on the citizen-soldiers of the Guard and Reserve. Mobilization is a given; capability is important, not which component it comes from, except in terms of the time it takes to make a unit ready and available. *The U.S. Army in Transition II* suggests an innovative force with the active as the role model, the Guard as a set of proud units capable of supporting national military strategy, and the U.S. Army Reserve as a talent pool of highly competent individuals possessing critical skills.

Doctrine must shape these changes. Our war-winning AirLand Battle has proven flexible and is based on sound principles. The Army is adjusting that doctrine to reflect changes in the security environment and the *National Military Strategy*. Through our doctrine—the way we think about winning the next battle and war—we can harness and leverage the power of the microchip.

The security of our nation is a shared responsibility. Americans have often failed to think about the unpleasant, failed to invest in a prudent insurance policy, failed to keep our military trained and ready, and failed to seize opportunities to improve the security of our interests. We have in our history a series of bloody debacles in which American soldiers paid the supreme sacrifice to teach us the error of our ways. It would be easy to continue into the next century victorious, complacent, and assured.

Citizens—those of us in private life, legislators, executives, and uniformed—must fight complacency. We must ensure that America's Army has a vision of the future and remains prepared to answer the nation's call and

deliver what the nation expects. *The U.S. Army in Transition II* presents an excellent and stimulating elaboration of the issues that we must consider to ensure our security into the next century. The Association of the U.S. Army is pleased to help provide this challenge to think of the future.

Gen. Jack N. Merritt, USA (Ret.)
President
Association of the U.S. Army
Arlington, Virginia

PREFACE

THESE ARE GENUINELY EXCITING TIMES FOR THE STUDENT
of national security affairs. The international political, military, and economic environments have been affected by the unpredicted demise of the
Soviet Union; by the demonstration in the Persian Gulf war of extraordinary attack capabilities at the strategic, operational, and tactical echelons,
using precision-guided, conventional munitions; and by the "information
revolution" now supplanting almost two hundred years of the Industrial
Revolution. The impacts of these new international forces are aggravated
by the reemergence of older forces and trends suppressed for decades—vir-
ulent nationalism, religious intolerance, and widespread starvation. These
are the ingredients and tinder for regional or global conflict, and the spark
could light as Eurasia destabilizes after the collapse of the Soviet Union.

Freed from persistent international concern about Soviet ambitions
and military capabilities, the U.S. government reexamines its national prior-
ities, while influenced by an electorate increasingly concerned about domestic issues. A profound restructuring of the U.S. economy is under way,
following the rise of the global economy. Social policy faces new public
concerns, in some cases uniquely American expectations, such as equal opportunity, which are yet to seize other nations. Few policy precedents are
available. Yet whether the United States leads or follows change, the results
are the same. Many of the familiar points of the policy and budget compass
seem to be spinning.

Faced with the specter of precipitous reduction of budget and force
structure, the military services—particularly the Army, the custodian of
landpower—fear reversion to an unwelcome past: then, in the euphoria of

victory, military capability was permitted to decline and led to defeat in the early stages of the next conflict. Victory in 1945 was reduced to defeat in Korea in 1950, when the first American reinforcements, Task Force Smith, were defeated by the North Koreans. The pain from the impacts of victory in one war, followed by defeat in the next, is embedded in the Army's psyche. This should never be permitted to happen again, because the long-term costs in lives and treasure are unacceptable. A crucial question faces the United States, the U.S. Army, and American citizens: At this latest major watershed in world and American history, how should the landpower military capability of the United States—a democracy, a people, a nation, a state, and most of the continent—be developed to meet the demands of the next several decades?

Here is *an* answer to this question. It is aimed at serious observers and those engaged in the development and sustainment of American landpower, represented by the U.S. Army. *The* answer can only come from the national security decision process and its diverse, powerful actors. It is hoped that this book can help frame a reflective professional debate so essential to sound decisions in this area of national significance.[1] This book is not an historical record of past events, laudable as they may have been; nor is it an explicit prescription for change. Rather, it is a description of major, new, international and domestic forces acting to influence landpower. It is intended to stimulate challenging, but responsible, discussion.

Detailed policy and program changes are only hinted at; explicit force structure recommendations are deliberately vague. I leave those to the many "experts" who discuss at great length end strength, weapon systems, and numbers of divisions. Debate over specific budgetary outcomes should not conceal much more important reflection on the long-term forces influencing broad landpower policy alternatives at a defining watershed in U.S. national military policy. This work does not address the overall national defense posture, important though it is to joint and combined operations by the United States as the global military power. Lastly, useful reflection mandates searching thought within the service. Assessments of critical functions such as structuring, equipping, training, manning, sustaining, mobilizing, and deploying the force are necessary to plumb the magnitude and azimuth of probable change within the Army.

This book, therefore, shuns proposing a future defense program. Rather, it establishes a broad framework for reviewing tough professional issues. It will probe the design of a new army from the foundation up, with most of the work on basic design and the foundation itself. To some it might seem no more than a cloudy vision of a new army, but I believe the magnitude of current change demands serious introspection. This is my purpose. Armed with a vision of the future, albeit cloudy, others can worry more effectively about the program implications.

Thus far, the current debate seems inadequate. There are some genuinely difficult issues that contemporary writing neglects. Examples include: the global economy has arrived; Japanese global corporations dominate the automobile and home electronics industries, and the availability of information and computer power has made a significant difference in the Air-Land Battle during Operation Desert Storm. Are the criteria for success of the global economy more relevant models for future landpower than those of the tried-and-true mass-production of the industrial age? Is, perhaps, structuring forces to exploit advantageous battlefield functions more important to success in regional coalition warfare in the post-industrial age than dispatching masses of conventional units with balanced functional capability? The current composition of the Total Force seems absolutely appropriate for constituted landpower in a democracy. Could it also possess the seeds for a substantial restructuring of landpower to accommodate requirements for more units (National Guard) and better, more competent people (Army Reserve) in the information age?

Clearly, officers today must master new, more complex battle tasks to fight the AirLand Battle. Has the information age brought new competency requirements that surpass traditional blue-collar–white-collar distinctions? If so, can the highly skilled themselves have become a new and significant element of deployable military power? Lastly, can highly intensive training and evaluation, distributed virtually to the home, permit new vistas of training and readiness proficiency? These are the kinds of issues that will mold the characteristics of future landpower. They need to be on the table and examined in the continuing policy debate.

This book is designed to stimulate discussion. Part 1 reviews the new security environment, which provides the rationale for landpower. Part 2 examines issues related to the long-term sustainment of landpower in a democracy. Part 3 selects several issues that can propel major changes in large organizations, while Part 4 suggests more specific, lasting changes—policies and programs to maintain national preeminence as a landpower.

I am indebted to the thoughtful comments of serving and retired Army leaders of all ranks, uniformed and civilian. I, of course, bear sole responsibility for the contents.

PART I

CHALLENGES OF THE
INFORMATION AGE

1 New Challenges to Landpower

FROM 1989 THROUGH 1991 THERE HAVE BEEN SIGNIFICANT successes in the national security policies of the United States and in the operations of the U.S. Army; the custodian of landpower on an island continent. Fifty years of direct confrontation with the world's major continental land powers, Germany and the Soviet Union, ended in decisive military supremacy at every echelon of military conflict—tactical, operational, and strategic. Three wars were won on three continents: the end of the cold war and the collapse of the Soviet Union and the Warsaw Pact; in Operation Just Cause intervention in Panama; and in the Desert Shield/Desert Storm operations in the Persian Gulf. These national victories were achieved by all U.S. services, combined with other instruments of national policy. They were international victories, too, gained with allies joined in both cold and hot war.

The triumphs were even sweeter, considering the Army's experience over those fifty years. Victory against the Axis was followed by sudden disarming after World War II, then by initial defeat in Korea. After Korea, the Army rebuilt to the Strategic Army Corps (STRAC)—"skilled, tough, ready around the clock" for contingency response from the continental United States—and the Seventh Army in Europe. Then came the nadir: the Vietnam War and rejection by some of the American people. Finally, there were twenty years of long, slow rebuilding to today's Army of Excellence. In the late sixties and early seventies, professionals and close observers saw the Army torn apart by drug abuse, racism, dissent, and the stresses of adjustment to the Modern Volunteer Army (MVA). The Army discovered it was a generation behind the Soviets in equipment and doctrine and suffering

from eroded policy and weakened resource support. The future looked really grim.

But then came its rebirth into a highly capable landpower force, created by superb civilian and military leadership. President Ronald Reagan, Secretary of Defense Caspar Weinberger, and Secretary of the Army John Marsh, Jr., led the way, supported aggressively by too many gifted military leaders to name. Of course success was primarily due to outstanding young soldiers well led at every echelon. The Army can be justifiably proud of its accomplishments across the board. Clearly, much has been done well in those years of sixty- to eighty-hour weeks. Perhaps it is time to relax a bit, to bask in the glory of it all.

Wrong. Today's Army faces what may be its most severe challenges to capability and professional ethos since the interwar period. As our nation addresses new challenges, the Army, with its renewed confidence, must face reductions some consider tantamount to a defeat. A world that the Army has clearly mastered is changing beneath its feet—as it has done before. The technological arbiter of landpower success has moved from the internal combustion engine and atom to the microchip. The international environment is undergoing profound, destabilizing change. The society the Army existed to defend faces grave systemic challenges. Thus, the Army needs to look about, assess where it must go, and start the anguishing process of "adapting." More critically, it cannot dwell on the achievements of the past; rather, it must build again, fortunately from a far better vantage point than the last such effort after Vietnam.

We should not be surprised at change. The Army is a conservative institution, as it should be, given its profound responsibility of unlimited liability—service to death. There has been little time for reflection in an institution not given to excessive soul-searching under any circumstances, even less during the intense pace of events of the past several years. Yet, the framework for the next several decades of national security policy is being formulated now. It is a critical time to "look about"; to reset the course for the years ahead. It is not the moment to hunker down and wait for all to pass. It is not the time to fight delays on successive positions, but rather a time for quick attacks leading to exploitation of known success.

Before we look at specific issues, it is useful to set the stage and to survey the big picture in order to assess the magnitude and shape of changes and how they may influence landpower. It is equally important to consider what has not yet changed and is unlikely to change in the future. Finally, we should remember and exploit some important landpower characteristics or capabilities often taken for granted.

The most significant influence is change itself, both in the nature of changes in many aspects of military capability and in the accelerating rate at which it occurs. The Army has undergone frequent alteration in the past. It was wrenched into the industrial age by the Civil War and then reener-

gized from frontier routine in intense change at the start of the twentieth century. World War I was traumatic, but with the National Defense Act of 1920 the Army returned to its "out of sight, out of mind" slumber. New manifestations of the industrial age had appeared in the form of the airplane, the tank, and chemical weapons, but they had little impact on an endemically impoverished army. World War II basically repeated World War I. Sleeping potential was rapidly converted to global performance in the best traditions of mass production in the industrial age.

The cold war brought a truly major change in the Army: It did not demobilize after the Korean conflict, but with the other services, the Army emerged as a deterrent force ready for global struggle. Now fifty years later, this post–World War II aberration in landpower, stimulated by the cold war, has become the accepted and comfortable "base case" of Army expectations. America's current success in the precipitous demise of the Soviet and Russian "empires" has destroyed this base case. It is not that the world is any more secure, nor the United States immune from sudden devastation by strategic attacks from hostile groups or nations. But the half-century rationale supporting substantial, sustained, ready landpower in a democracy is gone. If arms control is successful, there may be further beneficial force reductions in all the major democratic nations.

There is a new security environment emerging that will influence the employment of landpower not only within the United States, but also in the other democracies. The salient characteristic of this new world is that in the absence of a clear global enemy, national security against foreign threat is no longer perceived as the primary threat to the nation. As Gen. Colin L. Powell, chairman of the Joint Chiefs of Staff, describes it, "Demons are hard to find." The Soviet Union, always the nemesis to justify U.S. defense forces, no longer exists and successor republics are as yet undefined. New national military strategies are still evolving that may suggest capabilities to address possible contingencies rather than the traditional Soviet-generated threat scenarios. What will these necessary capabilities be?

The collapse of relative bipolar stability with mutually understood dangers has complicated, not simplified, the international security environment. The Warsaw Pact is gone; NATO searches for its role. Ad hoc alliances created to respond to particular regional threats seem to be replacing traditional alliances. For example, military alliance with Syria in Operation Desert Shield was wholly unexpected. Other ad hoc cooperation is surely in the offing as the United States contemplates the various regional orders. The splintering of Yugoslavia opens up sores of animosity centuries old. Inflation, profound religious tension, and opposing nationalities cause aspirations hidden since World War I to reemerge. Immigration challenges political and social stability across Europe. Local conflicts spread—annually, with more than a hundred of various sizes. The conditions of instability that fomented totalitarian regimes in the 1930s return. These are

hardly comforting prospects, but then America focused internally when this
happened before. Hopefully we have learned over these past fifty years that
our security is the world's security.

As the military threat to our national security appears to recede, the
economic threat grows. Presidential near-genius in the prosecution of Operation Desert Storm is eclipsed in the minds of many Americans by nagging
internal threats to domestic well-being. The riots in Los Angeles reflect serious economic, political, and social problems in the inner cities. And solutions transcend our borders. Competing successfully in the world market
is an increasingly important national goal.

But nothing described here is necessarily a rationale for sustained,
ready, U.S. landpower of the size maintained today or even for that currently programmed for the mid-nineties. Certainly not all conflicts require
U.S. intervention; nor, if there is intervention, should it necessarily be military. Political or economic actions can be credible, especially without Soviet
aid on the horizon. Ask South Africa, Vietnam, or Cuba. If military action
is required, it does not necessarily involve landpower. Airpower has
emerged as a truly decisive military capability, as was demonstrated in the
Persian Gulf. Libya-style strikes with precision munitions look even better
after Operation Desert Storm. We are the premier seapower, capable of
dominating the seas and projecting effective force ashore. Finally, if landpower intervention is required, significant military contributions from other
nations seem essential to ensure a desirable, regional political aftermath to
its use. Thus, endemic global instability, unwelcome as it is, is not a compelling rationale for major U.S. deterrent landpower capability, even were
there not important competing demands.

And there are. Economic competitiveness and well-being and the resolution of pressing social problems are seen by many Americans as the most
immediate threats to national security. The Council on Foreign Relations
and the American Assembly recently conducted a thoughtful assessment of
U.S. national security policy and concluded: "American security by the traditional military definition is less at risk. This circumstance inevitably brings
to the surface with fresh urgency the other dimensions of security, and in
particular, the need for greater attention to America's domestic agenda."[1]
The development of advanced military capability, for its own sake, is no
longer persuasive as the sole rationale to garner defense expenditures. Military ability to respond to other pressing national problems becomes increasingly important as security is defined more in domestic terms.

Traditional military aspects of national security are also influenced by
ongoing global transition from the industrial age, best represented by the
internal combustion engine, to the so-called information age driven by the
computer. National markets increasingly become global markets. During
the past five years, the United States has doubled the percentage of national
product developed through international trade. The pace of introducing

new products targeted to very specific demand "niches" increases as the flow of commercial information explodes. And there is an increasing premium on innovative applications of computers.[2]

Operation Desert Storm has been called the first war of the post-industrial or information age and was, in fact, dominated by the computer—from precision weapons to timely, complex logistics planning. We will return to the implications of the information age again and again, for they are of seminal importance in thinking about "futures." The concepts of Alvin Toffler and Heidi Toffler are useful, for example. They see the information age as the "Third Wave" in the evolution of human relations. The "First Wave" was the agricultural revolution with human conflict, or war, characterized by hand-to-hand combat. The "Second Wave" was the Industrial Revolution, represented by wars of mass destruction—World War I and World War II. The Third Wave is the ongoing information revolution reflected in the evolving information- and knowledge-based economy. Third-Wave war is knowledge-based war, as evidenced in Operation Desert Storm. "Third Wave violence is the extension of the mind, not the fist." To the Tofflers, Operation Desert Storm

> ... was not simply the use of quantitatively better technology but a truly revolutionary infusion of knowledge into violence, forcing changes in organization, training, tactics, battlefield management, intelligence, timing, along with fundamental reconceptualization of the relative roles of firepower, mobility, logistics, time, space and communications.[3]

For now, think of war as a combination of all three "waves"—primitive, industrial, and knowledge based.[4]

Change accelerates in military requirements for national security, competing domestic needs, and the nature of war itself—Third-Wave war. These are the "megatrends" that provide the backdrop of the future. More specific developments will also directly influence national military policy and programs during the nineties and beyond. Four stand out.

• *The nature of usable military power* is changing. Precision munitions proved capable of imposing extensive damage at the strategic, operational, and tactical echelons of war during Operation Desert Storm. The dreams of airpower enthusiasts were finally realized when near-nuclear effects were achieved with usable, conventional firepower increasingly employed by all services. Stealth fighter-bombers or cruise missiles remain the primary means of delivery, but no one can doubt the operational, if not strategic, potential of "brilliant" munitions delivered by the multiple launch rocket system (MLRS) or the Army tactical missile system (ATACMS). It is now entirely credible for the United States, unilaterally or with a United Nations or regional mandate, to threaten overwhelming destruction to deter or punish unacceptable aggression. The air capability postulated by air-

power enthusiasts such as Gen. Billy Mitchell exists as usable, precise strategic power that provides new potential for deterrence. The chairman of the House Armed Services Committee could state unequivocally that air power was the decisive weapon of the desert campaign.[5] Fortunately, these new deterrence systems have been proved just when more and more "poor man's" strategic weapons appear in the form of terrorist or missile-delivered chemical, biological, or even nuclear warheads. Strategically, there is an emerging requirement to combine the threat of new air-, sea-, or land-based conventional weapons with other sanctions, to be supported by the glare of hyper-communications, and so deter the use of strategic weapons as they spread through fragmenting empires like the former Soviet Union or rogue states like Iraq or Iran.

The basics of conflict deterrence have changed. Opportunities for arms control expand, as demonstrated by the proposed elimination of ground-based tactical nuclear weapons in Europe, and significant reductions in strategic systems proposed in negotiations between the United States and Russia. These decisions will lead to new opportunities and challenges for landpower at the operational and tactical echelons of war.

• *The computer* expands as a powerful aid on the battlefield, akin in the past to the stirrup, gunpowder, the internal combustion engine, and nuclear power. The computer permits an exponential increase in the power available to a single warrior, accentuating the continuing focus on the free individual in Western democratic societies. The ranges of battlefield acquisition and engagement double every five to ten years. The 3,000-person brigade of the eighties has the combat power of the 18,000-man division of the fifties and sixties. The 1,000-person battalion of the late nineties may routinely employ combat power associated with division formations in World War II. The computer offers to the nations that can develop its potential quantum improvements and opportunities in military organization, equipment, and training. Good or poor exploitation of the computer's potential will likely be a dominant discriminant of military capability in the Western democracies and probably in the world for the next several decades.

Armies are notoriously conservative organizations. There are genuine rewards and risks associated with accepting major changes generated by the computer. Target acquisition (Q36), fire direction (Tacfire), and firepower (MLRS) have revolutionized fire support. But, otherwise, Army experience has not been entirely successful. Good intentions and trying hard cannot compensate for the overly rapid introduction of technology. The M60A2 tank with Shillelagh missile was a clear case of "too much too soon." The technology had not matured sufficiently for field use. Today, some fear that the complexity of the Bradley infantry fighting vehicle has diverted the

ground focus of infantry. The Abrams M1A2 tank has revolutionary battle-management capabilities, but it requires new levels of computer familiarity. Will the Army be able to exploit such clear force multipliers? Accelerated assimilation of change is a new and unwelcome challenge to most military establishments, yet psychological and practical physical acceptance of accelerating change in warfare spawned by the microchip will be a major criterion of military success in the future.

• *Potentials of individual soldier performance change*—they change both what the soldiers do and how well they do it. More is now expected of the individual soldier. Soldiers working together, focused as a team, or the unit, remain the essence of military capability; but as computer-supported weapons increase the power of their users, the military has new reliance on the individual soldier's performance. For example, the infantryman armed with a laser target designator can direct devastating firepower. In this scenario, not only does the individual soldier become more important but the general focus of his or her activity is increasingly directed to support or deny individual needs. Certainly, group needs remain important: ecology, education, and public health continue to have competing national claims on resources previously allocated to landpower readiness. But voters in old and new democracies express their concerns regarding the satisfaction of individual rights and responsibilities.

Satisfying separate needs of individuals holds an increasingly important role in all aspects of public service, including that of the military in the information age. Major legislation supports improved facilities for the handicapped. "Politically correct" affirmative action targets an incredible range of initiatives potentially offensive to various people. Training the individual soldier for a productive civilian job, once a recruiting attraction, now becomes an expected civil benefit of military service. New Army missions seem likely to highlight individual soldiers responding to individual civil needs.

Accepting such new missions is only a part of the response expected from the Army. The new tasks must be done well. Demonstrated competence is becoming an increasingly important measure of general public confidence and esteem. As many governmental agencies demonstrate through an inability to execute complex programs successfully, competence itself becomes an expectation, if not an obligation, of service. The nuclear disaster in the Soviet Union at Chernobyl severely eroded Soviet public trust in authority when managers demonstrated administrative incompetence. In the United States, demonstrated military war-fighting competence became an important national theme during Operation Desert Storm. Public pride centered on the clear competence of the nation's military. That competence is expected to continue.

The message seems clear: Do more to support individual needs, and do it exceedingly well. This admonition applies not only in the United States but worldwide. In responding to national requirements during the past several decades, the Army has created a new and very effective weapon—the highly skilled soldier, deployable as a model of individual competence, supporting public needs.[6] Fielding competent soldiers and units that represent the results of the most far-reaching social programs of any military (equal opportunity, counterdrug), the U.S. Army has itself become a powerful model at home and abroad. This new aspect of a military competence has stimulated responsible commentary about new roles. David Broder expressed this well in his May 13, 1992, article in the *Washington Post,* extolling ". . . the U.S. military, which in the last two generations has probably done more and succeeded better in creating a nonracist, bias-free meritocracy than any other part of American society." Broder then went on to advocate creating a new Civilian Conservation Corps (CCC) from the thousands about to be involuntarily separated.[7]

Heightened international interest in individual rights and responsibilities has put a new premium on recent Army innovation and competence in addressing complex, national social problems. As it implemented equal opportunity for individual soldiers at home, the Army acquired a new ability to influence the policies and programs of local armies abroad, thus satisfying social and cultural needs in many nations. Highly competent soldiers of both sexes, of mixed races, and of various ethnic origins are important national ambassadors. The Army has always meant "people" formed into capable, trained, and equipped units. Now, in the information age, competent people, properly employed, are themselves a powerful weapon.

• *The presence of hyper-communications*—intensely focused information provided globally and almost instantly—has military significance at strategic, operational, or tactical echelons. The CNN-reported Scud attack on Israel, which triggered virtually simultaneous gas alarms in Saudi Arabia, is one example. It is an important byproduct of the information, or knowledge-based, age. Today, virtually immediate world feedback is available on important aspects of relations between nations. Feedback is much more than "news." It is "facts" converted and molded into visual images, which themselves become the collective global memory. The domestic impact of the visual image of Los Angeles policemen beating Rodney King is clear.[8]

With respect to military operations, CNN was on the drop zone during Operation Golden Pheasant in Honduras. There was detailed coverage of the 27th Chinese Army in Tiananmen Square. Instantaneous media communications clearly helped defeat the August 1991 Soviet coup. The media were equally important in Operation Just Cause, although more after the fact, when inquiring press looked for instances of military error concerning civilian casualties and excess collateral damage. Operation Desert Storm

was different with its intensive control of press access, but perhaps the terrain caused it to be an atypical example. It was difficult for reporters to strike out on their own, and there were tighter controls on everyone in Saudi Arabia. Despite extraordinarily skillful handling of the media by the Department of Defense, there existed numerous opportunities for "bad press" had not the operation been executed with superb, professional military skill. The microscope of world media—the glare of hyper-communications—was everpresent. The new and rising importance of communications was acknowledged by *Time* magazine in selecting Ted Turner as its "man of the year":

> What a computer message can accomplish within an office, CNN achieves around the clock around the globe: it gives everyone the same information, the same basis for discussion, at the same moment. That change in communication has in turn affected journalism, intelligence gathering, economics, diplomacy and even, in the minds of some scholars, the very concept of what it is to be a nation.[9]

The military implications appear equally profound. Skillful, rapid execution becomes a precondition, if the political objectives arching over most conflicts are not to be compromised by the glare of the world media. World hyper-communications erode severely the utility of conscript forces of average discipline and competence. Public confidence wanes as average units commit normal errors, magnified in the public eye by hyper-communications. Highly competent, professional, U.S. and other countries' forces seem essential for landpower to be effective in local or regional conflicts under the unblinking stare of hyper-communications. Yet, in the absence of credible threats, cost constraints will drive the nations to increased reliance on less capable reserve forces unlikely to withstand the glaring media spotlight. This is a genuine dilemma: Usable military power is being redefined to accomplish political ends, which are themselves influenced strongly by the media.

Hyper-communications promise to become increasingly powerful as more people expect to know information sooner. Wait and you will be passed by events or become less able to influence the "spin" of opinion. This is a far deeper issue than a conventional "dealing with the media"; it is an awareness of the need to gain and secure the information initiative in military affairs, in both peace and war in the information age.[10]

These four developments portend new challenges, and each represents a sea change in the military as it has existed for the past five decades. If not mastered, their combined impact could seriously erode U.S. landpower.

In many ways, the situation is much more difficult today than it was after Vietnam. Change was relatively easy to accommodate after the despair engendered by the uncertain military outcome many considered a defeat. Flushed from convincing victory in the Persian Gulf, change is now less

welcome. We won the first battle of the post-industrial period, but the infrastructure—doctrine, organization, equipment, and training—was from the industrial age. What needs to be adapted to today not just to respond but to exploit this new situation?

While change is accelerating, there are important constants, or enduring truths, that will continue to govern sustaining and using landpower. Any changes must be at least consistent with them.

Foremost, man is a land being and is dominated only when his land, resources, and people are controlled. Landpower is the ultimate application of military power whose cutting edge is the individual fighting soldier. This is expressed well in the 1981 edition of *FM 100-1: The Army*:

> Landpower—The imposition of territorial control, or the resistance to such control, has been the central military objective in the majority of wars of recorded history. Control of seas and of airspace is also vital in modern land warfare; without this extraterritorial security, land control is not likely to be achieved nor sustained. All military services thus make direct and essential contributions to the ultimate control of land and of its peoples.
>
> While the power to deny or to destroy is possessed by all the military services, the fundamental truth is that only ground forces possess the power to exercise direct, continuing, and comprehensive control over land, its resources, and its peoples. Land forces thus perform important, and largely unique, functions besides denial and destruction: landpower can make permanent the otherwise transitory advantages achieved by air and naval forces."[11]

The enduring nature of landpower carries special significance in the United States, and the Army occupies a particular place in the national ethos. This idea was so described by Gen. Fred C. Weyand, a former chief of staff:

> The American Army really is a people's Army in the sense that it belongs to the American people, who take a jealous and proprietary interest in its involvement. When the Army is committed, the American people are committed. . . . In the final analysis, the American Army is not so much an arm of the Executive Branch as it is an arm of the American people.[12]

The Army certainly cannot execute its mission without the concerted aid of the other services. In Operation Desert Storm, the decisive importance of airpower at strategic, operational, and tactical echelons was demonstrated convincingly, and Operation Desert Shield simply would not have occurred without control of the seas. Only the Army, however, can ensure absolute control of people—a truth rediscovered in the Persian Gulf War.

> When the war started I had 39 T72s; after 38 days of air attack I was down to 32. After 20 minutes with the 2d Armored Cavalry, I was down to zero.
> —Iraqi battalion commander[13]

The U.S. Marine Corps (USMC) might seem to be in potential conflict as a landpower alternative. As an island continent, the United States must project landpower by seapower or airpower if it is to work. Landpower can be introduced into a theater of operations by air, but its logistics requirements can be sustained over time only by sea. The USMC is absolutely necessary with its amphibious capability to project seapower ashore and thus make it possible to sustain landpower. Important in the past, this capability will be vital in the future to permit timely military interventions. The Marines, therefore, are an exceedingly valuable hybrid that expands the synergistic capability of the Army and Air Force in Air Land operations and helps the Navy maintain supremacy of the seas—no more and no less.[14] Working with the other services, *the Army must retain the capability to dominate land, its resources, and people consistent with the national military strategy of the United States.*

A second constant is the enduring nature of the Principles of War in focusing landpower on fighting. The capability to fight wars is the ultimate purpose of the Army, and the Army exists to support its most valuable weapon, the individual soldier. War-fighting capabilities must be consistent with the principles of objective, offensive, mass, economy of force, maneuver, unity of command, security, surprise, and simplicity.[15] Information-age changes should support and hopefully increase practical application of the Principles of War. *The primary focus of the Army is and must remain on the application of the enduring Principles of War to joint and combined war-fighting, to win.*

The third truth is that landpower can be sustained in the swirling competition for national resources only if it is managed responsibly. However the Army may change, it must remain efficient and effective in executing the functions of command and management in force development: acquire, train, distribute, develop, deploy, sustain, and separate.[16] Computer and other management aids should be drawn upon to foster efficiency and economy. Certainly, overhead structure can and should be reduced consistent with force reductions, but beware economies focused on and justified by the active force. *The Army management objective must be competent stewardship for the Total Force, for joint obligations, and for regional operations with allies.*

Simply stated, whatever change may bring, the Army must manage its resources to be ready to fight and win on land in AirLand Operations. This may be more difficult than some think in the tumultuous days ahead. Fortunately, the Army has significant consensus among the officer and noncommissioned officer (NCO) leadership on basic, important issues sometimes taken for granted. Consensus in these areas is a source of real strength in difficult days:

- The primacy of the Constitution and civilian control is unquestioned. The Army exists to support the civilian leadership of our nation.

- There exists an abiding ethos of service to nation—"Duty, Honor, Country"—that has been strengthened during the past decade.
- The Army *is* people—nationally based across race, gender, and ethnic origin. It must master machines, including computers, but its final strength is the individual soldier, disciplined yet encouraged to exercise imagination and initiative.
- The Army is a Total Force of uniformed and civilian, full-time and citizen-soldiers, all focused by task, condition, and standard of rigorous training.
- The Army simply cannot go it alone. It depends on all services and allies to fight and win.

On balance, there is a formidable array of challenges facing the U.S. Army. But the strengths are also significant. As an institution, willing or not, the Army is probably as prepared for major change as it has ever been. Although this is a superficial judgment, a more balanced one will emerge after a detailed review of several issues—challenges and possible responses—provided in the following chapters.

Chapter 2 addresses the characteristics of landpower in response to the evolving information age. It discusses the impact of new doctrine such as AirLand Operations. Relating the military situation to the global market, chapter 2 proposes that the basic building block for contingency operations is the functional battlefield operating system, which draws on national military comparative advantage.

Chapter 3 develops requirements for the Army's active component (AC) and reserve component (RC) forces and suggests allocations of functional responsibilities across the components. It describes new, desirable characteristics for the Total Force, including rapid transition through mobilization, ad hoc multifunctional forces, tailored component and personnel composition, and new cost sharing. Variable readiness is proposed, with new guidance for force structure allocation between active and reserve forces.

Chapter 4 analyzes the long-term sustainment of landpower across continent, nation, state, democracy, and people. It reviews the advantages and disadvantages in the information age of the regular Army, National Guard, and Army Reserve, describing different roles for each across the continuum of potential conflict. Various myths and realities of active Army and reserve relationships and the needs of both constituted units and trained individuals are discussed. A new formulation of the roles and responsibilities for the Total Force is proposed.

Reviewing the challenge of preparing for and fighting a multitheater "world war," chapter 5 considers the peacetime readiness state, the timeliness of reconstitution decisions, and the pace of force generation. Sustainment alternatives are proposed for the technological and industrial bases,

considering the decline of the traditional industry base and the onset of the information age. Both equipment and personnel policies are proposed. The chapter then addresses peacetime "steady state" policies and programs necessary to preserve reconstitution for the long haul in the face of increasingly globalized industry.

The concepts-based requirements system was extraordinarily successful in building landpower to readiness for Operations Just Cause and Desert Storm. New doctrine was complemented by synchronized organization, equipment, and training development. In chapter 6, we ask, how should the processes of integrating doctrine, organization, equipment, and training evolve for the future in preparation for possible operations with "ad hoc" allies in a joint environment of constituted active and reserve forces? How are we to sustain the national strategic advantage U.S. landpower possesses in the early 1990s?

Chapter 7 summarizes the major steps in renovating the Army training system after Vietnam, then extends current policies and programs to the future to accommodate the evolving army. It discusses improved task definition, performance assessment, structured training programs, and new requirements for mobilization and training of ad hoc allies. It emphasizes new training techniques, drawing on new technologies to intensify training even when distributed to dispersed units.

Chapter 8 looks at the changing requirements being placed on personnel by current doctrine and technologies and concludes that the Army is no longer a blue-collar (NCO) and white-collar (officer) organization. Many NCOs today are expected to perform traditional officer tasks on the modern battlefield, while officers are expected to perform complex integrative tasks made feasible by the power of the computer. These new battle problems give a mandate to white-collar noncommissioned officers and gold-collar officers—a new set of training and personnel development requirements for both active and reserve soldiers.

New leadership requirements are associated with evolving doctrine and the new world environment. Specifically, chapter 9 addresses new proficiencies demanded by coalition operations in the information age for military and other services supportive of national needs. Specific attention is directed toward new forms of preparation for gold-collar leaders.

Chapter 10 reviews the considerable achievements of competence-basing. It discusses the convergence of the training and personnel systems that made possible the Army of Excellence and points out the considerable challenges to be overcome in retaining excellence in the draw down of forces. Specific actions are suggested to reduce the effects of drawdown such as end-strength floors, separate budget costing in civil support areas, revised family-support programs, and new alternatives for reducing the support costs of combat forces. The last would be achieved by increased reliance on Department of the Army civilians, contractor support, and host-nation support.

Chapter 11 assesses systems acquisition and training opportunities currently available as a result of computer development and reviews the Army's ability to exploit this potential. Several examples are provided on how to draw more aggressively on the power of the computer.

Chapter 12 records the Army's remarkable achievements in institutionalizing profound social change and, in so doing, leading the nation. How could this success be applied in the future? The constituted force has clear opportunities and resources that could be applied to the problem to support variable readiness policies. Peacetime activities could be reinforced with models for regional change. Domestic local needs could be alleviated by trained leaders released early from the military. There appears to be a broad range of opportunities available as an adjunct of the information age.

A new professionalism is associated with a post–cold war Army immersed in the information age. Chapter 13 suggests that traditional formulations need to be modified as the constituted force continues to mature and the length of probable service decreases. New road signs are proposed for the professional ethos distinguishing active from reserve forces. Clearly, acceptance of global military responsibilities in the information age may mandate new perspectives of professionalism.

Drawing on the preceding work, chapter 14 proposes specific action programs to retain U.S. preeminence in post-industrial military capability. It suggests that implementation of seven specific, internal Army policies could virtually ensure that, should it be the national will, the current momentum of change is sustained for the next several decades and, with it, the dominance of landpower.

Chapter 15 summarizes the central thoughts developed here on the future use of landpower and offers insights for developing a new vision by uniformed and civilian supporters of U.S. landpower capability.

In sum, this book is a call for substantial change in U.S. landpower. Naysayers will insist that the change proposed here is excessive. Nothing is really broken; resist change. To them, I answer that this is the "second shoe" after two world wars and accelerating social change exacerbated by changing technology. For better or worse, the United States is entering into another major phase—unilaterally and in relation to other nations—of its evolution. Sage policy and wise programs during the last fifty years have created a military preeminence on land, sea, and in the air, unprecedented in modern times. The nature of military conflict itself, however, is now changing, reflecting global evolution from the industrial to the information age. As other national challenges press in, they deserve and will preempt the national priority formerly afforded defense.

This is not pessimistic counsel for either the nation or its military. Some national "crises" are self-imposed and, as such, represent policy issues, not intractable economic problems. Consider the costs of medical care. AIDS support could be reduced and abortion and the elderly's "right to die"

encouraged—three costly medical issues theoretically changeable overnight. These variables could have profound effects on the costs of national medical care. Consider the national budget deficit; it could be wiped out almost immediately by a gasoline tax or a value-added tax less than that borne by our major allies and competitors. Availability of resources is another vexing issue. California searches for water for its residents, yet most of the state's water is consumed by agriculture subsidized to thrive in a virtual desert. Consider how much arid soil west of the Mississippi is kept artificially green. I do not question any of these policies. They are important issues with strongly held national constituencies. I merely note that each is a one-time "good idea" now becoming a luxury increasingly expensive to maintain. As opportunity costs of current policies change, so will the vote of the electorate.

Opportunity costs, too, are changing within landpower. Some policies or programs represent the "nice"—like creating hundreds of economic and social "little Americas" for forward-deployed forces—that became necessary as expectations expanded during the forty long cold war years. Despite vociferous arguments for their continuation, some of the "nice-become-necessary" may not be affordable today. Good decisions during a time of affluence can produce unaffordable luxuries during one of relative poverty. Retrenching is terribly difficult, but reductions are a fact. Hard choices face every decision-maker. Each must review what is really necessary to fight and win in the post-industrial age. From a strategic perspective, what kinds of military power do we as a nation really have to be able to use to protect our vital national interests? And of total military power, what should be the landpower contribution? How much should be expended for what capabilities? How capable should the hedge be in case the estimate is wrong?

The Army needs to think these kinds of issues through. It is really a critical time to "look about," to reset the course for the next several decades. To repeat, it is not the time to hunker down and wait for all to pass. Nor is it the time for delay missions on successive positions, but a time for quick attacks to exploit success. Then, the Army should have the courage of its convictions to engage the Total Force in the national political processes to effect change. I hope here to stimulate these necessary thought processes.

2   Coalition Conflict

THE CURRENT NATIONAL SECURITY STRATEGY OF THE United States is all-encompassing. It addresses broad national interests and objectives, then describes political, economic, and defense agendas necessary to relate means to ends. It raises the substantial challenges of ensuring effective military responses to regional security threats:

> Because regional crises are the predominant military threat we will face in the future, their demands—along with our forward presence requirements—will be the primary determinant of the size and structure of our future forces.
>
> The regional contingencies we could face are many and varied. We must be prepared for differences in terrain, climate and the nature of threatening forces, as well as for differing levels of support from host nations or others. We must also be able to respond quickly and effectively to adversaries who may possess cruise missiles, modern air defenses, chemical weapons, ballistic missiles, and even large armor formations.
>
> —*National Security Strategy of the United States*, 1991, p. 28.

Readiness for regional contingencies seems certain to be a primary and lasting justification for maintaining landpower capability. This is confirmed in the recently prepared Joint Chiefs of Staff's (JCS) *National Military Strategy*, which prescribes crisis response as one of the four foundations of national defense policy, along with strategic deterrence and defense, forward presence, and reconstitution. The current *National Military Strategy* outlines the principles that will govern policy execution: readiness, collective security, arms control, maritime and aerospace superiority, strategic agility, power projection, technological superiority, and decisive force. These are backed by four supporting capabilities: transportation, space, reconstitu-

tion, and research and development.[1] These were generally self-evident, understood, and employed through the decades of the cold war.

Several, however, are new or have new interpretations. They describe requirements for military force in the post-industrial, or information, age. Essentially military analogs to economic measures now required to prosper in the global economy, they deserve special mention, for they will have profound impact on future landpower. Key parts are underlined.

> Collective Security—Increasingly, we expect to strengthen world response to crises through multilateral operations under the auspices of international security organizations. In the 1991 Gulf War, the United Nations played the role envisioned by its founders—orchestrating and sanctioning collective resistance to an aggressor. The new international order will be characterized by a growing consensus that force cannot be used to settle disputes and when the consensus is broken, the burdens and responsibilities are shared by many nations. While support of formal alliances such as NATO will continue to be fundamental to American military strategy, the United States must be prepared to fight as part of an ad hoc coalition if we become involved in conflict where no formal security relationships exist. We must, however, retain the capability to operate independently as our interests dictate.[2]

While we will be prepared militarily "to go it alone," at least for one major regional contingency, the preference is clear for coalition operations with traditional or ad hoc allies.

> Crisis Response—The capability to respond to regional crises is one of the key demands of our strategy. The regional contingencies we might face are many and varied, and could arise on very short notice. U.S. forces must therefore be able to respond rapidly to deter and, if necessary, to fight unilaterally or as part of a combined effort. This response might range from a single discriminate surgical strike to the employment of overwhelming or decisive force to defeat a regional aggressor.[3]

Executing complex operations is difficult under the glare of hyper-communications. Operation Just Cause was challenging as a unilateral U.S. joint operation. Rapid response to fight with ad hoc allies is even more demanding. At a minimum, remarkable competence and extensive doctrinal and organizational preparation seem essential to prepare allies for effective execution of the AirLand Battle or combined AirLand Operations. In retrospect, there is clear acknowledgment after Operation Desert Storm that common procedures, training, and friendships among senior leaders during years of association in NATO contributed notably to successful combined operations.[4]

> Decisive Force—Once a decision for major military action has been made, half-measures and confused objectives extract a severe price in the form of a protracted conflict that can cause needless waste of human and material resources, a divided nation at home, and defeat. Therefore, one of the essential

elements of our national military strategy is to assemble rapidly the forces needed to win—the concept of <u>applying decisive force to overwhelm our adversaries and thereby terminate conflicts swiftly with a minimum loss of life.</u>[5]

Decisive force was provided on Operation Desert Storm. Presidential guidance was explicit: General Powell told the field commanders: "Tell me what you need for assets. We will not do this halfway. The entire United States military is available to support this operation."[6] American military professionals will applaud this concept. Lessons from "limited war" in Korea and Vietnam are applied at last.[7] National intent is more explicit in the new JCS doctrinal publication:

> We should strive to operate with overwhelming force, based not only on the quality of forces and materiel committed but on the quality of their planning and the skillfulness of their employment. Properly trained and motivated forces with superior technology, executing innovative, flexible, and well-coordinated plans provide a decisive qualitative edge. . . .[8]

Those are remarkable objectives when the preponderance of crisis response operations are envisaged to be quick response with allies, some ad hoc. In fact, it would be incredible were it not for the superb precedents of Operations Just Cause (unilateral) and Desert Storm (combined). The national military goal clearly postulates future coalition-based, Third-Wave war—a formidable challenge during a period of declining military resources.

These strategic concepts address *how* we intend to employ military power. Equally important is *when*. Under what circumstances will the United States be prepared to employ substantial military capability? Practice of the past several years has confirmed the merit of Secretary of Defense Weinberger's formulation in remarks to the National Press Club in 1984. They were prescient; subsequent operations could have been scripted from them. The current national military strategy is absolutely consistent with his ideas. Based upon clear success in two major contingencies, they have established a policy precedent likely to last, despite changing administrations.

> . . . I have developed six major tests to be applied when we are weighing the use of U.S. combat forces abroad. Let me now share them with you:
> (1) First, the United States should not commit forces to combat overseas unless the particular engagement or occasion is deemed vital to our national interest or that of our allies . . .
> (2) Second, if we decide it is necessary to put combat troops into a given situation, we should do so wholeheartedly, and with the clear intention of winning. If we are unwilling to commit the forces or resources necessary to achieve our objectives, we should not commit them at all. Of course, if the particular situation requires only limited force to win our objectives, then we should not hesitate to commit forces sized accordingly . . .

(3) Third, if we do decide to commit forces to combat overseas, we should have clearly defined political and military objectives. And we should know precisely how our forces can accomplish those clearly defined objectives. And we should have sent the forces needed to do just that. . . .

(4) Fourth, the relationship between our objectives and the forces we have committed—their size, composition, and disposition—must be continually reassessed and adjusted if necessary. Conditions and objectives invariably change during the course of a conflict. When they do change, then so must our combat requirements. We must continuously keep as a beacon light before us the basic questions: "Is this conflict in our national interest?" *"Does our national interest require us to fight, to use force of arms?" If the answers are "yes," then we must win. If the answers are "no," then we should not be in combat.*

(5) Fifth, before the U.S. commits combat forces abroad, there must be some reasonable assurance we will have the support of the American people and their elected representatives in Congress. This support cannot be achieved unless we are candid in making clear the threats we face; the support cannot be sustained without continuing and close consultation. We cannot fight a battle with the Congress at home while asking our troops to win a war overseas or, as in the case of Vietnam, in effect asking our troops not to win, but just to be there.

(6) Finally, the commitment of U.S. forces to combat should be a last resort.[9]

These are practical guidelines. They have worked. The reasoning that brought us limited war in Korea and gradual escalation in Vietnam is gone. Clearly, the United States has no intention of entering a military conflict, particularly a regional crisis response—the most likely combat contingency—that it cannot win decisively and rapidly. And so strengthened, the credibility of U.S. military deterrence increases proportionally.

Having established how and when we intend to employ military capability, the next question is, *what* do we intend to do? The traditional spectrum of conflict has changed. Nuclear war remains the least likely, most destructive end of conflict, and the Army is in the process of divesting itself of tactical nuclear weapons.[10] Specific reference to low-, mid-, and high-intensity war has disappeared from the strategy. In their places are regional contingencies. This seems appropriate. Somehow, neither Operation Just Cause nor Desert Storm seems to fit into traditional conceptions of counterinsurgency or limited conventional war. Downtown Baghdad did not see nuclear, bacteriological, or chemical warfare, but the damage to important targets was equivalent to nuclear effects. Distinctions may seem academic to a potential target. Twenty-seven simultaneous night assaults, supported by extraordinary focusing of intelligence, fire support, and command and control, paralyzed Panama—not much low intensity in that operation. Panama was a small country, but it seems apparent that if it had been larger, the force would have been larger still. Perhaps the reason for the shift away

from low-, mid-, and high-intensity wars as clearly delineated alternatives is that each regional contingency will combine whatever is required at each level of intensity to win. This is Toffler's case. Future war is presented as combinations of First-Wave (primitive, hand-to-hand), Second-Wave (industrial, mass-production), and Third-Wave (knowledge-based, computer) warfare. The United States is declaring that it will employ what is required to prevail, rapidly. The old terminology has become inadequate.[11]

New terms are necessary. One has already appeared as planning and employment guidance in the *National Military Strategy*—forward-presence operations. It expands the range of military activities as it addresses combating drugs and humanitarian assistance:

> **Combating Drugs**—The detection and significant reduction of the production and trafficking of illegal drugs is a high-priority, national security mission of our armed forces. . . . A comprehensive program for attacking the flow of drugs—at the source and in transit—has been established. . . . The military . . . will encourage and assist other nations to develop aggressive efforts and capabilities necessary to stem the flow of drugs.
>
> **Humanitarian Assistance**—Not only must our forces be prepared to provide humanitarian aid, but, as seen recently in Northern Iraq, in some cases they must also be prepared to engage in conflict in order to assist and protect those in need.[12]

The nature of forward-presence operations is summed up as the *National Military Strategy* discusses the four general categories of operations requiring combatant commander-in-chief (CINC) planning. *Inter alia*, CINCs will need to "actively employ resources on a day-to-day basis to build military and alliance readiness; foster stability; promote peace, democracy, human rights, and the rule of law; protect lives and property; help our friends, allies, and those in need of humanitarian aid . . ."[13]

This is a broad charter. The United States seems prepared to assist selected nations in promoting "peace, democracy, human rights, and the rule of law." In return, we would presumably hope to receive general support in achieving our regional goals. Using the precedent of Operation Desert Storm, international support could include financial aid to execute regional contingencies. Some could see forward-presence operations as unwelcome military violations of national sovereignties, as the United States was so accused when conducting internal development operations in the sixties. These operations, however, seem no more invasive than are national economic operations by a global corporation to gain a market share or information penetration by CNN of the national media. Times have changed.[14] The strategy reflects well the changing world. How should landpower take advantage of this fact?

To answer this, we need to look into probable requirements and the needed "toolbag" of military capabilities, as aptly expressed by General Powell during Operation Desert Shield. What should the "adaptive planning

process" consider? There are several new ground rules that appear absolutely certain to govern future landpower operations. Based on the declared
strategy, tempered by Weinberger's practical, political guidance, adaptive
planning should assume that:

1. *The Army will not engage in major contingency operations without
   drawing upon individual soldiers or units from the reserves. Partial
   mobilization is a "given." The restraint will be whether or not requisite
   reserve unit capability is constituted and trained.* Mobilization is no
   longer a question; the political consensus required before a national
   military commitment will ensure political support to mobilization—
   as it did for Desert Shield. Les Aspin, chairman of the House Armed
   Services Committee, made this point well in a recent report on reserve
   forces: "The need for this principle (support of the populace before
   presidential commitment of force) is as great today as in the past. The
   prospect of a professional military available for foreign adventures
   without widespread public engagement is not one which America nor
   its full-time military is comfortable."[15] The issue is the size and mission
   capability of the constituted force. Dependent on the affordability of
   active forces, even lesser contingencies may require substantial reserve
   call-ups to ensure rapid, decisive victory.
2. *The Army will not deploy without interservice support even to the
   small unit level. "Joint" is not a slogan. Just as heavy, light, and special
   operating forces will fight together, so will elements from one or more
   services when a military force deploys for regional contingency operations.* The unique characteristic of knowledge-based combat is the
   synergistic focus of all national resources, including those of other executive departments, to achieve decisive results. That is what reorganization of the national defense structure (Goldwater-Nichols) is all
   about.
3. *Most, if not all, Army operations will be combined with allied elements present in tactically significant numbers performing some essential combat, combat-support, or combat-service-support operations.*
   The United States cannot afford, politically or economically, regional
   contingency operations without allies. Rapid, convincing victory
   through "overwhelming force" is certain to require allied support to
   achieve the necessary preponderance of military power.

Now, what are the requirements? *Where* would we be likely to commit
landpower? Consider some representative situations that might provoke regional contingencies or forward-presence operations. These are notional;
individually, they may seem fanciful, but, collectively, they portray a range
of threats well beyond those envisaged as of low, mid-, and high intensity
during the cold war.

• *Endemic global instability.* Regional and local violence is increasing as ethnic, religious, and racial tensions abound after the cold war. The breakup of the Russian "empire," with twenty of twenty-three borders contested in one manner or another, is the most immediate example of erupting regional and local conflicts that were suppressed during the cold war. It is less a disintegration of the existing world order than a reemergence of old tensions previously restrained by force. Consistent, however, with the acceleration of events characteristic of the information age, the pace quickens. That is dangerous. The most recent collapse comparable to that of the Soviets, the Ottoman Empire, took decades. Conflict such as the ethnic war dividing Yugoslavia appears virtually inevitable in the former Soviet Union.

It seems reasonable to assume that future relations between states and nations will be more rather than less acrimonious as ethnic and religious differences intensify and as they are communicated more effectively. People become more assertive in expecting that "their" group will be recognized in the local order when their grievances are fanned by hyper-communications.

But increasing local or regional conflict, which appears certain in both Europe and Asia, does not presage increased U.S. landpower intervention unless publicly acknowledged threats occur directly to the national interest. The Weinberger injunction seems relevant today. The United States might conceivably intervene to secure strategic nuclear missile sites in a renegade republic or region of the former Soviet Union. But, other than in explicit response to a direct strategic threat, U.S. intervention appears unlikely—no more Siberia expeditions. Only the Middle East with its oil looms as a credible trigger to U.S. involvement. Other nations may intervene locally, unilaterally or multilaterally, to rescue threatened ethnic neighbors if emerging alliances flex their military muscle, but there would seem to be few that pass the Weinberger test for U.S. intervention.[16]

Nevertheless, the prudent planner might select several likely regional scenarios where some landpower involvement would be plausible:

• *Overturning revolution from within.* Coups in Central America condemned by the Organization of American States could lead to a multilateral intervention. Alternatives abound in Africa (Organization of African States intervention), or the Balkans (NATO or WEU [Western Economic Union] or perhaps European Community [EC] intervention).

• *Stopping religious and ethnic violence.* There are potential bloodbaths on the periphery of the former Soviet Union. The plight of the Kurds was evident in Operation Desert Storm. Now they could be assailed in Iraq, Iran, or Turkey, requiring multilateral, humanitarian support of much larger scale than Operation Provide Comfort during the Persian Gulf War.

• *Peacemaking,* or imposing peace in a fragmenting state undergoing civil war such as Yugoslavia.

- *Peacekeeping,* or maintaining peace during an uneasy truce. The mission of numerous UN forces over the years, peacekeeping has been most recently considered for Cambodia and Yugoslavia.[17]

- *National stresses imposed by the international economy.* New international tensions will arise, based on global economies mixing with traditional industrial and preindustrial economies, as all compete for markets with traditional national work forces. Many more vital economic decisions may be taken out of local hands as the global economy expands. If democracy continues to spread, there will be additional national and local pressures on governments to support local needs or grievances that may be potentially counter to global understandings.

Toyota and Honda appear honorable in carrying out their obligations to American workers in their U.S. manufacturing facilities. But what about the Bank of Credit and Commerce International (BCCI) causing local bankruptcies yet remaining immune to regulation from its nominal host country? Could military action be appropriate if economic or legal sanctions fail? What if the U.S. savings and loans fiasco of the early nineties had been caused by an international, foreign financial industry? These situations should be resolved by economic or legal actions, not military. But what about predatory trading practices such as an embargo of the oil trade? The Japanese found that intolerable in 1940. The United States came to the same conclusion in the Gulf in 1990. In each case landpower was brought to bear in major operations.

- *Information* itself promises to stimulate tensions in new ways. The global language of American-English has become the general business language. Corporations based in non–English-speaking countries have adopted English as their business language. French uneasiness about the spread of the use of English will reach new heights now that the new Disneyland-France has opened. English seems to dominate the information-processing and entertainment industries. Effective rioters now print their grievance signs in English for the "world market," as was done recently in Beijing and Moscow. These are not frivolous issues. American culture is world-dominant—a considerable economic and social advantage. These are vexing but not fighting sorts of issues.

Other areas associated with the information revolution may be less harmless. Could preserving communications "lanes" become the modern version of protecting sea lanes, with appropriate military significance? Satellites and major communications nodes are developing increasing economic importance. The General Agreement on Tariffs and Trade (GATT) negotiates piracy of copyrights and other "gold" of the information age. As the flow of information accelerates emerging global markets, serious national interests are certain to be threatened. What if a renegade state began to pirate valuable software as state policy? Would that piracy constitute

grounds for unilateral or multilateral intervention? Economic conflict appears certain; military conflict may follow.

• *The international ecology* is another matter entirely. Another Chernobyl in an Eastern European nuclear facility would stimulate grave international concern. Uncontrolled nuclear fallout could mold international "consensus" for the use of force, if necessary, under UN or regional mandate to preserve the international ecology. Imagine the collapse of a Hungarian reactor, followed by uncontrolled fallout across national borders, then local rioting and mass population movements to avoid the fallout. This is a grim yet possible scenario. Few civilian agencies have the capability and discipline to handle a crisis of this magnitude. Earthquake experience, challenging as it has been, is simple by comparison.

• *Gross disparities in social or economic status* provide great potential for strife with possible landpower involvement. Different standards of living (exacerbated by comparisons on global TV) create potential for mass migrations wholly destructive to national standards of living. Migration flows could be North Africans into western Europe, Russians into Poland, Albanians into Italy, eastern Europeans into the European Community. Vietnamese boat people, Kurds, Croatians—the list grows. Mass population movements create both local and national tensions. Russian Jews fleeing to Israel have created a new strategic situation in the Middle East. Migration impacts would be primarily political, economic, and cultural, but there could be military need to reinforce the rule of law and to distribute resources.

When mass migrations add to serious economic dislocation such as unemployment and serious inflation, budding democracies are threatened. The world has been in the same spot before in the twenties in Germany. Timely contingency interventions could become necessary to restrain adventurous totalitarian regimes created out of the frustrations of economic and political uncertainty.

Another manifestation of gross economic and social disparity is the international drug trade. Current Department of Defense (DoD) drug-suppression efforts demonstrate what can be accomplished by peacetime activities in forward-presence operations. Extensive military support to domestic law enforcement and external aid to foreign governments appear to be effective efforts. The so-called drug war is more than fighting an agreed internal threat to national well-being. DoD involvement in drug suppression is, in fact, military involvement in support of national and international efforts to eliminate crime organized beyond the capabilities of conventional law enforcement. Operation Just Cause itself could be seen as a massive military effort in law enforcement in support of the Departments of State and Justice, necessary because government itself had been corrupted.

• Last but perhaps most serious in maintaining international stability is the *proliferation of arms,* which can take many forms. The most dangerous threat is from weapons of mass destruction created by a rogue state in violation of international agreement. The best and worst example is Iraq. International persuasion has proved ineffective. Intrusive onsite inspection by UN agencies supported by the United States revealed massive Iraqi deception and violation. Iraqi chemical and nuclear threats are chilling examples of the results of inadequate international safeguards and the many difficulties of conducting effective inspections. Even after decisive military conflict to ensure generally open ground access, intrusive inspection has been extremely difficult. This is primarily a political issue, but military expertise and rapid-intervention capability seem essential factors for successful inspection.

The danger is not limited to so-called special weapons—nuclear, bacteriological, and chemical. The computer promises dramatic upgrades in capability, which can be retrofitted clandestinely to old military equipment or even to "nonmilitary" items. The United States has extensive programs to make modular improvements to equipment. Over thirty different warhead packages are possible for the multiple launch rocket system (MLRS). The Abrams tank has been upgraded modularly in gun, armor, and vetronics (vehicle electronics). Some improvements can be quite difficult to detect, such as internal reconfigurations to permit adding power, cooling, and, eventually, unanticipated weapons to a basic combat vehicle.

Improvements extend to commercial equipment that innovative armies have discovered ways to upgrade. Antitank guided missiles (ATGM) on Toyota trucks were effective in Chad. Hellfire missiles also can be launched from a truck. MLRS can be fitted to a variety of transport. Effective use will be governed by doctrine, training, and maintenance—the traditional criteria of military success. The end result, however, is unsettling. There are many effective "poor man's weapons" that could appear in a broad range of conflict scenarios.

This has been an extensive list, reflecting a remarkable breadth of challenges. Many political, economic, ecological, and social tensions emerge to further expand the broadening array of possible military threats. And prospects of unwelcome surprise seem excellent, caused by unexpected technological advances or unanticipated applications of existing technologies. Unforeseen combinations of primitive, industry- and knowledge-based conflict (First-, Second-, and Third-Wave warfare) appear likely. All in all, requirements for landpower seem to be a growth industry in the post–cold war era. The capability "toolbag" will have to be formidable. It is to that "toolbag" that we now turn.

Doctrine is the generator of landpower tactics, organizations, equipment, and training. Doctrine makes possible the Army's role in war. That

role is defined as ". . . to apply maximum combat power against the enemy center of gravity and through swift, synchronized joint and combined action to destroy the enemy's will to resist."[18] In effect, doctrine is the source of the "toolbag" of capabilities available to support national military strategy. The current version of AirLand Battle doctrine was articulated in 1986 after almost fifteen years' gestation.

> AirLand Battle doctrine describes the Army's approach to generating and ap-
> plying combat power at the operational and tactical levels. It is based on se-
> curing or retaining the initiative and exercising it aggressively to accomplish
> the mission. The object of all operations is to impose our will upon the en-
> emy—to achieve our purposes. To do this, we must throw the enemy off bal-
> ance with a powerful blow from an unexpected direction, follow up rapidly
> to prevent his recovery and continue operations aggressively to achieve the
> higher commander's goals. The best results are obtained when powerful blows
> are struck against critical units or areas whose loss will degrade the coherence
> of enemy operations in depth, and thus most rapidly and economically accom-
> plish the mission. From the enemy's point of view, these operations must be
> rapid, unpredictable, violent, and disorienting. The pace must be fast enough
> to prevent him from taking effective counteractions.[19]

Four basic tenets govern execution of the doctrine: initiative, agility, depth, and synchronization. "Initiative means setting or changing the terms of bat-tle by action," forcing ". . . the enemy to conform to our operational pur-pose and tempo while retaining our own freedom of action." Agility is ". . . the ability of friendly forces to act faster than the enemy. . . . Depth is the extension of operations in space, time, and resources. . . . Synchronization is the arrangement of battlefield activities in time, space, and purpose to produce maximum relative combat power at the decisive point."[20] All in all, this doctrine is a rather good description of what happened in both Oper-ations Just Cause and Desert Storm. A thoughtful participant in Desert Storm commented that ". . . this form of warfare elevates the tactics of fire and movement to a new structure of warfare where the integration and synchronization of redundant, multiservice war-fighting systems results in simultaneous attack on the enemy throughout his entire depth." That is Third-Wave war.[21]

Operations Just Cause and Desert Storm were the proof of the doc-trine, now in the process of revision. New technologies and experience in two contingency theater campaigns counsel change.

The revised doctrine—once AirLand Battle Future, now AirLand Op-erations—has been evolving for several years. As it matures, it appears to extend the basic tenets of AirLand Battle to take advantage of new tech-nologies, particularly at division echelon and below.[22] Future operations are grouped in four stages: detection-preparation; establish conditions for de-cisive operations; decisive operations; and reconstitution. The intent is to open up the battlefield to favor more nonlinear (maneuver) operations,

much as operations proceeded in Desert Storm. As it continues to mature, the new doctrine should be influential in shaping further requirements for organizational change, new equipment, and revised training. Cost may be a stumbling block. A recent description of the doctrine by one of the authors is revealing in its reference to knowledge-based Third-Wave war:

> Besides being more open and fluid, future battlefields will also be much more lethal. Ironically, the growth in lethality relates less to the enhanced capabilities of direct-fire systems than it does *to the tremendous advances in the ability of military forces to acquire information about the enemy; to fuse and distribute it on a real-time basis; and to engage high-value targets at great distances with exceptional accuracy.* With these capabilities, any force, friend or foe, whether deployed in position for a significant time or on the move, can be detected and attacked well before it gets within direct-fire range.[23]

With different words, this doctrinal expression could describe the emerging global economy: ". . . *to the tremendous advances in the ability of military forces (global industry) to acquire information about the enemy (market); to fuse and distribute it on a real-time basis; and to engage high-value targets (niche market opportunities) at great distances with exceptional accuracy.*" Obviously, the analogy cannot be pushed too far. These are two different activities, although the aggressive businessman sometimes uses combat terms to describe a highly competitive business opportunity. Nonetheless, it does suggest the possible applications of some post-industrial business lessons learned in adapting to the global corporation in the world market. After all, use of landpower is also adapting to a new world market (regional contingencies and forward-presence operations).

Pursue the comparison. As landpower strategists contemplate change to support the new *National Military Strategy* in the information age, there may be provocative parallels to the automotive industry, since it has addressed similar changes. U.S. industry's "Big Three"—General Motors, Ford, and Chrysler—have been accused of high production costs, inadequate quality, sluggish market responsiveness (infrequent model changes), and general indifference to the consumer. They have been rapidly losing their market share to a knowledgeable buyer who votes with his feet to go elsewhere. "Elsewhere" is often to the Japanese automobile producer. The Japanese auto industry provides generally lower cost, steady quality, frequent model changes, and intense concern about customer satisfaction. They are clearly winning in the United States and are about to challenge the European Community.[24]

Now, what about adapting landpower to dramatic change in the world security situation or military "market"? Current U.S. landpower is configured to handle a conventionally defined market consisting of low-, mild-, or high-intensity conflict. The basic "product" is the division—a group of combat, combat-support, and combat-service-support capabilities

designed to cope with almost any anticipated or unanticipated military market requirement. Since most of the market share has been in NATO, the product is generally configured to win in past European, mid-intensity scenarios. Because the world market can vary greatly, some variety is provided here. The Army can offer armored, mechanized, infantry, light infantry, airborne, and air assault divisions, as well as assorted special forces, all in various combinations of light and heavy forces. To respond to unanticipated requirements, landpower has also developed packages of supporting units, generally sized to support a deployed corps, all prepackaged in advance. While not matched to any specific situation, there is enough general capability to hold on in the contingency area until tailored reinforcements can develop the superiority to win. Most packages today were configured for past NATO requirements. They seemed responsive to the new requirements of Desert Storm but were not tested for months. This luxury of time to modify the force to local requirements probably will not be available in the future.

I suggest, however, that this process has about the same market responsiveness to changing opportunities and challenges as does that of the traditional U.S. automobile industry, which has been basically designed looking inward to organizational imperatives rather than outward to changing consumer (market) desires. It is hoped that landpower will not meet the same fate. Let us return to the kinds of situations previously discussed that could provoke regional contingencies or forward-presence operations, like establishing order after another Chernobyl. Corps- or division-force packages do not seem to be a particularly efficient answer to many of these contingency requirements, yet we postulate that such contingencies will dominate in the future. To be sure, landpower must be prepared to fight and win unilaterally against capable landpower formations anywhere in the world in joint operations. Large multipurpose corps (JTF) and division formations are required, but are they enough? I believe not. They are a necessary but not sufficient relic of the industrial age.

An answer to the many diverse military needs (niche markets) of the post-industrial age lies in finer tuning of landpower contingency-response capability. Complement the general all-purpose utility of the division with very precise, deployable combat power in the form of battlefield operating system (BOS) force packages tailored for explicit contingency requirements. Just as dominant world industry (Baldrige Award-class) knows that it must attack highly segmented markets with precise quality the first time, so must landpower be prepared to provide rapidly very precise, tailored capability, not only to respond but to overwhelm. An example:

- *Contingency*: IRBM-Scud threat to an ally, Israel.
- *Traditional Response* (Second Wave): a brigade or division, reinforced with corps-support Patriots deployed to Israel.
- *Information Age Response* (Third Wave): one or more Patriot battalions, with appropriate command and control and combat-service

support, rapidly deployed from the Army in Europe to Israel. This was the excellent response on Operation Desert Shield, the first post-industrial major contingency.
* *Information Age*⁺ *Response* (Third Wave): predesignated Patriot units, to provide area as well as point defense, with modular additions capable of handling known, regional air-defense threats. The units are trained to be integrated into the regional air-defense structure. They are joined en route by preassigned soldiers conversant with the local language. The unit may or may not be assigned to a corps troop list, but it knows that it is an elite air-defense entity, with mission-planning responsibilities for one or more regional contingency areas. It could be an active or reserve unit.

Now we are looking into the capability "toolbag" in detail. Using adaptive planning, we just generated a rather specific requirement. The key is not relating contingency force packages solely to the all-purpose unit (Second Wave), but rather to the functional capability or BOS (Third Wave), which will be required for particular contingencies.[25] The new AirLand Operations concept seems to appreciate this new opportunity and force the challenge:

> *Combined and Joint Operations.* Combined operations occur either within the framework of traditional alliances or in emerging coalitions. The latter is characterized by diversity of doctrine, levels of readiness, and equipment, especially where a high/low technology mix exists; or where requirements for liaison augmentation of combat/combat service support (CS/CSS), command, control and communications (C³), and fire support will stress our abilities. Plans must optimize the strengths of each partner, and avoid duplication, which suboptimizes the total force capability.[26]

That is the doctrinal requirement. Recent practice confirms its importance. In a well-documented series of articles on Desert Shield, the *Army Times* described the initial defense challenges faced by XVIII Corps in September 1990:

> One solution [to ground defense] was to try to bolster the Saudi forces covering the border, and in September, the Corps expanded its operations planning to try to coordinate with the Marines and the Royal Saudi Land Force—the Saudi regular army—and the Saudi National Guard. . . . The Saudis recognized their land forces were neither equipped nor trained to conduct the main fight. *The US concepts of combined and joint warfare were light years beyond Saudi practices—as they were to prove with other allies—and required liaison teams, largely consisting of Army Special Forces, to coordinate fire, close air support and command and control measures.*[27]

Later the series describes "parking" allied contingents at King Khalid Military City ". . . safely out of the line of fire."[28] For the policies outlined in the *National Military Strategy* (1992) to succeed, allies clearly must go from uncertain liability to welcome strength. Thoughtful focus on battlefield

functional responsibilities may assist. The BOS concept is central to an understanding of coalition-war requirements. It is described well in the Army capstone training manual:

> The seven battlefield operating systems (BOS) are used to systematically ensure that all elements of the organization's combat power are directed toward accomplishing the overall mission. BOS are the major functions which occur on the battlefield and must be performed by the force to successfully execute operations. The systems are as follows:
>
> * Maneuver.
> * Fire support.
> * Command and control.
> * Intelligence.
> * Mobility/survivability.
> * Combat service support.
> * Air defense.[29]

The sum of potential requirements is contained in these seven functions. Of course, prudence would dictate that several functions would have to be represented in most force packages in some degree, but *the basic building block for regional contingency operations and forward-presence operations could be the function, not the unit.* To return to the Israeli air-defense example above: if the threat had been greater, the air defense could have consisted of enough Patriot battalions, national intelligence units (intelligence BOS), theater command and control (command and control BOS), and logistics (combat-service-support BOS) to be designated as an air-defense division (Middle East) when activated for contingency employment.

Another example of the need for functional capabilities could be a massive nuclear accident in Eastern Europe, a Hungarian "Chernobyl." Here, the requirement might be five or six engineer heavy (construction) battalions, a composite NBC (nuclear, biological, chemical) reconnaissance and decontamination battalion, two battalions of military police, and four mobile hospitals. With appropriate command and control and combat-service support, this could be an engineer division (nuclear accident). Similar such troop lists could be prepared for the other requirements suggested above.

The logic does not necessarily end with smaller contingencies or forward-presence operations. By similar process, combat and combat support could be furnished for major contingencies. Ground maneuver units were critical to success in Operation Desert Storm. U.S. conventional deployment planning quickly put airborne infantry units on the ground—"speed bumps," as they were labeled in the *Army Times*. These units were reinforced as rapidly as possible with maneuver aviation and fire support. Basically, units were reinforced by BOS. To approach the problem a bit differently, perhaps the original wave could have been maneuver (Apaches),

fire support (MLRS), and CSS (logistic support for Apaches and MLRS), with appropriate command and control and local security—all initially supporting Marines landed by seapower. Needed BOS can be formed into ad hoc units, based on the specific requirement as it occurs. Not only does this concept provide greater flexibility to respond to various regional contingencies, but also, it has U.S. landpower providing joint and combined support to allies in areas where landpower has a clear advantage.[30]

The U.S. Army today has the "toolbag" to provide remarkable Third-Wave capabilities. Doctrine is solid; it is war-tested. The concept-based requirements system (CBRS) has produced organizations, equipment, and training designed to boost the individual and synergistic effects of the various BOS. The Army has superb people. Competence-basing and liberal immigration policies permit the Army to match virtually any language, ethnic, or racial characteristics in a contingency area with competent leaders of the same characteristics. Then, the combat training centers can add the mission-related training. They can provide tough, realistic analogs of likely contingency requirements to test new combinations of BOS blended into contingency-specific units. Such training facilitates the assimilation of innovative applications of BOS combinations by imaginative leaders. These are confident, competent leaders, assured because they have been able "to fight" the various combinations in realistic situations before deployment.

This solid potential, in being able to respond rapidly with a high-quality product, to very specific contingency (market) requirements, describes success in a prospering global corporation. The responsibilities of landpower are far more serious than those of commerce, involving service to death and national survival. It is encouraging, nevertheless, to see how landpower has already most of the components required for executing regional contingency and peacetime activities in the information age. The challenge is to shift conceptual gears from industrial-age units mass-produced to precise application of battle functions, focused in time and space, to achieve specific results in joint and combined contingency operations. Some would say that is precisely what was envisaged in AirLand Battle doctrine. The analogy is not football; it is soccer.[31]

The how, when, what, and where of regional contingencies and forward presence have been discussed in some detail. The "toolbag" has been described sufficiently to illustrate new concepts. It seems clear that the Army today has most of the components necessary to make the plans outlined in the new *National Military Strategy* work. There are a number of policy actions that would have to be taken to make the concepts real. Several included here further describe the kinds of actions required; they are mostly initiatives in the combined area, as both Army and joint planners are actively pursuing new alternatives.

- Expand military coordination mechanisms in the United Nations, structured under the direct guidance of the United Nations itself and

by various international regional organizations created under the
auspices of the UN Charter. It would seem sensible to have all the
world covered by regional security organizations, as originally envisaged after World War II.[32]

- Consolidate and expand existing UN and regional (such as NATO
  and the Organization of American States) military standardization
  agreements to encourage common techniques and procedures, particularly for command and control and combat-service support.
- Confirm English as the global language for peacekeeping, as it is for
  commerce.
- Develop common protocols appropriate to new operational techniques involved in intra- and inter-BOS coordination. For example,
  is there a UN or regional standard operating procedure (SOP) to
  coordinate ground-air attack—a joint air attack (JATT) transformed
  into combined air attack (CATT)? There would appear to be similar
  need for SOPs for other collateral, multi-BOS operations. Thoughtful review of former Warsaw Pact protocols is probably necessary
  to ensure that new procedures are as simple and effective as possible
  across military cultures.
- Encourage BOS specialization by state or region. This is a very sensitive area but, clearly, there are some functions best accomplished
  by certain nations. Should ground rules be established by the UN
  Military Committee?

Another group of issues relates to applying the Army concept-based
requirements system (CBRS) toward improving Army readiness to execute
the new national military strategy. First and foremost, there is a need to
restructure landpower analytical capability to relate to regional tensions. At
present, other than a general threat orientation to the former Soviet Union,
there are no focused means to ensure integrated application of the CBRS to
likely regional contingencies in support of the various CINCs or potential
allied commanders. Excellent regional training facilities have been created
for army leaders in South and Central America in the School of the Americas, formerly in Panama, and in the InterAmerican Defense College located
in Washington, D.C. Similar theoretical and practical military training and
education could be developed for other regions.

The heart of CBRS rests in integrating responsibilities of the U.S.
Army Combined Arms Center at Fort Leavenworth, Kansas. It may be useful to create regional institutes at Fort Leavenworth, tied to regional special
operating forces (SOF) groups, to provide area expertise. Regional institutes
could also assess, as an element of contingency planning, national military
comparative ability of potential allies by battlefield function. In a multinational force, national contributions would take advantage of national military strengths. For example, the United States clearly has dominant

intelligence capabilities, and the U.S. contribution would exploit this fact. Then, if the planning results in an actual contingency operation, SOF could facilitate the introduction of BOS into the particular region. This could be quite similar to SOF training responsibilities with allies in Operation Desert Shield.

The issue here is not regional alignment, as during the cold war, but the development of local military associations in step with political, economic, and social "realities" of the information age as they evolve in these places. While the focus here is landpower, clearly seapower and airpower should have similar concerns. Some mechanism seems necessary to provide joint focus.

The issue of social "realities" is particularly important and sensitive. U.S. landpower is an outstanding model of the institutional change sought by people in most nations. The global "victory" of democracy underscores the importance of the Army's (particularly SOF's) role in encouraging competence and developing equal opportunity. Because forward-presence operations seem to offer great peacetime opportunities, an institutional structure would be needed to focus these efforts.

In sum, as we move into the post-industrial age, the opportunities for landpower in coalition operations are genuinely exciting. And the Army is already more prepared than its soldiers may realize.

PART II

LANDPOWER FOR THE
LONG TERM

3　A Total Force

S USTAINING LANDPOWER OVER THE LONG TERM IS PER-
petually challenging in a democracy normally preoccupied with political,
economic, or social issues. Defense is expected to "be there" when called
but, otherwise, generally out of sight and out of mind. But when defense *is*
needed, the public expects almost immediate military readiness. Generating
a rapid response really has not been a problem since the forties. World War
II and the cold war period demanded that a major landpower capability be
kept available for unforeseen contingencies. Despite the past fifty years,
however, ready landpower remains an aberration in our military history.
Traditionally, when crises pass, the nation's landpower is disarmed.

The post–World War II capability, generated by the Soviet threat and
generally kept strong by forward-deployed troops in western Europe, was
exceedingly useful in providing a significant source of landpower readily
available for emergency deployment elsewhere. This capability served well
in multiple crises: Lebanon in the fifties; Vietnam in the sixties; Israeli support after the Yom Kippur War in the seventies; Grenada and Panama in
the eighties; and Seventh Corps, from the NATO force to the Persian Gulf,
in the nineties. All came out of the deployed cold war "reserve" of readily
available active forces. Now we seem about to return to the historical level
of interwar inattention to defense issues. The comforting "cushion" of a
deployed, ready active force to meet contingencies—no matter varying public interest—is disappearing. Yet, the list of possible trouble spots grows.
How can we justify, then sustain, the needed landpower capability? Clearly,
the answer lies in a combination of active and reserve forces, the Total
Force, which would be sustained in the future with fewer forces.

Some decline in resources is certain. What is the likely reduction? The general trend is for less support following the "high" of Operation Desert Storm and the demise of the Soviet Union. The initial glide path is an overall 25 percent reduction during a five-year period; this was established during the dissolving of the Soviet empire but before the fragmentation of the Russian empire. Now, another, steeper glide path appears certain. After the 1992 U.S. elections, politicians of both major parties see in the Department of Defense a surplus of world-class military power that can be drawn down safely as the nation turns its energies to solving economic and social problems. One hopes that there will be left in the arsenals of the world enough capability to control rogue states, such as Iraq. But to politicians and people preoccupied with other issues, military sufficiency, despite increased defense cuts, seems a reasonable expectation for a clearly competent military bureaucracy to meet.

We the people, however, intuitively know the result: less defense capability than enjoyed at present. So the current challenge for U.S. and other democracies, therefore, is determining what to discard and what to retain. What essential deterrent forces must be maintained immediately available (as little as is prudent), and what forces can be relegated to a less ready, less costly position (as much as is possible)?

Traditional landpower backup has been reserves, now institutionalized in the United States as the Total Force, composed of units and individual replacements in state and territorial National Guards and in the U.S. Army Reserve. Abiding uneasiness about day-to-day readiness of reserve units was tempered by the realization that there would be a cushion of time before the units would actually deploy.

The logic was compelling: ready active forces would go first, and endemic shortages in strategic air- and sealift would place all deployments on a phased and lengthy schedule to respond to force requirements generated by an elaborate war plan.[1] Rigorous, detailed planning ensued to coordinate the deployment, manning, equipment, and training required to bring units to war-fighting readiness. This deliberate, time-phased, unit mobilization schedule is the successful product of the industrial age, very much in the model of the traditional production line but, in this application, turning out military units rather than cars or refrigerators. National mobilization policy essentially consisted of "business as usual" in peacetime, then with crisis, turning on the production line. Eventually, sufficient numbers of capable units come "off the line" to fight and win.

But that is not the model of knowledge-based Third-Wave war envisaged by U.S. doctrine, at least in the early stages. The *National Military Strategy* calls for rapid, precise, overwhelming force—air-, sea-, and landpower—to be applied in crisis-response operations anywhere in the world against a broad range of regional contingencies or forward-presence oper-

ations. With the national strategy so defined, the Total Force needs reshaping; it must cover near-term contingencies requiring overwhelming force and meet the long-term production-line requirement now defined as reconstitution. *The National Security Strategy of the United States* and the *National Military Strategy* documents address both. After it acknowledges the success of the Total Force policy over the cold war years, the *National Security Strategy* (1992) charts a course that would rely primarily on highly ready active forces, at least for most crisis-response contingency operations.

> Over time we will move to a Total Force that permits us to respond initially to any regional contingency with units—combat and support—drawn wholly from the active component except for a limited number of support and mobility assets. Since many support functions can be more economically maintained in the reserve components, we will still rely on reserve support units in any extended confrontation. The primary focus of reserve combat units will be to supplement active units in any especially large or protracted deployment. To hedge against a future need for expanded forces to deal with a renewed global confrontation which—though possible is less likely and clearly less immediate than previously calculated—some reserve combat units will be retained in cadre status.
>
> This approach will allow us to maintain a Total Force appropriate for the strategic and fiscal demands of a new era: a smaller, more self-contained and very ready active force able to respond quickly to emerging threats; and a reduced but still essential reserve component with emphasis on supporting and sustaining active combat forces and—in particularly large or prolonged regional contingencies—providing latent combat capability that can be made ready when needed.[2]

Note the critical assumption that active combat forces will be sufficiently large to handle most contingencies. In the overarching *National Security Strategy* (1992), the reserves are clearly relegated to a subordinate combat role. The *National Military Strategy* is restrained on the issue of reserves. Reference is limited to indicating the numbers of Army Reserve divisions in the base force. In discussing the base force, it does acknowledge that regional contingency forces ". . . will be drawn in large part from the active components, with essential support from the reserve components. If these crises become larger or more protracted, we will increasingly rely upon the reserve components."[3] This is confirmed by the substantial role of the reserves in Operation Desert Shield, particularly in combat support and combat-service support. Of 539,000 people in-theater at peak strength, 303,000 were in the Army. More than 1,000 Army Reserve units of all types were called to active duty; 139,500 Army Reservists served worldwide— 74,000 in Southwest Asia in eight combat, 175 combat-support, and 509

combat-service-support units. At one time, 70 percent of the units assigned to the theater-support command were reserves.[4]

The *National Military Strategy* (1992) is more detailed in discussing the major land war hedge, reconstitution:

> FORCE RECONSTITUTION. As we reduce the size of our military force structure in response to the demise of the global threat, we must preserve a credible capability to forestall any potential adversary from competing militarily with the United States. This "Reconstitution" capability is intended to deter such a power from militarizing, and if deterrence fails, to provide a global warfighting capability. Reconstitution involves forming, training, and fielding new fighting units. This includes initially drawing on cadre-type units and laid-up military assets; mobilizing previously trained or new manpower; and activating the industrial base on a large scale. . . . Preserving the potential for expansion of air, ground, and maritime forces will require extraordinary foresight and political courage to lay away infrastructure, stockpile critical materials, protect the defense industrial base, sustain a cadre of quality leaders, and invest in basic science and high payoff technologies. . . .[5]

Reconstitution provides a welcome perspective to the Total Force. Extending well beyond constituted units to address the possibility of global world war, it stimulates a long-term view of national landpower policy. The implications of force reconstitution itself and the structure of landpower reserves, therefore, should be reexamined from this latest strategic perspective.[6]

Several aspects of the new strategy stand out. Minimizing any real need for combat reserve units in crisis operations, reserve force requirements focus on combat support and combat-service support for regional contingencies and peacetime operations. It remains to be seen whether the active combat units will be sufficient to handle likely contingencies. If not, reserves will have to supplement them. To the extent that the United States develops the ability to deploy functional BOS force packages to support knowledge-based Third-Wave war with allies, however, the reserves could still exercise a dominant role in contingency operations. The reserves maintain the preponderance of functionally oriented combat-support and combat-service-support units. Some 70 percent of support units are in the reserves. So, although the reserves may seem to fade into the background because their combat units will not be called, they can expect to be more, not less, active—perhaps even more so, if long-term force constitution and reconstitution are considered.

Looking to the future, a key question would seem to be how much active capability should be maintained as combat-ready in each area? Demanding active soldiers for all combat units and reservists for all combat-support units is an inappropriate oversimplification for Third-Wave war dominated by functional BOS capabilities. A sliding scale, based upon "best" AC/RC ratios for war fighting seems appropriate and necessary for

each battlefield operating system. The most politically acceptable ratio would probably be that most supportive of long-term force sustainment. This fact weighs the ratio to favor the reserves. Ready, active BOS capability is clearly necessary for the immediate readiness requirement. After that, acquiring, training, and sustaining long-term BOS capability could be the next highest active Army priority. Reserves may have to be ready much earlier than many believe today, particularly if the active percentage of Total Force BOS capabilities declines.

The second major change is more in the mindset than reality. Employment of the reserve components is no longer a major "go-no go" national decision. Partial mobilization and current reliance on reserves by all the military services may require some mobilization before contingency deployments, involving even relatively small tactical organizations, can occur. The deploying maneuver unit is only the "tip of the iceberg" when considering the formidable combat-support and combat-service-support units necessary for deployment. The range of reliance is so comprehensive because AirLand Battle doctrine stipulates that units being committed "to win" in combat require overwhelming support. This is the Weinberger injunction about national support being required before even lesser regional contingencies can be implemented. In other words, the United States is not going to commit forces unless vital national interests are involved and unless the nation supports such action. Then, we will engage with overwhelming force, to win, quickly and decisively.

With respect to reserves, the issue will be their constitution. To the layman, the question will be, are they ready? It will not be, should they be mobilized? Mobilization would not be an issue to an American public that has agreed to Uncle Sam's "going in." In fact, mobilization could be considered a positive indicator of American support as with appropriate media fanfare, citizen-soldiers are called up. Partial military mobilization may become a sought-after opportunity to meld national support for regional contingency operations. Mobilization then shifts from being an impediment to being an accelerator for decisive national action.[7]

Reserve landpower usefulness is not hostage to possessing ready major combat formations or to uncertainties about national decisions to mobilize. Both issues have been traditional concerns about reserves. In the new strategy, *reserve usefulness will be determined by contingency-ready, functional BOS capability organized in constituted units*. In other words, if you are concerned about reserve readiness to fight, do not worry about armor or infantry brigades. Worry about Apache attack helicopters, MLRS, maintenance units, or hospitals. Are they ready? Next, do not worry about timely mobilization. If the active force goes, partial mobilization will have already occurred. Debate should focus on how many of what kind of units will be constituted in peacetime to fight what kinds of regional contingencies with which BOS and when? These are new and rather different issues.

The new issues crop up when one looks at the Total Force from this perspective and considers the implications of the pragmatic adaptive planning model by the JCS, which generates ". . . a range of preplanned options, encompassing all the instruments of national power (diplomatic, political, economic, and military)"[8] for potential contingency situations. The Total Force may be quite different from what it is today, with such differences as rapid, almost perfunctory, transition through mobilization; task organization and deployment; ad hoc force composition seeking not only highly effective landpower capability but also deliberate component mix and a tailored composition by race, language, or ethnic background; designation of multicomponent, multifunctional organizations, trained for probable contingencies, and grouped by specific levels of readiness to deploy based upon days of notification before departure; and lastly, new cost-sharing rules for allocating Total Force expenses.

During the cold war, mobilization became a ritual almost to itself—an elaborate minuet—that allowed moving many units to NATO in a short reinforcing period. To European nations, conditioned for decades to look at mobilization as an integral step in going to war, it also demonstrated the seriousness of U.S. intentions. In fact, in the industrial age, mobilization was a military equivalent to setting up a new line for mass production. Operation Desert Shield was the proof of the system for all the services. Significant changes from the precontingency scenario were introduced while mobilization and deployment were under way. Times, destinations, and units, to include unforeseen allies, changed routinely. Finally, VII Corps—an absolute wild card in all planning—was added. The successful strategic deployment owed its success to solid prewar planning, highly professional people, and the data-processing capabilities of the information age.

The United States has demonstrated its ability to form new organizational configurations (task organizations) quickly and effectively on the move. This is precisely what is needed to respond to the broad range of requirements envisaged in the *National Military Strategy* (1992). The diversity of potential regional contingencies, combined with an adaptive planning process and the need to build up rapidly for quick, decisive victory, means that unanticipated change will be the rule, not the exception. In one smooth flow, units will have to mobilize, restructure dependent on BOS requirements in the contingency area, and deploy. The major variable in the deployment sequence for all constituted units, active and reserve, may be the steady peacetime readiness level declared for the unit. That is, time for final readiness preparations, from notification to deployment, will be the major factor driving readiness requirements between units. Improved by computers and explicit, verifiable, training to standard, the processes of mobilization, organization, and deployment should become routine.[9] This is a rather different way of looking at the Total Force, caused by the information age.

The range of potential contingency operations is extraordinary. Equating the array of possible commitments to comparable market possibilities in the world economy during the information age, landpower faces an almost infinite set of niche markets to master. Each contingency will have its own *METT-T*. Missions will arise across the range of doctrinal possibility. Enemies will be capable of fighting at the primitive, industrial, or post-industrial levels of war. The *Terrain* is global. *Time* will be always variable and usually limited; that is the challenge. The good news relates to *Troops* available. The Army now has the ability to tailor the force precisely in response to very different situations. The all-purpose unit can do all things well. Yet, in any given situation, it has an excess of capability. This is, of course, desirable for any commander uneasy about the unforeseen, which always seems to pop up. But in very precise situations, U.S. ability to "flood" the contingency with specific BOS capability appears to provide decisive information-age assistance to the force commander.[10] Sustained access to the contingency area by strategic transport would be essential, of course, to permit substituting or adding BOS, should that be necessary as the campaign develops. The point is to be able to tailor contingency forces by BOS as events require rather than to rely uniquely on the all-purpose, balanced-unit force of traditional, industrial-age war planning.

Tailoring a force extends to people. The training of precise individual tasks to standard, superior people and increasing the knowledge of team-building, or bonding, could permit ad hoc composition of units for contingencies as they occur. High-value personnel (world-class expertise) could be assigned en route to units.[11] Quickly bonded to the unit, they would ensure that the best individual skills in the Army are available to the contingency military force. The teamwork of cohesive teams, with each soldier confident of the ability and reliability of his fellow soldiers, is clearly very important, as it has been for centuries. But bonding has become easier. Competence-basing individual soldier development ensures common task training to a precise task, condition, and standard. The result has been a remarkable standardizing of soldier proficiencies. The bonding process has been studied intensely in recent policies and programs to improve unit cohesion. The combined result permits rapid team-building, as was evidenced in Operation Desert Shield.

Other criteria could govern. It may be appropriate to adjust the racial, gender, or ethnic balance in a unit or to assign personnel to increase linguistic proficiency in foreign languages. Note that what is described here is the extreme: constituting, then deploying a competance-based, functional capability, rather than a traditional, balanced combat unit. The objective is to smother the crisis with overwhelming superiority in selected functional areas to permit rapid, decisive victory. When seeking this "world-class" overkill, does it really make any difference whether that very valuable soldier or section or even platoon is active Army, National Guard, or Army

Reserve? Indeed, if we want the American people to be more attentive and supportive in a contingency crisis, perhaps trained citizen-soldiers should be called upon, instead of active soldiers who may be needed anyway for reconstitution. Often, citizen-soldiers have extensive experience from their civilian jobs and could serve as models for both military and civilians in the objective contingency area. Could the use of citizen-soldiers be preferred over that of regular soldiers? This is a rather different way of looking at the Total Force in the information age. As debate builds concerning the future active/reserve mix of the landpower force, these sorts of considerations should be weighed more heavily; but they will not be unless an information-age, reserve forces rationale is prepared.

The *National Military Strategy* (1992) mandates landpower poised to execute joint and combined regional contingency or peacetime operations. It seems essential that uniform ground rules be established to describe the readiness of formations. Clearly, it is neither necessary nor affordable to have all units ready for almost immediate deployment. Some must be instantly ready; other units may not be needed for several months. To permit rational allocation of resources, peacetime readiness assessments and resource needs should be related to days required of additional preparation (manning, training, equipping) before deployment for contingency operations. There is no distinction in support between active and reserve, so long as they are constituted units. As allocations have been made in the past, resource priority would go to those first to fight.

Some broad time bands seem necessary. The first, most ready level could be deployment in one to fifteen days. This seems unattainable for constituted reserve units, although it may be feasible for selected individuals or small detachments or by very high levels of full-time manning and increased training time. Another level could be deployment in fifteen to sixty days, consisting of mostly constituted active units but with some constituted reserve units in important, functional (BOS) packages, particularly combat-service support. The next level could be deployment in sixty to 180 days, consisting of mostly constituted reserves but with some unconstituted active units, such as school units not organized for war during peacetime. These would be programmed to deploy on the "second wave" of strategic transport. The last level could be 180 to 720 days, made up of constituted reserve units, such as the National Guard, some of which could be maintained more for state than federal service.[12] After 720 days, the force would consist of units or functional capabilities that would be reconstituted after the war began. Once these bands are established, divisions or corps with associated combat, combat support, and combat-service support would be composed entirely of units sharing the same readiness band. Similarly, based on staff analysis of various regional contingencies and adaptive planning, functional BOS packages could be composed of units sharing the same time-readiness level.

Landpower force requirements would be based not only on traditional unit contingencies, such as one or more corps-size joint task force sustained anywhere in ninety days, but also on functional contingencies. For example, consider air defense in a potential contingency. The following kinds of questions have to be addressed: How much joint air defense is required for the deployed U.S. forces? How much for allied forces deployed with us? How much residual air defense will be necessary to cover the unanticipated, such as protecting a targeted ally? Then, how much air defense *must* be active to meet deployment deadlines? The balance should be in the reserves. Analysis such as this, across the range of functional capabilities (BOS) and applied to possible contingencies, may demand new landpower capabilities, particularly when comparing our landpower advantage with that of our allies. More MLRS, AHIP/Apaches, Patriot, and command and control (multiple-subscriber equipment) support may be needed than the traditional, unit-based, force-generation process—the corps/Division "slice"—can currently justify.

Review of likely regional contingencies and peacetime operations may generate a more plausible functional landpower requirement than traditional, unit-based planning. Then, time-phasing deployment requirements will clearly show the advantages and risks associated with various active-reserve ratios, because it will be contingency based. As BOS requirements for support of U.S. landpower, joint support, and allied support are added to the range of possible contingencies discussed under "coalition conflict," there will be a substantial total. This sum may be more than appears necessary at present. This is another rather different way of looking at the Total Force in the information age.

The growing absolute and relative importance of reserves is apparent. There is an excellent case to be made that the United States—as a people, a democracy, a state, a nation, and most of a continent—has in its current landpower components a perfect blend of federal and state, national and regional, and professional and militia.[13] There is another equally compelling case to be made that reserves are less costly than active forces. Estimates vary, based on the specific characteristics of the unit, but savings range from 26 percent to 40 percent for comparable units.[14] During a period of reduced threat and severely constrained defense resources, it would seem cost-effective to rely more heavily on reserves. This may be true, but it really depends on how one costs out reserve support requirements.

First, there may not be practical alternatives. As the active force becomes smaller, it will be increasingly difficult to retain all of the skills essential to execute the highly effective but complex doctrine. High-value, gold-collar skills may not be attracted to full-time military service. The contribution of the reserves is already vital, with linguists, technical intelligence experts, and highly specialized engineers. As the force becomes smaller, the physical and psychic rewards of active service may be insufficient to retain

certain skills. Requirements for gold-collar personnel prepared for know-lege-based war go up as we foresee more coalition operations. Matching the unique requirements of "niche markets" in the international military environment by active personnel will be more difficult as the active force declines. It would seem prudent to analyze carefully the bank of skills that the active force can sustain and then move aggressively to capture projected shortages in the reserves.[15]

The cost-accounting rules could be modified to have reserve funding accounts "billed" directly, rather than carried as overhead for the active force. Assume the result of the force-requirements review by BOS develops a need for considerably more Patriots for allied support than can be justified for joint support during conventional joint task force (JTF) operations. Allied support could be put into the Guard, with enhanced full-time manning authorized to maintain fifteen- to sixty-day deployment readiness. Assume that 50 percent to 75 percent of the Total Force Patriot capability is in Guard units, aligned to contingency operations in the various regions. Today, the active force would directly "pay" for all of the institutional training structure and the very substantial development costs. Why not have some of those costs be borne by Guard funding, perhaps by separate title? This is another rather different way of looking at the Total Force in the information age.

These are five significant changes in the Total Force as we enter the information age: rapid transition through mobilization; task organization and deployment; ad hoc force composition, with highly functional land-power capability; deliberate components mix and tailored personnel composition; designation of multicomponent, multifunctional organizations grouped by levels of readiness; and new cost-sharing rules for allocating Total Force expenses. Adopting these policies could make a major impact on current policies and programs. They really open up new opportunities for innovation in the Total Force more suited for the information age. Other opportunities seem possible.

There are two real breakpoints in the time-based readiness: one, deployment in fifteen days or less; the other, deployment during the six-month to two-year window before reconstitution. In the first case, any company-size or larger unit would have to be active. There would hardly be time to conduct refresher training. In the latter case, there would seem to be considerable flexibility in the peacetime composition of the forces. Fifteen-day-readiness is the most ready end of the active Army–reserve mix; 180 days is the far end. One could designate forces in the fifteen- to 180-day window as ready forces. They are all constituted units with designated replacements from the Individual Ready Reserve—those discharged from active service within the preceding twelve to twenty-four months who have retained their skills. These ready-force units would conduct some individual skill training, such as weapons qualification or higher-echelon unit training after mobili-

zation. Unit funding would be federal, with state funding of some portion of the Guard—perhaps 10 percent? Individual replacement policy would remain as it was for Operation Desert Shield.

Units in the over-180-day category could be sustained in a far different manner. Training emphasis could be limited to individual skill training with most collective training conducted after mobilization. U.S. Army Reserve (USAR) focus would be on developing and sustaining proficient soldiers—blue-, white-, and gold-collar. While all supporting funding would be federal, USAR personnel with civilian-related skills could work until they mobilize for federal departments other than defense—such as education, housing and urban development, transportation, or interior—and be supported through those departments as they implement federal programs addressing important domestic needs. The Guard could focus on units maintained at varying levels of peacetime readiness. Some, not required for eighteen to twenty-four months, could be maintained at reduced strength and organized to support state needs. For these units, much of the funding could be state, with the ratio determined by whether the responsibility was federal or state. This could be the standby force—Guard units and Army reservists able to serve domestic needs, as they demonstrate the pride of landpower service across the United States.[16] This view is purely hypothetical. The point is that *National Military Strategy* (1992) indicates new ways to consider national military service. Reliance on old, unit-based precedents may preclude taking advantage of useful new opportunities.

Decisions to "band" unit readiness to create some form of variable readiness could open up a broad range of supporting policies. Based upon time to deployment, units could be focused on specific training-readiness ceilings. Units deploying in fifteen days would be mission-capable at premobilization. Reserve units deploying in sixty days should be proficient at all times to platoon level and higher for commanders and staffs, with proficiency validated by outside evaluation. At the next level, sixty- to 180-day units would sustain competent soldiers, sections, and crews before mobilization. The very-high-priority units could be funded for more training days, sustained at a higher level of full-time manning or maintained at higher overall strength. There would seem to be many possibilities once the general proposition of variable readiness and resultant variable resourcing is accepted.

Dual focus on a Total Force of combat unit–based forces, such as the corps joint task force represented by XVIII Corps in Operation Just Cause and function (BOS)-based forces represented by air-defense Patriot support to Israel in Operation Desert Storm, permits consideration of new ground rules for allocating capability between active and reserve components. The first decision rule is stated explicitly in the *National Military Strategy* (1992): "Our strategy for the 'come-as-you-are' arena of spontaneous, often unpredictable crises, requires fully-trained, highly-ready forces that are rap-

idly deliverable, and initially self-sufficient. Therefore, such forces must be drawn primarily from the active force structure, and tailored into highly effective joint task forces. . . ."[17] Presumably, the Army contribution to this force would be in the force-structure range of a light corps, a heavy corps (not committed simultaneously), and Army special operations forces, with doctrinally appropriate combat support and combat-service support. In effect, this force would be the unit core of the active Army.

Where the unit has highly civilian-related skills, it might be put it into the reserve components, unless it supports absolutely critical functional BOS requirements for fifteen-day readiness contingency forces or assists in reconstitution.

If the complexity of unit equipment causes rapid decay of skills, the unit should be active or, if reserve, have very high full-time manning.

If the unit's basic mission is to support very early deploying joint or allied forces, it should be an active unit.

If a capability is clearly required for the long term, such as acquiring new equipment, training, or sustaining the force, the personnel should be active.

Other constituted units or individual personnel would be reserve.

The active Army support structure, such as Training and Doctrine Command (TRADOC) and Army Materiel Command (AMC), would have to be restructured, consistent with the new landpower requirements. There are major, overdue management reviews under way throughout the Department of Defense. It appears that new considerations would be appropriate in light of likely changes to the Total Force, fostered by the ongoing transition to the information age.

TRADOC could be reshaped to permit intensive educational and training opportunities to citizen-soldiers and regional allies. These could extend from larger BOS-oriented schools to accommodate potential allies to expanded combat training centers for functional (BOS) forces and potential regional allied units; the expansion would provide contingency operations training. The relative percentage of TRADOC devoted to supporting allies and international organizations such as the UN should be increased. Increased support (TDA) structure is worrisome, but it is inevitable in a smaller active Army due to the range of Army management functions—procuring, developing, training, and the like—that must be accomplished for reserve, joint, and allied forces.[18]

Army Materiel Command (AMC) would also have to change to improve support to joint and allied constituted forces. Contingency troop lists will vary significantly for each crisis. Foreign equipment employed on coalition operations presents new sustainment problems. Reconstitution will require entirely new policies and procedures for sustaining a force in the face of a much smaller production base and increased reliance on global manufacturing.

These examples should convey the magnitude of the conceptual and practical changes that the new national security strategy and the national military strategy will bring to the landpower Total Force. Other implications, such as the impact on personnel policy and the professional ethos, will be considered separately. Chapters 4 and 5 address reserves ("Reserve Force Challenges") and reconstitution capability ("Reconstitution: Revisiting Global War").

4   Reserve Force Challenges

SINCE THEY MAKE UP MOST OF OUR MOBILIZED LAND-power, the reserves are important.[1] They promise to become even more so as our nation surveys its military policy for the future. Operation Desert Shield now seems both a timely "test bed," confirming the wisdom or error of the Total Force, and a lodestar for future reserve policies and programs. Despite continuing and predictable differences between the government branches on the size of the reserves, increased reliance on them appears inevitable. This reliance, in fact, is the choice of the Atlantic Alliance, faced as it is with more immediate instability in Eastern Europe and the former Soviet Union.[2]

Timely prototypes of major contingencies envisaged by the new national military strategy, Operations Desert Shield and Just Cause will be scrutinized for topical "lessons learned" regarding future reserve responsibilities, policies, and programs. As could be expected, increasing evidence reflects results both good and poor. Yet, focusing only on the immediate past can overlook longer-term challenges that may govern decisions on major national security policy. There is a pressing need to sort the systemic from the anecdotal evidence. The challenge is to focus on key levering issues of the reserve forces and their role in long-term sustainment of landpower in the information age.

Since I look for problems, my focus tends to be negative. The bottom line, however, is not. There has been remarkable improvement in reserve readiness during the past two decades. More competent, better motivated people, provided specific mission focus and the necessary equipment, have responded exceedingly well. Today, the United States has the most ready

reserve force our nation has possessed since World War II, perhaps in our nations' modern military history. Building an all-volunteer Army was a successful but difficult national effort; above all, the resources provided during the Reagan years and the outstanding vision and perceptive guidance of Secretary of the Army Marsh added to this success story.

Today, reserve forces equal, if not exceed, the professional competence of the active force in the seventies. They are more capable than the active forces of many other nations. Fortunately for the United States, unfortunately for comparisons, the active force today has improved even more rapidly than the reserves; thus, a long-standing "delta" of greater active capability has remained and in some areas increased. Without the perspective of personal experience over time, younger active Army officers see and are deeply troubled by reserve forces' inadequacies—a source of great frustration to many deeply patriotic, extraordinarily hard-working citizen-soldiers. At a minimum, effective communication between components has to be improved. The Total Force can, perhaps, merge complementary strengths and vulnerabilities to make a more capable "whole" at this pivotal time for the nation's future landpower.

The purpose of this chapter is to lay out some tough issues that should be addressed while the long-term missions, policies, and programs of reserve forces are debated in both executive and legislative branches of government. It reviews the various myths and realities that underlie every serious discussion of reserve forces but that are too seldom put on the table. It is often assumed that all understand and, therefore, the underlying assumptions do not have to be raised. Sometimes, discussion is muted through natural politeness, that is, unwillingness to raise distasteful or controversial issues that could mar completion of the "action" in question. After laying out myths and realities, I will propose some specific policy or program alternatives.[3] Some of these actions will require legislation. Regulatory changes, while helpful, will not be sufficient. This is not bad. The political processes should be activated, for the issues at hand go to the fundamentals of sustaining landpower in a democracy.

First, from a national strategic perspective, the Total Force policy is a resounding success, particularly suited for the national military landpower capability. As a maritime power, we have found in the Total Force a superb combination of federal or state governance; national or local representation; and professional or citizen-soldier competence, uniquely suited to America—a state, a nation, and a democracy—all of which reflect the diversity of a continent.

The regular Army is highly competent, ready-to-project decisive military capability to win as a strategic force anywhere, anytime. Operations Just Cause and Desert Shield are recent examples of combat, but holding the line against major threats in Europe and Asia for decades has been an

equally important mission. The regular Army is a federal force. It is nationally distributed and is fully representative of region, minority, and economic status, although with shortages at both ends of the economic spectrum. Neither the affluent nor the less-capable poor serve as national demographics would dictate. The Army is absolutely subordinate to civil direction, because it is responsive to the president as commander in chief.

This federal force is complemented by the National Guard of the various states. Commanded by the governor in peacetime and manned by citizen-soldiers who are motivated to serve state as well as national interest, the Guard represents integral and absolutely critical elements of the republic—the pride and diversity of the various states. The Guard provides ready-state capability to support in civil disaster or to reinforce state law enforcement. Recent examples are earthquakes, the war against drugs, and the 1992 Los Angeles riots. As a state entity, the Guard responds to the governor, not the president; however, through state representation and national associations, it leans heavily on the U.S. Congress for political and economic support, particularly when preparing for federal missions.

The National Guard, a state and regional force, is well complemented by the Army Reserve, a federal and regional force. The USAR can recruit across state boundaries. Its federal status permits the USAR to access functional talent in a highly mobile work force generally unconstrained by local politics, particularly in major, multistate urban metroplexes. This capability, perfectly suited to attract talent in the emerging information economy, has resulted in exceptionally capable individuals and units. There are Army Reserve units with technical competence unmatched and unattainable in the active Army such as specialized engineer units and technical intelligence and psyops units with world-class talent. Although the USAR is commanded by the president as a federal force, it joins the Guard in relying on Congress for political and economic support. This causes great frustration to the active Army, but it is inevitable until the active force provides more effective day-to-day control. For a combination of reasons to be discussed, the active force does not routinely provide sufficient governance today. Concerned reserve commanders, inured by years of inconsistent direction yet charged as commanders to provide ready units, go where they can get help—Congress.

While many may look at what I have described as a disaster in divided command, it is, in fact, absolutely consistent with the intent of our Constitution, relying as it does on division of power with the checks and balances essential for governing our diverse peoples, regions, and needs. When the Army goes to war, no citizen-soldier questions the absolute primacy of the chain of command. In fact, the increase in support to individual and unit missions mandated in the mission-essential task lists (METL) of current Army training programs and the added readiness responsibilities of the "go-to-war" chain of command (Capstone) acknowledge this and are actively

supported by both National Guard and Army Reserve. The concern about shared command arises from active Army uneasiness about the "untidiness" of divided responsibilities during peacetime.

Yet, looking to a future of declining public concern about defense, if the competitive marriage of active Army, National Guard, and Army Reserve did not exist, we would probably have had to invent it. This would be particularly true during a period of diminished threat, when, protected by dominant seapower and perhaps airpower, a democracy uneasy about maintaining large land forces looks for lower-cost defense "insurance." It is incumbent on all, particularly the often nearsighted active force, to realize this and not fight the problem of the Total Force. The issue is how—not if—to support the 1992 national military strategy.

In addition to the division of peacetime authority and responsibility particularly suited to the United States, a second major advantage to the Total Force is found in new technologies and applications that permit effective programs, despite extraordinary decentralizion and continental distribution of units. The training revolution has brought about the task, condition, and standard. No army has defined with such rigor the individual and collective task-training requirements to execute its war-fighting doctrine. *The Soldiers Manual* and the Army training and evaluation program (ARTEP) define training requirements in detail. Dragon gunners or Bradley crewmen know exactly what is needed to be battle-ready, whether they are on active duty in Korea, in the National Guard at Gowen Field, Idaho, or in the Army Reserve at Fort McCoy, Wisconsin. This rigor permits standardization, despite peacetime dispersion of wartime chains of command.[4] The systems approach to training is complemented by advances in distributed communications, which permit networking geographically spread units to "train together" over a common war model or virtual reality (simulation networking, or SIMNET). These technologies, combined with comparable advances in achieving accelerated bonding, provide absolutely revolutionary opportunities for reserve forces' training.

A third advantage is the sheer quality of today's Total Force. The reserves are as "volunteer" as the active force. Americans are serving because they want to. There is a fundamental strain of patriotism, a basic desire to serve the country, present throughout the force. There is no draft inducement, but like the active force, many citizen-soldiers are recruited because of educational benefits. Despite some heart-wrenching stories of personal, family, and financial sacrifice, there has been remarkably little citizen-soldier dissent about Operation Desert Shield made evident by searching microphone and camera either before or after the experience. By their actions in Desert Shield, the reserves have earned their "spurs" for a broad range of important landpower tasks. Their demonstrated competence and local political power should be very persuasive in shaping the future force structure

of the Army. In fact, it seems fair to speculate that the reserves will have had a greater role in determining the future Total Force than will the active force, after the last congressional subcommittee has had its say.

So, although there are good reasons for being bullish on the future Total Force, the path is not clear. There are profound misunderstandings among and between all three components of Army landpower. These will not be solved quickly, but they do need to be on the table and weighed as the tough decisions are made on the design of the post–cold war Total Force. Several differences are routine requirements too intense for citizen-soldiers' time; faulty resource analysis in planning, programming, and budgeting (PPBS); inadequate full-time manning support; and general lack of active Army understanding of reserves, particularly the imperatives of political support and the reserves' suitability for social missions.

• More appears to be better for the active Army, which is clearly mastering increasingly complex doctrine and equipment. In its enthusiasm, it expects comparable competence across the Total Force. In the absence of an effective screening mechanism at Department of the Army (National Guard Bureau [NGB] or Office, Chief Army Reserve [OCAR]), requirements have gradually, but inexorably, grown for citizen-soldiers. The pressure is such that it is becoming more and more difficult for the genuine citizen-soldier to become a senior leader. Such a leader is expected to attend regular courses; the year-long course at the war college becomes virtually mandatory for line-officer candidates for general officer positions, particularly in the National Guard. Senior officers are increasingly state civil servants—school-teachers, State Department of — employees, and so forth. Key positions are occupied by full-time, quasi-professionals. Senior competence is genuinely increasing, although at an agonizingly slow pace from the perspective of the regular Army; but we no longer have as many units motivated by the ethos of citizen-soldiers. The uncompromising intensity imposed by the regular Army is driving out many young leaders, who are striving to succeed both in the IBMs and Motorolas of competitive industry and in "growing" a successful family. This situation is exacerbated when the spouse works, either from conviction or to support a college education for the children.[5] When these quality young people cannot prosper in the reserves, we have done something fundamentally wrong for the future security of our nation.

• The imperatives of resource allocation in the reserves are nearly a mystery to the PPBS world. Comptrollers and systems analysts everywhere relate to effectiveness and efficiency. These are good, solid concepts of economic analysis, permitting rational decisions based on the critical resources of money and people. The process has conditioned all, from the Office of

Management and Budget and the Congressional Budget Office down, to regard tough policy decisions in these terms. There are often controversial but generally valid results. That said, much of this analysis becomes fundamentally defective when applied to the reserves, because the vital, scarce resource is neither money nor people; rather, it is time for unit-readiness preparation. The federal bureaucracy generally asks the right questions but often comes up with the wrong measures of effectiveness. As a general proposition, people and money can compensate for a time shortage. For example, remarkable improvements can be made in heavy-maneuver unit readiness if modern training technology and qualified leaders are available at each armory or reserve center. Neither the training support analysis nor a strategy to provide much more time-efficient training to the reserves has been implemented. The sole restraint to an expectation, in fact demand, for higher levels of training readiness through more time-efficient training is physical conditioning. It simply takes time to get in shape, although even here investment in hardware, such as Nautilus and Nordic tracks, and trained instructors can clearly speed up the process. Until there has been serious negotiation across the resource bureaucracy on this issue, significant improvements in reserve-unit readiness will be very difficult to achieve. In PPBS terms, to ensure effective analysis, the true marginal cost of time for reservists must be incorporated in every cost-effectiveness study in nearly every area of program review.

The problem is not only lack of management appreciation for the criticality of time or the intensity of the active force. Reserve force leadership, particularly but not exclusively in the National Guard, is unyielding in its desire to be "just like" the active force. Thus redefined, "RC friendly" requirements are regarded with suspicion. For example, reserve "train-to-level-organized" multiechelon training becomes a major objective, despite regional or local shortcomings that can invalidate this strategy. Some proficiency evaluations after Operation Desert Shield call-ups demonstrated serious shortfalls. They reflected concentration at higher levels of command, when the basics clearly had not been mastered down in the squad and platoon. This is a known hazard of multiechelon training, particularly with inexperienced, young leaders. Such training assumes a chain of command competent to train at all levels. For understandable reasons, this competence is difficult to achieve in many reserve units. Also, active-force training philosophy is biased toward decentralized training to strengthen the chain of command. Inefficiencies associated with decentralization are accepted; there is time to correct, if training is offtrack. Neither trained leaders nor time are as available to the reserves as they are to active forces. Frequently, centralized training—often single-echelon, small unit training and evaluation—is the most effective, efficient training strategy. Few commanders are sufficiently confident to do it, because it is "nonregulation."

Motivated to be "just like" the active force, the reserves have evidenced a strong reluctance to adapt training policies and programs to the different training environment.[6] At times, there has seemed to be an almost paranoiac fear of being judged "second class," as a result of doing anything different. This is unfortunate and doubly so because it lets the active Army off the hook about seriously examining its policies and procedures. The relevancy of multiechelon training should sometimes be questioned. The perceived judgment also provides fertile ground for compromises of integrity by junior reserve leaders. Statistics-oriented higher headquarters, out of touch with small-unit "reality," can measure subordinate performance against unrealistic objectives. Well-intended "just like the AC" objectives, which are beyond the capability of the average unit to achieve, are absolutely corrosive to integrity. Impassioned appeals to be "just like" need to be viewed with great suspicion.[7]

• While the vast majority in reserve units are and should be part-time citizen-soldiers, the complexity of unit administration today is such that there must be a cadre of full-time people available to support the commander. These soldiers attend to the day-to-day administration at every command echelon from captain to major general. The expanding demands of readiness have increased this requirement to the point that both National Guard and Army Reserve have thousands of vital people in positions ranging from sergeant in charge of company administrative technicians to full-time recruiters and ROTC (Reserve Officers Training Corps) detachment members, to colonels in key staff positions in field commands and at reserve and Guard headquarters (OCAR [Office, Chief of Army Reserve] and NGB [National Guard Bureau]). Some are former active Army members.

Full-time manning policies vary between the National Guard and the Army Reserve, but the basic dilemma is the same: how to develop competence while the most important positions, including command, are reserved for citizen-soldiers. Individual development programs for full-time manning are spotty at best, although members are increasingly required to attend full-term schooling conducted by the active force. Citizen-soldiers' concerns about competition for positions are predictable. If key command positions are allocated to full-time people, why devote all those funded and unfunded days away from job and family as a citizen-soldier—often averaging eighty to one hundred days a year—with slim prospect of command? The result is continuing morale and competence problems, often resulting in high turnover of the less capable into full-time positions or in stagnation in these positions by those who have "found their niche" and are resistant to change. There are clear exceptions in the National Guard, largely because some state headquarters have attended to personnel development and demonstrated a willingness to absorb key Guard leadership into the state administrative bureaucracy. The Army Reserve does not have the luxury of such a sepa-

rately maintained bureaucracy, which underwrites operating costs in many states.[8]

The result of all this is generally inadequate full-time manning support and understandable tension between part-time and full-time people competing for important professional development opportunities.[9] Political support to technicians notwithstanding, a near-term answer to this is to draw on the active force to provide full-time personnel support as required. More of the active force need to understand the reserves. An active, ready backup of competent, full-time soldiers would give breathing space to the reserve leadership. Additionally, more active force members would understand reserve problems.

For the long term, there should be only two kinds of soldiers: full-time professionals of the active Army in support of reserves when required and part-time citizen-soldiers, commanding, staffing, and serving in units. Guard and Army Reserve members at all echelons should be citizen-soldiers, with explicit limits on reimbursement that they will need other civilian employment. Active officers and non-commissioned officers would be available only as advisers or to fill selected staff positions in the reserve unit when specifically requested by citizen-soldiers, with all active positions renegotiated on a specific schedule. Such policies could provoke an outcry from the current full-time reserve bureaucracy, including most of the "higher headquarters" of the reserve establishment and their congressional support. The active force would be reluctant to provide such extensive support to the reserves. The status quo, however, is unacceptable. More and more, citizen-soldiers are being replaced by full-time people of greatly varying competence who are trying to master an increasingly complex war-fighting doctrine. Over time, this practice will ensure mediocre units, out of touch with local elite groups. This is precisely the worst situation for landpower in a democracy relying on "militia" forces.

• One of the greatest problems facing reserve readiness is the paucity of active Army understanding of the reserves. Very few senior leaders in the Army have seen much service with reserves. Because the readiness region, an active major general command, was disestablished, there is today no seasoning assignment for active general officers—brigadier general or major general. There are colonel assignments in readiness groups or as senior advisers, but promotion from these positions has been extremely rare. Often active Army senior officers will say "they understand" because of associations under Capstone or after multiple evaluations during annual training; but, although these are relevant experiences, they are grossly incomplete and simply not representative of the ethos, the challenges, and the satisfactions of service in reserve forces. As a result, active leaders come to rely on false "instincts" derived from incomplete personal experience or on the advice of the full-time reserve personnel discussed above.[10]

The result of all this is a steady stream of solid, active force policies and programs often misapplied to the reserves. Cases in point are personnel and training policies formulated by active-Army people, then translated to the reserves. Multiechelon training was discussed earlier. Many programs succeed "in spite of" this or are selectively ignored. Unfortunately, the negative feedback follows a difficult path to the leadership in Washington, D.C., screened as it is by the full-time reserve "experts" in OCAR and NGB who are available to the Army staff to explain what it was "that the —— meant to say." These full-time experts may be disposed to expect the reserves to perform at the same level as the active force. They are responsive—supported and with resources—up to the headquarters, not down to the field units. This is precisely the situation alluded to in reviewing the problems associated with being "just like" the active force. As a result of the tensions between full-time manning and citizen-soldiers already described, many active Army reserve "experts" back in Washington lack the sensitizing influence of unit-command or recent troop experience. So the active force's lack of "gut experience" with the reserves is not corrected by the reserve advice available in Washington. Normal feedback loops are not working.

At present, this is a flawed process, probably resistant to correction, unless Congress steps in with a reserve equivalent to the Goldwater-Nichols legislation that would mandate service to ensure understanding of the Total Force within the active Army. The best short-term correction would be to form a reserve command responsible for formulating policy and programs for the Army Reserve similar to the responsibilities of the NGB for the National Guard of the various states. Able to "resubmit" poor decisions to Congress for correction, these reserve commands can patch together benign policies that are at least sensible. This is no way to develop policies and programs that will use to the fullest the great potential of citizen-soldiers during a time of severely constrained resources. The long-term answer must address both the developmental experiences of active leaders with the reserves and the nature of full-time support to the reserves. Neither is adequate today.

• Reserve-force structure and disposition are not the result of a totally rational analysis of national defense requirements. Size and location of reserves influence federal construction and subsidized jobs throughout the United States. Predictably, they are subject to political pressures similar to traditional river and harbor works managed by the Corps of Engineers. The corps has handled this exceptionally well over the years, with a system of division and area engineers accustomed to responding to local political pressures. It has resulted in superb control of an important resource on a continental scale. This is how our country works; it is the political process made possible by the Constitution the Army exists to defend.

The same process governs in configuring reserve forces, although the active force has consciously or unconsciously granted the decision leverage to OCAR and NGB. As river and harbor works have moderated, running out of uncontrolled water, the pork barrel has moved to reserve readiness. Consistent with base closures, for a combination of good and bad reasons, the executive branch has displayed limited flexibility. There is a floor on federal support to states and localities. As social costs have shifted from federal to state and local jurisdictions, strong resistance has developed to reductions in other federal programs. Active-force drawdowns and the policies outlined in the *National Military Strategy* (1992) notwithstanding, the chances of significant reductions in reserve-force structure are slim. Congressional formulations of national security strategy consistently envisage an increased reserve role. Reserve credibility, at least in combat-support and combat-service-support units, has been increased by Operation Desert Shield. This is reinforced by the National Guard's performance in response to urban disorder. Rather than be in anguish about the rationale of too many units, ill-distributed to support today's operational planning, which will change regularly because of global instability and the adaptive planning process, the active force might focus more on a way to capitalize on an assured resource-generating capability. Combat-support and combat-service-support force structure and materiel to support allies in regional contingencies and forward-presence operations are examples of genuine and highly salable needs appropriate for reserves. There are significant requirements for functional units to provide quality BOS support to joint or allied forces.

• Nor should the active Army be uneasy about reserve acceptance of increased social responsibilities, particularly in later-deploying units that are expected to conduct considerable unit training after call-up. Since the Total Force is credible to average citizens, reserves can demonstrate important military concern about and willingness to support priority social programs. This can relieve some public pressure for active-force support. More important, demonstrating an ability to attack pressing problems, such as drug suppression or systemic economic and social problems in the inner city, can be a useful stimulant to local recruiting of motivated, capable young people. They are the quality "gold-collar" officer or "white-collar" noncommissioned officer whom we need to serve the country. Their service can provide a basis for understanding national defense needs, to be drawn upon when they advance to important economic and political positions later in life. Finally, the so-called diminishing threat may require us to accept more locally relevant responsibilities if we wish to attract enough volunteers to sustain the force. In this vein, there may be new and genuinely important opportunities for the military to expand existing training capabilities to up-

grade training suited to the information age. Reserves are, by definition, sensitive not only to local needs but also to the military's potential to alleviate them. The active force needs to listen carefully.

These are complex underlying issues. It seems apparent that there are some broad, fundamental systemic challenges of purpose that need to be addressed as we ponder new policy directions for the Total Force in the emerging information age. Against this backdrop, consider three major reserve force policies in which substantial change may be in order: missions and appropriate force structure; developing the unique strengths of the active Army, the Guard, and the Army Reserve; and modifying active policies and programs to further support reserve readiness.

Traditionally, reserves have been seen as a supplement to active forces or a source to "roundout" understructured active divisions. More often, reserves provide backup to complete the full range of supporting units needed to field a balanced expeditionary force. The backup was necessary because the nation could not or would not sustain capability in active forces. These requirements remain, and they will persist at whatever level of active force. Now, with the release of the *National Military Strategy* (1992), there is a new range of opportunities for employing citizen-soldiers as individuals or units. Contingency and peacetime operations in AirLand operations provide new requirements for functional BOS support in addition to the traditional all-purpose, deployable contingency unit, the corps or division.[11]

Thus, besides conventional reserve units "traced" to CINCs over the years, there are opportunities for other units that could be structured to provide expanded support to deployed air and naval formations. There could also be new units constituted to support contingency combined-force headquarters. This would appear particularly useful to CINCs, with their expanded responsibilities and authorities under Goldwater-Nichols. I suspect Gen. H. Norman Schwarzkopf could develop a healthy list of capabilities he would have liked to have had available, as he thought through tactical, administrative, and logistical support requirements for the allied hodgepodge that rushed at our call to Saudi Arabia early in Operation Desert Shield.

Another form of valuable reserve backup for contingency operations could be to provide support for allies in those areas of combat capability where we have clear comparative advantage. In the past, we have structured our Total Force to execute AirLand Battle in various war plan scenarios. By and large, the underlying rationale for force structure has been the requirement to support all U.S. forces. Exceptionally, we have created forces explicitly to support allies, for example, nuclear weapon custodial units in NATO. But now, in the absence of a clear, focused threat, we use an adaptive planning process keyed to the development of interrelated military, eco-

nomic, and political capabilities prepared to respond to increasing regional instabilities.[12] As we have seen in Operation Desert Shield, there are often important combat or combat-service-support augmentations required to enable our allies to fight AirLand Battle alongside U.S. forces. Improved intelligence, modern command and control communications, highly effective new fire support, and expanded logistics are all needed to improve our allies' ability to fight coalition contingency operations. It would seem that high-priority National Guard and Army Reserve battalions of multiple subscriber equipment (MSE) for corps communications, MLRS, or intelligence battalions could be valuable additions to the Total Force. It may be better rapidly to deploy fire-support battalions needed urgently by our allies than round-out infantry battalions more difficult to keep ready. In addition, by their battlefield mission, combat units are subject to heavy, highly localized losses in the event of hard combat. This could be a hyper-communications disaster in a sensitive contingency situation.

There are other, more conventional needs for reserves in reinforcing units, both constituted and cadre. These kinds of units, maintained at a long-term sustainable level of readiness, determined by time available to train before commitment, seem exactly what both the Department of Defense and Congress have been describing as desirable variable readiness. There would appear to be a wide range of important missions suitable for reserve units at every level of readiness.[13] Once the necessary force structure is determined, the major challenges will be placing the units on the ground in peacetime to ease readiness preparation. One alternative is to organize so that like units are collocated across components on the ground. This would encourage economies of scale in concentrating training infrastructure. Similar active, Guard, or Army Reserve technical maintenance units could be concentrated in one part of the country to facilitate training. Alternately, units could be collocated so that all on a particular contingency mission plan are in the same geographic region. Thoughtful positioning is nice for the active force attempting to find the most cost-effective mix of units; it is absolutely critical for reserves with severe time constraints.[14]

Individual replacement requirements offer equally broad opportunities for reserves. There are many areas in which the reserves possess virtually unique skills critical to unit readiness in peace or war. Language skills developed for missionary service and technical intelligence resources developed by selected industries are examples of capabilities always in short supply. As we move to an information economy, an increasingly complex active force will require more individual skills available only through the reserves. Mobile, knowledge-based competence will be at a premium across industry. We may or may not be able to compete directly with industry to retain active people. Reserve affiliation may be the best long-term source of certain skills; that is, if the Army can prove sufficiently imaginative in structuring service opportunities to attract and retain them. We are limited only

by our imagination, particularly with the reserves. There should be flexible organizations or policies counterbalanced by absolute competence in meeting objective performance standards. For example, if high-tech processor programmers are needed, an answer could be a programmer team of a carrier information management grouping, based in Silicon Valley, with each soldier having mobilization orders as an individual filler to a deploying unit. The annual training could upgrade individual skills or have them serve in a field exercise with the wartime gaining unit. Organizations would be flexible, whatever was appropriate to attract and retain. Frequent, "hard-nosed" proficiency testing in basic military skills and physical fitness would be nonnegotiable.

We have explained the distinctions between the components—federal and state; national and local—and the need to take advantage of these differences. Next, we discussed issues of comparative advantage in relation to our potential allies. For the United States, it is high-tech intelligence, fire, support, and command and control; we do that exceedingly well. For many allies, comparative advantage may be in infantry. It would be better to leave the infantry to our allies whenever we can for a number of good reasons.

There are other comparative advantages in the Total Force within the framework of total-mission capability. We really need to seek and capitalize on the internal advantages.

• *Regular Army: Soldiers and Units—the Standard of Excellence.* Those advantages of the active force seem evident: ready, virtually instant responses, limited only by political will and strategic transport. The active force is a professional model—a developer of doctrine, organization, equipment, and training. Regulars serve as mentors, instructors in schools, and the repository of joint and combined lore. Beyond the demanding requirements of elite, highly "projectable" strategic units, the regular Army's focus is mostly the business of officers and senior noncommissioned officers.

• *National Guard: Proud Units.* The Guard is different: soldiers formed with care into many, many cohesive units; here, smaller is better. Guardsmen are proud to be serving their unit, their locality, and their state in time of disaster or need. They are deeply patriotic and proud if their unit can serve with "the regulars," particularly overseas; but they are equally proud of their special state license plate, the tuition program at the state university, and the social bonding. The focal point is the local unit, a disciplined home, a mainstay in many communities. The Guard is an important, respected link between the American people and their highly professional regular force.

• *Army Reserve: Competent Soldiers.* The Army Reserve is people: mobile, joined not only by patriotism but also by skills, particularly those of white- and gold-collar officers and noncommissioned officers. Reservists

are people, located regionally but able to train in national units. They can be viewed not so much as an organization as a source of talent unrestricted by state boundaries in the emerging information age.

The comparative advantage is this: when we view and count the three components as troop lists of such and such units, we miss a valuable perspective. Active forces are role models, the yeast that allows dramatic expansion in national need. The Guard is units, cohesive teams that embody the spirit of towns and suburbs. The Army Reserve is people, intelligent, motivated and skilled. As we think through future policies, we need to reinforce these complementary strengths, try not to make each in the mold of the other, and make the best of the active force as models, the Guard as units, the USAR as highly skilled people. Three different sets of organizational configurations, policies, and programs are highly possible.

Before elaborating on differences, let me say a few words on ensuring uniformity—federal control. There is agonizing within the reserves, particularly the Guard, about federal control—read federal dictation—in areas that should be under the state. At least, that is the challenge seen by many Guardsmen. On the other side, there are staunch believers in reserves' doing only what the "fed" checks. More checking is better; less federal presence is intrinsically bad. Neither should be concerned, for, practically, this is almost not an issue. The function of the Army inspector general is much more effective today; it seeks systemic problem areas, which becomes a proactive, rather than reactive, process. By virtue of major, automated management systems in place and building, the level, timeliness, and detail of data available to higher headquarters grows consistently. Second, the rigor of the task, condition, and standard to assess individual and unit performance provides unprecedented detail for federal review of reserve readiness. The system is there, and it can be tuned to any desired intensity. Finally, in the National Training Center and comparable facilities, superb opportunities exist to train and evaluate unit performance in a quasicombat environment. The tools, policies, procedures, and trained people are present to ensure responsible control. There may be risks of startling diversity between active and reserve forces, but they do not lie in maintaining control or in prescribing uniform practices.

There are some differences we may want to encourage to optimize inherent strengths of the active Army, the Guard, and the Army Reserve.

• *Regular Army*: Not much change in force projection capability, the Army is made of skilled, tough, proud, and ready units, prepared to fight anywhere, anytime, in conjunction with the other services and allies. The size is determined by the aggregation of regional threats and a national decision as to how big the United States wants the landpower "insurance policy" to be. These units, however many, are the primary models for reserves and allies who would join in AirLand operations. Deployable units would

be complemented by increases in nondeployable support (TDA) units, strengthened to provide quality training for the leaders of the Total Force as well as for probable allied leadership. Improved training would be matched by increased capability to develop and implement doctrine, organizations, materiel, and improved unit training. These changes would be appropriate for the various combinations of reserves, services, and allies necessary to fight together if our overall military strategy is to be credible. This is a formidable task. Lastly, there would have to be many more senior officers and noncommissioned officers to support cadre units and joint and combined organizations. Potentially, this could involve UN forces as well as regional ones. The overall allocation of more senior personnel would be considerably above that justified solely by the relatively small regular Army in units. Modification of existing statute and regulation would be required.

• *National Guard*: In contrast to active Army's focus on smaller size but with extraordinary excellence, the National Guard could sustain units— as many as are geographically sustainable—across the United States. The Guard would draw on the sinews of industrial and rural America, as it has with distinction over the years. It is not just a question of "flags" of greatly varying readiness that could be rapidly improved on mobilization, but also one of maintaining the presence of a proud, patriotic organization to provide a positive military experience. The Guard is also available to reinforce local authority in disasters and civil disturbances; in addition, it could help address local and regional problems, as authorized by federal or state authority. Some Guard units would have to be maintained at very high readiness levels to reinforce joint or allied formations. Others could be virtual skeletons but perform vitally important state or local missions as highly competent groups, able to make things happen.

• *Army Reserve*: Recruiting and retaining quality people wherever they may be in an evolving information economy would be the purpose of the Army Reserve. To achieve this, it would maintain close relationships with national industry and perhaps with multinational industry conducted by major allies. Examples could be media, transportation, or information processing, with specific industry and size determined by mobilization needs. Relations very similar to this exist in some strategic intelligence units today. More examples exist in basic industries; such as how should "Mr. Goodwrench" go to war? It would seem entirely possible that progression in industry could be matched by promotion in the Army Reserve. These people would become the reserves' leaders during war, a situation analogous to certain industrial responsibilities in World War II, when AT&T had a direct and beneficial association with the Army Signal Corps. Of course, there would have to be baseline military structure and training along with regular evaluation of military skills and physical condition, but these should

not be significant problems. Practical ties between the civilian airline industry, the Civil Reserve Air Fleet and the regular Air Force may provide timely examples. Current USAR responsibilities for the Individual Ready Reserve, individual mobilization augmentation, and postmobilization institutional training would be largely unchanged.

There are three different ways of looking at sustaining the current Total Force in the future. Obviously, it is not all that easy: What is right from a military perspective must merge with what is acceptable to the myriad interest groups involved in change.

It seems evident that the active force really needs to scrub some of its longstanding policies and programs, more or less taken for granted, for the reserves. The most pervasive problems are those associated with the differences in relative importance of various resources: dollars and people are most important for the regular Army, but time is the critical resource for the reserves.

The regular Army has had severe challenges to manpower and funds for several years. The resource competition became particularly intense in the eighties as the active Army expanded from sixteen to eighteen divisions. The mechanism for squeezing was the organizational redesign called Army of Excellence (AOE). The reserves were swept along in management enthusiasm to conserve personnel spaces and, where possible, to garner funds as new, higher technology, "more productive" organizations were introduced. Maintenance people were cut; assumed advantages of high-tech diagnostic equipment and better training for senior mechanics permitted substantial reductions in their numbers. Such was the planning. Reality has been less benign as has been discussed frequently in reviews of maintenance problems in Operation Desert Shield. Some support was cut just too much.

The bottom line is that much of the robustness essential to reliable performance in adversity has been "managed" out of the Army. The bill to restore it will be a significant increase, particularly in combat-service support at all levels. The unfortunate part of all this is that the reserves did not have a problem of money or people in the first place. Both have been in plentiful supply but provided generally from congressional pressure rather than DoD initiative, so they have been applied reluctantly. But the reserves did, and do, have a time problem, now exacerbated by the lean organizations imposed on them. In retrospect, when AOE was laid out, the reserves should have been given more rather than fewer people to compensate for the unique challenges they faced. New organizational documentation procedures and data processing made such variations feasible; it obviously was not deemed necessary for the reserves.

Another problem is the design of a reserve soldier's career progression. Career development, including promotion, assumes a succession of increas-

ingly responsible assignments. Implicit is the mobility of the soldier, his ability to move from one developing assignment to another, as is done in the regular Army. For many reserves in rural settings or with limited personal transportation in urban areas, this mobility is simply not possible. You grow and are promoted in whichever unit is available. Therefore, there are unusual out-of-pattern assignments, governed more by the chances of regional proximity than rational career development. Should there be much broader job patterns for the reservist, with very specific job training upon arrival in an organization? These are complex issues with no quick solutions. The easy ones have already been taken, after prodding by conscientious reserve leaders.

This problem applies to design of organizations, of military occupational specialties (MOS), and as mentioned, of all the training for individuals and units. It is absolutely pervasive. A common past answer has been to assign the problem to the full-time reserve force to advise the active proponents. This is the full-time reserve force already discussed, that which is precluded from becoming commanders and without a comprehensive career-development program tolerable to competing citizen-soldiers. It is the blind leading the blind, another defective loop in feedback.

There are now other major actions under way within the Department of Defense that may bring these kinds of issues to the fore. The Defense Management Review is conducting an important and searching check on service practices. It would seem appropriate to review the allocation of responsibilities among the various components of the defense force. Clearly, there will be new responsibilities associated with the post–cold war Total Force, and several examples come to mind that would reinforce them. The regular Army could need a disproportionate number of people to permit expanded training and intensified support of reserves and regional allies. The Guard would probably need recognition of its support to locally important federal programs like the war against drugs. The Army Reserve could need special authorities and resources to ensure cross-industry coordination of "gold-collar" support, including overseas coordination with multinational businesses.

These are hypothetical examples, but they are truly serious issues for the Total Force. They should be addressed by leadership "first-team" members to ensure policy direction and consistency in program resources. They have not been addressed in the past.

This is written not in frustration at facing change, nor from uneasiness about the complex political decisions that must be pursued to stimulate change in the Total Force. Rather, it is with great respect for the complex makeup of nation, state, people, and democracy, thankfully involved in decisions concerning American landpower. That diversity ensures our grandchildren and their offspring the same benefits of competent landpower we have had, and also it will suggest innovative ways to draw on the talents

and energies of the citizen-soldier, one of our strongest national assets. But diversity is really tough to acknowledge and stimulate, if we disagree on the presence of problems amid the obvious general success of the Total Force. There can be no persuasive case for "business as usual." There are serious internal challenges, and few easy solutions—all the more reason to bring issues of the Total Force to the national "front burner."

5 Reconstitution: Revisiting Global War

PRUDENT LEADERS CONSIDER THE UNLIKELY CONTINGEN-cies. None seems more improbable today than a World War III—a massive land campaign in multiple theaters of operations, involving much of the manpower of the industrialized nations. After Operation Desert Storm, the goals of civilian leaders, the general public, and the military establishment appear focused on winning fast and clean. War is unwelcome. When provoked, make it sudden, short, and violent; keep it as far from our shores as possible; and above all, achieve a clear victory. Involvement in prolonged land conflict appears both definitely undesirable and highly improbable.

The world scene can change remarkably rapidly. August 1990 saw Saddam Hussein invade Kuwait. Clearly, this was a miscalculated and perhaps irrational destabilization of the status quo in one of the world's most sensitive areas. In August 1991, both the Communist Party of the Soviet Union and the Soviet empire collapsed, with the tentative emergence of a shaky Russia. The southern borders of Russia touch emergent Islam. The western borders approach the fragmented and irredentist Balkans.

As the preeminent power, the United States has abiding interest in the current world order. We also have a great deal to lose should it change significantly. Many more uncontrollable forces are surging about than we have seen since World War II. It seems prudent, therefore, to consider how ready we are to defend, should we fail to deter another world war. What floor of national military capability must be maintained if we are to be able to respond to future crises of global magnitude? How can we sustain this floor? In the *National Security Strategy*, it is stated succinctly when discussing reconstitution:

Beyond the crisis response capabilities provided by active and reserve forces, we must have the ability to generate wholly new forces should the need arise. Although we are hopeful for the future, history teaches us caution. The 20th century has seen rapid shifts in the geopolitical climate, and technology has repeatedly transformed the battlefield. The ability to reconstitute is what allows us safely and selectively to scale back and restructure our forces in being.

This difficult task will require us to invest in hedging options whose future dividends may not always be measurable now. It will require careful attention to the vital elements of our military potential: the industrial base, science and technology, and manpower. . . . The standard by which we should measure our efforts is the response time that our warning processes would provide us of a return to previous levels of confrontation in Europe or in the world at large. We and our allies must be able to reconstitute a credible defense faster than any potential opponent can generate an overwhelming offense.[1]

The last sentence says it all. Reconstitute to create defensive then presumably offensive capability more rapidly than the potential threat can create an offense. There is no specified period. The challenge is to be able to recognize the enemy buildup and then catch up, or convert latent potential to actual capability faster than the enemy.[2] The critical variables are how "unready" the peacetime steady state is; when national authority perceives the threat and "sells" rearming to the people; and last, the rapidity of the pace of rearming. What is the glide path of reconstitution?[3]

In view of the historical record of World War II, these are not comforting measures. Years of peace almost destroyed the expansion base, the regular Army, despite the articulate protests of gifted leaders like Gen. Douglas MacArthur. The clarion call for national mobilization was one vote for extension of the draft. National attitudes did not support intervention until after Pearl Harbor. It was midwar before we achieved conversion and necessary growth of the production base. This is not a comforting recollection, but is it a fair comparison? World War II was the quintessential industrial-age war. Sheer quantities of mass production ensured eventual victory. Landpower conflict today has moved to a new paradigm—information-age war, as described doctrinally in AirLand Battle and AirLand Operations. It is the intense violence and accelerated tempo seen in Desert Storm. It is shorter, quicker, and more violent than the previous industrial-age breakthrough in land combat, the German blitzkrieg. Accelerated movement of information (command and control, intelligence, electronic warfare), combined with the intensified massing of firepower generated by precision munitions, creates battlefield violence akin to nuclear weapons. Perhaps, therefore, preparation for this new type of war invalidates the World War II mass-production model.

Future land conflict does not seem likely to be high-, mid-, or low-

intensity war. Rather, it may be all of the above, combined as required to win quickly with overwhelming force, at least in the early stages of conflict. It is focused military power ". . . permitting operational and tactical activities in three-dimensional space and time . . . to decisively overwhelm the enemy and exploit the advantage of initiative," all designed to accelerate the pace of operations to achieve the "cascading effect of each new success."[4] As described by Toffler, future land war is likely to be combinations of conflict: First Wave (agricultural revolution—hand-to-hand), Second Wave (industrial revolution—tank, artillery), and Third Wave (information revolution—accelerated tempo, "brilliant" munitions). Land forces will be employed in conjunction with other military services and regional allies, probably in a combination of all-purpose combat units, divisions and brigades, and highly specialized combat, combat-support, or combat-service-support capability. All will be integrated by BOS to support specific joint or allied war-fighting requirements.[5]

Excepting strategic nuclear initiation, World War III is likely to begin as one or more regional contingencies whose outcome is failure to deter general war; as regional contingencies spread, the conflict becomes global. Further, it seems reasonable to assume that when we become involved in regional contingency operations, the United States will shape the battle to national advantage. If deterrence fails, the United States will initiate Third-Wave war fighting as the current and emerging doctrine prescribe. Failing quick victory, we would regress to Second-Wave and then First-Wave warfare, as stockpiles of more capable equipment and supplies are exhausted. Meanwhile, we would have reenergized the industrial base nationally and with our regional allies.[6]

Credible capability to fight this kind of war is not sustained by amateurs. It will require the maintenance of very professional forces to enable the contingency forces mandated during peacetime by the new national military strategy. It would seem highly unlikely that we would return to the qualitatively inferior forces we had before World War II. Stocks may be drawn down so that there are fewer days-of-supply of "smart" and "brilliant" munitions, and much smaller professional forces may be capable of winning only operations smaller than Desert Storm. But what we have should be very good. The constituted peacetime "steady state" will be highly professional. It will know exactly what it needs to have to carry out the doctrine (Third-, then Second-, then First-Wave war fighting), although the means (days-of-supply of "brilliant" munitions) will be severely limited. This situation is different from pre–World War II, when the military and nation awakened to a revolution created by others.

The second critical variable is when the nation begins to rearm for global conflict. Operations in Panama and the Persian Gulf confirmed the wisdom of the national military strategy articulated by Secretary Weinberger and subsequently codified in the *National Military Strategy*. As a super-

power, the United States is and will remain an active member of the global economy. Regional trade dislocations will have increasing economic impact in the United States as reliance on international trade increases. Stimulated by hyper-communications, public unease about negative economic impacts at home should ensure some U.S. contingency response. The response might be primarily political and economic, but any threat significant enough to provoke a contingency response like an embargo should stimulate a complementary military backup. Public debate is an integral part of the national consensus-building necessary for a major contingency response. This is a lesson relearned from Desert Storm. Partial mobilization is likely to have occurred to enable reserve participation as an element of the consensus-building.[7] Serious debate about contingency commitment should be sufficient provocation to reactivate a levering industrial capability, assuming relevant mobilization planning has occurred. Continuing attention to issues of reconstitution assures detailed planning. Thus, it would not seem to be parallel to the inability to mobilize public consensus faced before World War II. The problem, however, may be that there is not much to turn on.

The likely glide path of reconstitution is another situation entirely. As our defense industrial base erodes, the current problem may prove as challenging as it was before World War II. National planning is under way to address key issues: retention of a national and international industrial base, identification of national critical technologies, development of manufacturing-process technology, and use of dual-use technologies. A recent defense report to Congress summarizes the various initiatives:

> In order to ensure that industry remains capable of producing the weapon systems DoD requires, the Department of Defense must manage a range of industrial base activities: the peacetime business of equipping and supporting military forces; ensuring industrial preparedness to deal with potential regional contingencies and conflicts; and planning for the reconstitution or expansion of military forces in response to a potential future, global threat. The most significant of the peacetime activities is for DoD to work with industry in managing programs and limited resources as wisely as possible.
>
> DoD has taken a number of steps to promote effective resource management—to get the most from defense dollars. Robust levels of R&D funding will be maintained and the Department has supported raising the cap on industry IR&D funding to sustain the nation's capability to develop and ultimately produce first-class weapons systems. These actions are complemented by the preferential funding of those critical technologies that are most important to future forces. Efforts to sustain the technology base and increase the use of dual-use products will have a positive effect on the businesses that are important to defense technology and production, as well as provide benefits to DoD. The Department is now reevaluating many of its acquisition practices to lessen private-sector risk and to ensure that essential suppliers remain strong, viable, and capable of providing high-quality products for defense.[8]

This focus is complemented by useful analysis of the desired defense technology and industrial base prepared by the congressional Office of Technology Assessment (OTA). OTA postulates that the following are desirable characteristics of the future base:

- Advanced research and development capability
- Ready access to civilian technology
- Continuous design and prototyping capability
- Limited, efficient, peacetime engineering and production capabilities in key sectors
- Responsive production of ammunition, spares, and consumables for theater conflict
- Healthy, mobilizable, civilian production capacity
- Robust maintenance and overhaul capability
- Good, integrated management

The study then identifies several broad, national strategic choices: autonomy versus interdependence (global market); arsenal system versus civil integration (internal structure); and current capability versus potential (military capability). Subordinate tactical decisions identified are *inter alia* "dual-tracking," or development of upgrades for current equipment, while sustaining continuous prototyping. All in all, OTA has produced an excellent summary of policy alternatives.[9]

This is all commendable, clearly required, but probably unrealistic, because it presupposes a continuing, reasonably robust defense industry in the United States. Current efforts, based on existing DoD planning for an orderly drawdown of some 25 percent by 1995, assume that ". . . current and projected defense spending will be maintained at roughly the levels that were experienced during the 1970s . . . government procurement for 1993 is projected at about the 1973 level."[10] This is simply not a credible projection. The seventies were cold war years. Granted, there was the search for a "peace dividend" after Vietnam, but those days simply are not comparable to the present. The American people are now convinced that the country's most serious problems are domestic. Popular support for defense readiness deteriorates; if you consider, too, the increasing globalizing of national economies, the result is enormous change in the traditional, Second-Wave, national defense industry. Even U.S. Third-Wave industry erodes from rationalization of global markets and skillful economic manipulation (warfare?) by the Japanese. The traditional, national-defense industrial base is disappearing.[11]

To a certain extent, the U.S. defense industry is victim of the exceptional successes of the Reagan years. But, at least for landpower, enough modern fighting platforms—the Abrams, Bradleys, MLRS, and advanced command and control—have been purchased for the next twenty to thirty years. This is confirmed by the lessening of credible world-class threats on

land, sea, or air. If there is an arms race for the near term, it will be with ourselves or perhaps the Japanese. But even if the Japanese intended to compete militarily, it would take years, if not decades, for them to develop a balanced global capability. The initial threat to the United States would be to seapower or airpower, not landpower.

Information-age technologies offer opportunities for substantial product improvements to existing systems. If produced, the Abrams M1A2 will be much more effective than the original Abrams, and the improvement appears sufficient to justify upgrade, in lieu of moving on to a new series of combat vehicles early in the next century. Product improvement can be profitable, but platform production remains the bread and butter of the Second-Wave defense industry.

There is clear opportunity to upgrade existing fighting systems, but that will not reinvigorate the industry competing in the international market. It is difficult to foresee any major new landpower systems this decade. Nor, as major programs vanish, is there much ahead for airpower or seapower. The bow wave of procurement for all the services today exceeds budget projections. The projected 25 percent reduction is probably optimistic as the grand budget compromise of 1989 runs its course. Which market forces will sustain the industrial base postulated by the Department of Defense? For practical purposes, assume that there is no major, industrial-age, defense industrial base in the future.[12] Now what is required for reconstitution?

Assume that the unthinkable has occurred: the world slides toward conflict, hopefully conventional warfare, surrounded by spreading major contingencies. What should our landpower posture be? What force-generation capabilities should we retain in the substantial drawdowns of the nineties to ensure that we do not face the time-consuming obstacles to readiness confronted by Gen. George Marshall before World War II? Today, we have the option of retaining dated equipment as we drawdown. What should we preserve, either nationally or within the regional or global community of nations?

General Marshall had no useful residual equipment base from which to start. Today, we should be very reluctant to sell equipment until we have determined whether it can be used for future product improvement. The overall challenge is much larger: to suggest long-term policies and programs that will preserve the options of timely reconstitution ten, twenty, or thirty years from now with a virtually nonexistent, industrial-age, defense industrial base. The programs should be as inexpensive as possible to improve the odds of sustainment over the years. They should also preserve as many options as possible for the moment of truth. The Total Force—the professional force combined with those citizen-soldiers prepared to lead the peacetime constituted forces—can be relied upon to provide the bank of militarily relevant expertise, if global war approaches. While the size of each com-

ponent may vary, particularly as the active forces reduce and the reserves expand, the combined total should approach a half million or more under arms. The crucial policies, therefore, are those relating to force generation—equipment and manpower availability. How could the United States man and equip an expanding army preparing to fight a Third-Wave, then Second-Wave war? If we have a clear ability to do this, the act may be unnecessary. We may have deterred the conflict.

First, equipment must be provided. Where the materiel is generally comparable to civilian equipment, the Air Force Civilian Reserve Air Fleet (CRAF) sets a highly desirable precedent. Civilian airlines are subsidized to use airframes that can be reconfigured for military transport. Civil air carriers know what their contribution might be under various contingencies; the CRAF was used quite successfully during Operation Desert Shield. Similar policies could be established for landpower needs. For example, civil transport could be given subsidies to provide military characteristics such as high-clearance, all-wheel drive. Similar incentives could be offered to ensure military utility in telecommunications, medicine, fuel-handling, food service, and other civilian-related, combat-service-support capabilities. The military could subsidize the addition of selected "tactical" characteristics which would make the equipment tactically useful even under restrictive conditions. Lest this seem "unmilitary," remember that host-nation support and U.S. civilian logistic support to sustain complex equipment were invaluable during Operation Desert Storm.

Weapons such as tanks, artillery, and air defense are more difficult. It seems highly unlikely that a civilian defense industrial base can be maintained at the low levels required for constituted forces, even considering foreign military sales.[13] One answer appears to be the same as in past times of reduced military capability: The nation has relied on a government-owned, government-, or contractor-operated arsenal. Critical, absolutely unique military requirements—such as gun tubes, night-vision aids, or ammunition—are produced and stockpiled, or standby facilities are maintained for production. Military requirements extend beyond end-item production. Competent systems integrators and design teams should be employed for these and other possible innovative approaches. Where feasible, offense and defense design teams should be placed in direct competition.

Positive incentives could be offered so that the services adopt common weapons for joint and coalition use in force reconstitution. This incentive occurs naturally today with dominant weapons like Stinger or Hellfire or the Blackhawk utility helicopter. The global market may help. MLRS is now a global product, with over thirty distinct warheads. The base system is manufactured in several nations and production costs could be spread globally with production facilities remaining national. Other weapon systems could be global, such as the Russian T tanks or the NATO 155mm tube artillery. Comparable multipurpose weapons could be declared DoD stan-

dard for reconstitution for U.S. forces or allies until the wartime production base comes on line. Preparatory planning in CBRS could modify organizations or training to accommodate equipment mandated by current doctrine.[14]

A key issue for future systems acquisition should be the expectations and rigor of the requirements documents. This is not merely an issue of increasing the suitability of civilian production for military needs; rather the issue is to slow deliberately the pace of new weapons development. The momentum of the arms race during the cold war demanded costly "breakthroughs" with every new generation of equipment. In addition to the obvious battle effectiveness of advances in weaponry, the fight to field, despite hostile bureaucracy and media, was so acrimonious it just was not worth the struggle for marginal improvements. So a breakthrough momentum developed. As the war in the Gulf revealed, we were extremely successful in our development efforts. Media sensationalism over the years notwithstanding, most of our advances work, in some cases even better than we expected. Soviet capabilities—some first-line, some second-rate for export—failed the test of combat.

Our competitive strategies appear to have been inordinately successful. Now, Soviet landpower is coming apart at the seams to a much greater extent than U.S. power did after Vietnam. In every dimension, the parts of the former Soviet Union, or Russia, or both face tough military issues:

- federal forces or republic guards?
- conscript or volunteer?
- creation of a noncommissioned officers corps?
- command and management, as communist infrastructure is dismantled?
- equal opportunity or the nationalities' equivalent?

These choices must be made despite continuing uncertainty, as political reliability is defined and redefined; substantial loss of face; and lessened recruiting and retention potential for the "best and brightest." Each is a formidable challenge. Together they seem overwhelming. Although the Russians possess undeniably great residual strengths, they will not loom as a credible, major military landpower with modern fighting doctrine for several decades. There are just too many internal and external schisms interacting simultaneously. So who is the United States now striving to best by sustaining a breakthrough momentum in systems acquisition? Then, if a breakthrough effort is required, should it be sought on the land or sea or in the air? We appear on the verge of an arms race with ourselves.

This may be an opportune time to stop and really take stock of our systems acquisition objectives. Perhaps requirements documents should place far greater emphasis on surge and long-term production capabilities by global industry. Less detailed and demanding requirements could en-

courage civil-military hybrids. Civilian equipment could be designed so that some agreed percentage could be converted to military use. For example, the military could create more CRAF alternatives, as discussed above and as the Navy is doing for logistic shipping. This may be the opportunity of the century to change the face of acquisition and to support new force-generation strategies that reinforce deterrence through regional landpower.

New strategies could benefit from the past fifty-year arms race. Then, the service lifetimes of equipment used by either superpower or client was expected to be long, so built-in growth potential was essential. This is a useful characteristic when we think of stretching the utility of old equipment. Much of the existing worldwide glut of military equipment is amenable to qualitative upgrading to exploit processor-based advances. Some of a general "world war" weapons shortfall could be alleviated by maintaining stockpiles of obsolete equipment. Continuing research and development (R&D) could be supported to permit rapid upgrade capability during periods of crisis. For example, armor kits and improved 105mm ammunition could be developed for M60A3 tanks stockpiled in the desert or improved armor and powertrain designed for stockpiled M113s. There is excess 155mm tube artillery with major reserves of diverse munitions. What high-technology, "brilliant" capabilities should be stimulated? The same logic is applicable for new warheads for tens of thousands of antitank guided missiles such as TOW (tube-launched, optically tracked, wire-guided) missiles. Production would begin only as triggered by a deteriorating situation. Tanks like the Abrams M1s in reconstitution storage could be modified to add data buses, which in turn would allow the drop-in of new capabilities introduced with the M1A2. Only high-value, long-lead, critical systems would be produced until the threat of war.

Aggressive R&D might also develop militarily significant features to insert into existing equipment, such as old helicopters or air-defense missiles. This would be encouraged if one of the development criteria was the ability to insert the improvement rapidly into stored equipment. The Department of Defense envisages this in its critical technologies plan committed ". . . to developing a broad range of highly leveraged breakthrough technologies that will be inserted efficiently into military equipment, as well as technology 'trump cards' that will allow the United States to sustain its long-term dominance in the technological arms race."[15] Other efforts could be initiated to use common components such as common chassis and power train whenever possible. This has been a consistent goal of the armor systems modernization program. Clearly, the primary focus of systems acquisition should be to retain the supremacy of the largely active deterrent force. As various threats diminish, force supremacy may be much easier and less costly to sustain than we currently believe, provided we do not provoke continuation of the arms race with ourselves. This focus, however, should not preclude sensible reconstitution programs.

Global industries may provide novel opportunities for ready standby production for coalition operations. Major international producers such as IBM, Toyota, AT&T, Siemens, Du Pont, GM, or EXXON could be encouraged by the major industrial powers (G-7 nations[16]) to keep certain on-call production ability available for regional or UN operations. Global stability, which provides market access, stable exchange rates, and the flow of trade, is as economically desirable as it is politically important. Tax or tariff advantages for global corporations based on innovative production support of world readiness for UN or regional security operations might stimulate considerable reconstitution potential.

Another, more controversial initiative could be G-7 subsidizing of common-end items of equipment. When military force levels recede, the political power of defense industry declines. When the decisive and increasingly costly weapons can be adapted to modular, national insertions—called preplanned product improvement by modular retrofit—perhaps the base weapons carrier, aircraft, or ship could become a multinational common item, at least for reconstitution. Some less affluent nations might choose this base capability for their constituted forces in peacetime. There is a consistent record of both multinational production of a national weapon (F-104G, MLRS, F-16) and multinational development for multinational use (airbus and European fighter–EFTA).

Foreign production of important national defense weapon systems is controversial. National self-sufficiency is a political "must." This became evident recently in the proposed sale of LTV to French-owned Thomson. The Department of Defense objected on security grounds.[17] A recent Association of the United States Army (AUSA) report on preservation of the defense industrial base did not discuss international production as a credible alternative.

Engine, protection, and weapon remain important as vestiges of the industrial age, but the decisive capabilities today are precision munitions and the processor-based guidances of the information age that can be applied by module to the base common carrier. Perhaps an answer to the materiel requirements of continental land war would be a contract with GM or Toyota to provide X thousand "universal tracked-weapon carriers" to designated allies from its global production capability within Y months of notification. Appropriate national subsidies could be established. After delivery, each nation would then add its own, computer-based capability. Such a strategy would reduce reliance on the receding metal-bending, Second-Wave, domestic industrial base and favor our Third-Wave capabilities such as IBM, INTEL, and Motorola.

These thoughts may seem fanciful or politically unacceptable. I would argue that change already under way in world security requirements is fundamentally altering defense industries. What the onset of the information age has not done to disrupt the old "metal-benders," the breakup of the cold

war has. As I hope is evident from various thoughts in preceding pages, more may be possible than we think. If we intend to maintain insurance or a hedge against another world war, we need innovative programs to sustain deterrence at the most likely levels of conflict.

What are other equipment alternatives? Several ground rules seem appropriate:

- Focus critical technology development to extend and exploit areas of national military advantage, or the capability for Third-Wave war.
- Avoid self-generated, self-competing arms races. National military supremacy on land, sea, and air is today so pronounced that we can afford to risk surprise in one or more technology areas. Do not introduce new technologies unless and until there is a clear need. It is not in our interest to further degrade the military potential of our stockpile of platforms, our obsolescent weapons. As the credibility of our "sunk-cost" stockpile declines, so the credibility of our reconstitution hedge recedes.
- To reinforce reconstitution potential, encourage Third-Wave component advances, not Second-Wave platform development. Component advances should concentrate on improving performance of reserve and potential allies on equipment likely to be available in global war.[18]

Personnel readiness may be almost as challenging as equipment availability. Trained personnel associated with constituted forces, active or reserve, will be drawn down as world war approaches, either in regional conflicts presaging a global war or in the cadre of reconstitution forces being generated. The Individual Ready Reserve will replace initial casualties. The manpower challenge is to determine the source of the millions of soldiers necessary to prosecute global war, particularly if Third-Wave war regresses to Second-, and First-Wave conflict. Involvement in destablizing civil wars almost certainly involves regression to First-Wave war. Croatia and Bosnia reflect the bitter conflict of the Middle Ages. We hope the United States will not become involved in conflict such as this, but prudent planners consider the worst eventualities. What should be the national manpower pool to support potential First-Wave war?

It seems unrealistic to assume that defense readiness alone will justify maintaining a costly pool of manpower as a contingency hedge. Alleviation of other, more immediate, national social needs is a better rationale for generating competent manpower for the long term. In World War II, General Marshall benefited from the Civilian Conservation Corps, although the Army had to divert a sizable portion of its professional army leadership to execute the program in the mid-thirties. Nevertheless, the CCC work experience was a valuable source of noncommissioned officer leaders early in

World War II. There may be parallels today. Purposeful CCC kinds of experiences can be excellent training for high school students uncertain about personal ability or career goals.[19] The ROTC basic camp course today provides similar training to develop college students who consider joining ROTC programs. Both types of programs provide excellent potential for long-term development of blue-, white-, and gold-collar leaders to the national manpower supply in peacetime and to the military in the event of global conflict.

The challenge will be long-term resource support. A much smaller Army simply cannot undertake something of this scale out of constituted forces. It seems an appropriate mission for the reserve forces. Whoever accomplishes the mission, the Army should be supported—in funding and manpower—by separate title so that there would be less competition for resources with already small and over-extended constituted forces.

Assuming that these programs could support expanded leadership manpower needs during world war, the challenge then becomes qualitative requirements for individual soldiers grade E5 and below. Today's constituted forces, active and reserve, have become practically dependent on acquiring very capable soldiers.[20] They are the most qualified by any measure that the nation has brought into the service, during peace or war. The Army has profited from the presence of a more capable force by reducing the length of training courses and shifting more training responsibility to an increasingly competent chain of command. More equipment requires mental category II or III personnel to operate to standards, which have, in turn, been raised to increase equipment capability. It seems fair to assert that, during these last several resource-constrained years, the Army has conserved resources and capability by basing doctrine, organization, equipment, and training on the presence of highly competent, motivated soldiers. These programs have been resounding successes, as demonstrated in Operations Just Cause and Desert Storm. They also conceal a great potential vulnerability should quality give way to quantity in general war.

Fortunately, the mobilization manpower strategy was not tested during Operation Desert Storm. Stretched to the limit, the constituted force satisfied requirements. Casualties did not materialize and members of the Individual Ready Reserve recalled to service retained many military skills when released from active service within the past twelve months. There was a modest, trained manpower cushion. This would vanish quickly in a global war preceded by regional conflicts. As the prewar constituted force suffers attrition, landpower would convert to a conscripted force, and the quality problem emerges.

Whatever the mental category of those conscripted in the event of global war, the Army's share of brighter people, relative and absolute, will be considerably lower than it is today. It will be much lower if we recruit a straight percentage of each mental group and lower still if national manpower policy favors the other services, as it has in every war. Several actions

appear prudent, irrespective of the eventual force-generation policies planned for reconstitution:

• Training effectiveness analyses need to be conducted on major pacing items of equipment to determine the resources required to train soldiers of various mental capacity to be proficient. Studies should consider both initial and sustainment training. Some of this has been done already in impressive ongoing efforts like the long-term Soldier Research Project to assess career performance. More needs to be done to study the trainability of people in mental categories IV and V—all brought into service in previous world wars.

• Where the training to current standard is impossible and when the equipment is expected to be still on the battlefield when post-mobilization troops arrive, develop aids to encourage acceptable performance. Aids could be automated and appended to the equipment; if this is not possible, lower the performance standard to what can reasonably be expected. Commanders need to know these probabilities before battle.

• Review training doctrine, practices, and procedures for large-scale training conducted by less capable cadre. They will be conducting the training in general mobilization. The quality of the current process is simply unattainable without highly competent trainers—officers and noncommissioned officers. The World War II model—basic combat training (BCT), advanced individual training (AIT), basic unit training (BUT), and advanced unit training (AUT)—was developed in consideration of a high-quantity, relatively low-quality input. This strategy should be accepted or rejected and then replaced for intense post-mobilization training as a result of conscious planning and testing before the crisis occurs.

• As the nation scrapes the barrel of trained manpower, tough policy issues result from lack of English proficiency in substantial minority groups; trainability of the so-called permanent underclass, and accession standards for offspring of addicted or AIDS parents. Decisions here can only be made when the crisis occurs. However, new training effectiveness analyses should be done now, well in advance, for recent work has focused on justifying higher quality and not on determining the lowest quality floor.

With respect to personnel requirements for global conflict, the bottom line is that the Army simply has not done enough basic research and analysis to recommend realistic policies and programs. For two decades, the focus has been on quality, not quantity. The Army just does not realize what it does not know in this area.

It seems fair to assert, however, that AirLand Battle or AirLand Operations seem neither qualitatively nor quantitatively sustainable if there is an industrial-age world war. As threats appear to recede and U.S. land-

power declines, replication of resounding AirLand Battle success with combat forces in Panama and the Gulf appears unlikely in multiple regional contingencies using less capable constituted forces. It would seem clearly beyond the capability of much larger but less capable forces during a world war.

Conflict seems certain to degrade from Third-Wave to Second-Wave and First-Wave war. If this is so, the concept-based requirements system tells us that we need to review the doctrine for employment of reconstitution forces. After that, more specific equipment and personnel requirements will flow. To be specific, in reconstitution, peacetime doctrine may no longer drive landpower composition. Less capable equipment and personnel will dominate landpower capabilities. Doctrine will need to be adjusted accordingly. Obviously, there is much more thinking to be done on reconstitution.

PART III

ENGINES OF CHANGE

6   The Concept-Based Requirements System

QUALITY OF PERSONNEL IS FREQUENTLY AND CORRECTLY identified as a critical factor in the regrowth of the Army. Less frequently is the other major ingredient cited, that is, the success of the concept-based requirements system (CBRS). The CBRS formula sounds simple: Determine your war-fighting doctrine, then ensure that your personnel, organizations, equipment, training, and leader preparation are all tailored to support it. It is not simple. Just determining what is required can and usually does involve hard choices. Then, traditional interests, certain of the wisdom and experience of the past, merge inevitably to resist change. The transition from horse cavalry to motor mechanization—armored fighting vehicles (AFV)—consumed decades. Even today, AFV, specifically the Bradley, remain anathema to many infantrymen, who recognize the need for greater ground mobility and protection but are concerned that they distract the infantry soldier from his basic mission on the ground. Even if there is broad professional agreement about what has to be done, there is no assurance that the necessary resources will be available over time to accomplish the objective. So, a clearly advantageous process does not in itself ensure success. But without it, failure or, at a minimum, slow and uncoordinated change, appears certain.

It has been a twenty-year struggle to achieve what U.S. landpower has today: the world's best "engine" for effecting change. With landpower primacy intact in the aftermath of Just Cause and Desert Storm, it is an engine now superbly suited to move further into the post-industrial age. Considerable change appears in the offing as "lessons learned" are digested. That

is the necessary aftermath of success. Fortunately, the change processes seem well-institutionalized, at least for now.[1]

The essential parts to establish the CBRS were evident well before the synergistic effects were realized. The most significant act was the creation in the early seventies of an Army major command focused on the problem of effecting change, Training and Doctrine Command (TRADOC). For the first time since World War II, all of the parts associated with design and implementation of change were placed under one commander. In addition to combat developments, this included much of the education and training of the leaders who would institute the changes. About the same time, the need for doctrinal change became evident in the 1973 Yom Kippur War. This conflict was perfectly timed to force institutional admission of the need for change and to provide a rational, practical, and analytical launch platform for TRADOC to initiate the process.

The record of accomplishment of TRADOC could alone be a separate history of effecting dramatic change in a large organization. Led by secretaries of the Army and chiefs of staff, who all shared and supported the vision to varying degrees, and executed by leaders of vision and imagination, particulary Gen. William E. DePuy and his many protégés, two decades of rebuilding began in the early seventies.[2] The scope of interrelated change was enormous. Doctrine was the centerpiece, the "driver," of all else. The active-defense concept expounded in *FM100-5* began the necessary intellectual ferment. Debate matured the doctrine through the integrated battlefield to AirLand Battle and now continues to AirLand Operations. Along the way, serious attention was directed to analysis of competing development processes. This was institutionalized in the Soviet battlefield development plan, so there was credible forcing pressure on TRADOC. Equally important, day-to-day doctrinal development was tied to the Air Force at Tactical Air Command, located next door to TRADOC at Langley Air Force Base, Virginia. The importance of airpower in AirLand Battle was acknowledged from the start.

Technology was and is the companion to doctrine. Technology, too, frequently leads the process, resulting in, "We have (name the weapon); now how do we use it?" After Vietnam, doctrine led. Once the need for virtually immediate deterrent readiness, the "come-as-you-are war," was agreed upon, the broad doctrinal direction was set in successive versions of *FM 100-5, Operations.* The next strategic decision was to focus the energies and resources available on the most important "levering" weapons systems necessary to execute the doctrine. The "Big Five" were designated: Abrams, Bradley, Blackhawk, Apache, and Patriot. Other critical new weapons emerged such as MLRS and joint-surveillance, target-attack, reporting system (JSTARS), but the wisdom of the basic choices and the focused discipline necessary to mature capability over decades was evident to all in Operation Desert Storm. Now the process continues with AirLand Opera-

tions, although the equipment will probably be information-age additions to the Big Five, rather than new systems.[3]

Organizations had to be modified to accommodate both doctrine and equipment. Objective organizations were constructed in Division '86, then the Army of Excellence, to ensure a balanced combined-arms capability across the tactical echelons from squad to corps. Probably the best example of the overall process at work was the design, then creation, of the light infantry division. It evolved in an interactive process of doctrinal requirement, to organization on the ground (high-technology, light-division test bed), then to revised doctrine with improved training, on to prototype division [7th Infantry Division (Light)], and finally, to a fielded force of several light divisions. All were subsequently tested successfully first in combat training centers and later in combat during Operation Just Cause in Panama.

Throughout, increasing attention was directed toward ensuring competent, motivated, disciplined soldiers led by trained leaders. In time, the training system was modified to produce soldiers who, at all grades, could exploit the doctrine. AirLand Battle war-fighting requirements were carefully dissected to define the individual and collective performance required by task, condition, and standard. It was a Herculean effort, undertaken across heavy, light, and special forces, all tied together by the CBRS. All of this was accomplished as the operational force continued to man the forward ramparts in Europe and Asia, while the Army in the United States prepared for global contingency employment.

The CBRS caused substantial change at every echelon in every unit. As the light infantry improved, armor forces modernized, following the CBRS sequence. The evolving modern battlefield set the requirements for the Abrams tank. Anticipated improvements in the survivability, new mobility capability, and night-fighting potential of the Abrams triggered reorganizations at platoon, company, and battalion. Training standards were tightened to ensure that potential for fire-on-the-move fighting became realized performance in the fielded Abrams unit. New forms of low-cost simulation were created as effective training. New personnel selection and training programs, such as excellence in armor, were developed to enable tankers to exploit the equipment. Officer and noncommissioned-officer courses were all changed significantly. Each of these actions was major in itself. Synchronized with other changes through the CBRS, the aggregate was revolutionary. Everything was not done smoothly; there were severe disagreements among professionals. In some areas, change was coordinated only in retrospect. Nevertheless, the deployed Army modernized. It was a significant achievement in focusing change, all powered by the CBRS.

The clarity of hindsight reveals some errors, most of them relatively minor, although they did not appear so at the time. The AOE reorganization cut too deeply into the robustness of combat formations and the requisite logistical support. Division '86 reorganizations had a devastating impact on

unit stability, when quality-of-life programs were just coming on-line. Coordination of equipment and personnel changes remained poor for years. This became a continuing frustration in force integration. A major education program was required in "how the Army runs" for both commanders and staff, so that aggressive unit leadership could sort out on the ground what had not been foreseen by swamped staffs.[4]

Some valuable experiences were lost; others came too soon. Some genuine innovation emerging in the high-tech division at Fort Lewis, not embedded in the bureaucracy, was not institutionalized. Several innovations such as feeding soldiers in the field were forced into units too quickly and before they were ready. Light and heavy forces diverged, as each focused on self-improvement to the detriment of combined-arms proficiencies. Reserve forces, constrained by time, found only partially useful active-oriented programs designed to conserve manpower or money. Professionals can each think of more examples in areas of personal competence, but in sum, the Army had 80 percent to 90 percent of the answer the first time.

These few errors are really insignificant, compared to what had been achieved from the early seventies to the late eighties.

- Traditional values, professionalism, personal competence, and confidence were restored to officer leadership, and an outstanding noncommissioned officer corps was recreated.
- A thoroughly advanced war-fighting doctrine was formulated and assimilated across a deployed army. Then, the doctrine was employed successfully in two major national contingency operations, one "light" and one "heavy," on different continents in less than a year.[5]
- Major Army capabilities such as logistics and communications were automated and modernized remarkably rapidly with labor-saving devices and innovative restructuring.
- Technology, computer led, was introduced across the force, including the combat arms, traditionally areas of understandable conservatism. For example, night-fighting became routine, often preferable, in many battlefield situations. Assimilation is incomplete, but the process is firmly embedded, thanks to Operation Desert Storm.
- The entire personnel and training systems were restructured from a conscript force-mobilization base to a volunteer force-deterrence base—the "fight-as-you-are" Army.

All this was done while maintaining forces ready for virtually immediate combat throughout the world. The result, a world-class army in its own class of one, is a significant achievement of the CBRS but one that the Army will not have time to relish in the future. For the next major shift, transition to landpower readiness in the post-industrial world is equal in

magnitude to the post–Vietnam War rebuilding. We may already be behind in adjusting to its demands. The Army will have to move to post-industrial readiness during a depressing era of drawdown and not the heady resource atmosphere of the Reagan years. Furthermore, results are needed in five years, rather than the fifteen or twenty years required after Vietnam. The CBRS now faces a second major test. How should it be employed in addressing this new challenge?

First, catalog the potential applications, which are significant, of CBRS. The CBRS today can be used to force change, be it discarding the old or embedding the new. It is invaluable to be able to write the doctrine and then develop integrated capability to actualize it, with synchronized organization, equipment, and training in a respected combat "crucible," the combat training centers (CTC). For innovative captains and sergeants, evidence of the use of the new in "battle" overrides the mind's eye of senior officers jaded by important but dated personal experiences. No other nation has such a fielded capability to stimulate innovation in war fighting today.

The benefit extends further. With the CBRS, doctrine has moved technology. Deep attack created the requirement for JSTARS and the Army tactical missile system (ATACMS). Extending the depth of the close-in, direct-fire battle to neutralize the mass of the breakthrough attack created the requirement for the hypervelocity missile. This ability may be decisive as new drop-in capabilities are developed and tailored in the information age. The increment of equipment capability required to ensure rapid, decisive success can be defined with relative precision and then inserted in generic equipment, overtly for deterrence or covertly for battlefield surprise. Conversely, a genuinely new breakthrough development can be more rapidly accommodated, because the doctrinal, organizational, training, and personnel implications can be determined, the necessary changes quickly made, and the new product validated by "war fighting" at the combat training centers.

CBRS is understood and respected by both uniformed and civilian leaders and, inferentially by the general public. CBRS is accepted as a rational process to be used by competent professionals to achieve the results promised in combat. It worked beyond expectation in Operations Just Cause and Desert Storm. This confidence is an important and pleasant change from the distrust made evident after Vietnam in public debate on Abrams and Bradley and, in fact, on most of our major systems. We clearly know what we are doing.[6]

While focused on the proper "bottom line" of any military organization—success in war fighting—the CBRS can shorten the development cycle. The rigor of task, condition, and standard combined with the technological ability to "trial by fire" in subsistent, virtual, or constructive tactical engagement simulation conserves time and narrows the requirements

for full, live-fire trials. This permits accelerated development in every aspect of the CBRS. Precision in defining then visualizing the new, along with ability to assess and evaluate in a "fighting" context, permits the accelerating development and assimilation "loop" essential to staying on the front edge in the emerging information age.

CBRS is embedded in the bureaucracy. A process exists that can be accelerated. The importance of this institutionalization can hardly be overstated. It provides potential to sustain current success in force integration, and perhaps even to accelerate the process, to compensate for the certain coming deterioration of capability in the national landpower industrial base.[7] As some form of arsenal system evolves, with inevitable pressure to reduce the support army, the CBRS—including the intellectual center of gravity at Fort Leavenworth, and the combat training centers—needs to be considered and conserved as straight combat power. In terms of long-term ability to influence constituted reserves, as well as to integrate joint and allied resources, vibrant, innovative, institutionalized CBRS is worth the battlefield capability of an active constituted corps. In other words, sacrifice structure, if necessary, up to one corps, assuming a potential four-corps Total Force, active and reserves, in order to maintain proactive CBRS in the years ahead.

We are fortunate to have this process in place, for the analytical requirements associated with the post-industrial age are substantial and growing. Three future challenges stand out: normal evolution of capability within the constituted active force; unique modifications associated with mobilization, primarily, but not exclusively, the reserves; and changes in coalition operations. We need to accelerate the application of the CBRS to each of these areas.

Constituted active forces undergo almost continuous force-composition changes. Producing "lessons learned," from either combat operations or ongoing training, is practically a cottage industry, for all the right reasons. "Lessons learned" about measures of effectiveness usually suggest improvements in existing doctrine, organization, equipment, or training—CBRS. Doctrine itself, the driver of the CBRS, evolves routinely in continuing processes of review. As AirLand Battle is fielded, the emphasis shifts to AirLand Battle Future, now AirLand Operations.

As each of the battlefield operating systems reassesses potential threats and new technological opportunities, new intra-BOS requirements are generated.[8] For example, introduction of an effective, hypervelocity, direct-fire missile or an air-defense "flyable," nonline-of-sight missile available to the mechanized infantry battalion could partially remove the requirement for a long-range, antitank capability on an infantry fighting vehicle. Similarly, extended-range tube artillery, improved by advanced propulsion like liquid propellant, can change significantly the best missile-versus-tube artillery mix. That changes significantly the direct-fire support available to maneu-

ver units. These are relatively routine trade-offs, made more evident more rapidly through CBRS. More substantial improvements are desirable and possible.

Today as resources decline, we should focus more on collateral operations, seeking synergistic effects of geometric increases in force-effectiveness by interacting BOS, and make much better use of existing capability. Arithmetic increases in capability, achieved by incremental improvements within a BOS, can become geometric increases cross-BOS. For example, an improved, top-attack missile directly increases the expected defensive capability of an infantry company. The same missile employed to destroy air defense, joint suppression of air defense (JSEAD), may produce a much greater battlefield effect, since it permits rotary or fixed-wing aircraft to better defend the infantry company. A nonline-of-sight missile guided by optical fiber (NLOS) is suitable for destroying helicopters. Its "brilliant" guidance may be better applied to destroy high-value command and control. Of course, the challenge of adaptive use is often more in solving bureaucratic turf problems than it is in improving actual capability. The proponent, or his military-industrial constituency, may not encourage or tolerate cross-BOS applications. This is another challenge for the CBRS methodology.

There are also certain synergistic effects that can be expected from computers, and the various combined-arms teams currently on the battlefield could be made to interact more effectively. The basic combined-arms teams are light, heavy, and aviation. The combined-arms heavy team focuses on the tank-infantry team as the combat element. All else—combat, combat-support, and combat-service support—is there to support the tank-infantry team. For combined-arms light, the primary combat element is the individual infantryman. For combined-arms aviation, it is the attack helicopter and the air-assault infantryman. CBRS, directed at multiplying the battlefield effectiveness of each of these three combat means, could develop different capabilities and combinations of arms and services from what we have at present. Improved, direct-fire, mutual support between Abrams and Bradley could be a good starting point: the CBRS could effectively force more integration by mandating joint Abrams–Bradley training tables.

Then CBRS could be applied to light-heavy, heavy-aviation, and light-aviation combinations, now including special operating forces. Surprising new tactical capabilities would be revealed without requiring major new investments, particularly as traditional "stovepipes" are broken. Stovepipes—communications from subordinate to superior—are inevitable in large bureaucratic organizations. Major defense firms, TRADOC, and other Army commands all have them. Stovepipes are often a deceptively efficient way to operate. As a general proposition, significant economies or synergistic new capabilities can be created by forcing horizontal coordination where it has not previously existed. It forces bright, capable people to look at

problems from new perspectives. CBRS can help to break down the stove-pipes impairing cross-BOS applications.[9]

The same analysis should extend to joint operations. Some of the best results of Operation Desert Storm involved exploiting new CINC powers, born in the Goldwater-Nichols legislation to produce new combinations of joint capabilities. Notable examples were merging search and rescue (SAR) and SOF, Army maneuver-aviation with Navy surface warfare for maritime intercept operations, and the interactive use of fixed, rotary-wing, and un-manned airpower in a single air-tasking order. There appears to be ample opportunity for intensified CBRS to achieve considerably more "bang for the invested buck" with our constituted forces.

The payoffs appear even larger if the CBRS were to be applied to reserve forces. This is yet to occur in any significant manner.[10] The primary resource for the citizen-soldier is time, for both pre-and postmobilization constituted units. For the regular force, it is people and money. The Army of Excellence was designed to fight and win AirLand Battle while conserving personnel spaces in order to generate new units. It was also designed to save money to purchase more equipment. These new active-Army organizational designs were trimmed to the bone to conserve personnel, and then applied without modification to the reserves. The number of mechanics in reserve Apache battalions was severely reduced, as it was in active units; yet there was no manpower need to reduce the number in the reserves. In fact, there may have been a case to increase the number of reserve mechanics over that of the active force because of dispersion, turnover, and the time required to train and sustain a mechanic's skills in the reserves. For years, additional tankers have been sought as individual trained replacements in tank companies. Creating a security squad of ten tankers in tank company head-quarters was the recommended method. Denied the active Army in the competition for manpower spaces, the addition has never been permitted the reserves. The computer has allowed flexible tables of organization (LTOE); there simply has never been the demand to structure uniquely reserve organizations to facilitate either peacetime readiness or wartime mobilization.

Personnel development and training for the reserves have been equally neglected in the CBRS. The development and flow of MOS assumes an individual soldier's mobility in a succession of assignments that would permit professional development; that is, the individual can be assigned where required to progress in his or her professional development. This flexibility is simply nonexistent for most citizen-soldiers. Their MOS progression is limited to assignments available in their immediate geographic area. Lack of consideration in development opportunity is pervasive, even in MOSs where most of the total capability is in the reserves. The same inadequacies exist in training, where there has been persistent inability to make substantive adjustments to training doctrine or be responsive to the vastly different cir-

cumstances of reserve training. The regular Army is too engrossed in genuine, immediate, force-readiness requirements for deterrence to address the
issue. The reserves simply do not have the level of professional competence
and confidence necessary to fight active-Army bureaucracy.

To the best of my knowledge, the CBRS has yet to be applied substan-
tively to the reconstitution force generated from scratch after mobilization.
Uncertainties about the availability of new equipment and particularly
about the capability of the national production base have seemed so great
that everything else would have to be solved when production resumed.
That estimate may need revision. The global economy emerges with new
production opportunities for potential allies, and the processor may permit
rapid wartime modification of peacetime production.[11] At a minimun,
CBRS should review force generation with personnel of lesser quality. Also,
it would seem appropriate that the methodology be applied to wartime upgrade of previously outdated equipment. What could be rapidly upgraded
with new technologies? The result may not be elegant, but it could be workable on mobilization. What would the training package be? Is a new organization required? As constituted active forces are reduced, there would
appear to be increasing need for these kinds of applications of the CBRS.

If we think the reserves—the majority of our Total Force—have been
slighted in the CBRS, that inattention is dwarfed by our lack of focus on
planning associated with coalition operations. Here, there appears to be an
entirely new set of factors that need thoughtful analysis. We should consider
areas of comparative U.S. advantage, where U.S. units need to be designed
to reinforce BOS shortfalls of prospective allies.[12] As we foresee the potential for contingencies in regional areas, CBRS should address the total requirements for successful war fighting with likely allies. Could we have
foreseen the need to structure rapid-response, regionally oriented U.S. Patriot capability?[13] Are Patriot units, organized and trained for rapid-response support of allies, justifiable? If circumstances convert a former threat
(Syria) into a regional ally, does that change the doctrine, organization, or
training of the hypothetical rapid-response Patriot unit? Are we prepared
today for similar regional operations with allies of relatively comparable
capability, such as cooperative air defense with Russian units in the Far East,
under the control of UN rules of engagement? What about sophisticated
U.S. intelligence support of a regional ally in South America? As threats and
the world order change, special-purpose intelligence units may be easier to
justify for the constituted force than the traditional corps force package for
U.S. contingency operations.

There are other cases where U.S. equipment will be provided to allied
units. Training in operations and sustainment become vital. Culturally correct material must be prepared before the event. This happens today. Creation and conversion of U.S. training packages for the M1A2 tank are under
way for the Saudis as potential purchasers. But this is almost entirely equip-

ment oriented, related to the foreign military sale itself. Yet, if the vehicles were to be employed in a regional contingency, national interests far transcend just equipment-operational rates. We should consider the full CBRS in assessing how a significant capability such as the M1A2 could be integrated into our regional contingency planning. Are there special training exercises appropriate to probable missions—likely threat, local weather, or terrain? Do the Saudis need new organizations appropriate to their social structure or new organizations to be able to plug in rapidly to our command-and-control systems? Should we design these organizations for foreign military sales or potential contingency use? The same questions should be asked for each BOS if we anticipate fighting AirLand Battle in that contingency theater.

There is yet another variation that deserves thoughtful review. We need to assess the capabilities of various military equipment that permeate the world. The Army is used to doing this as part of threat analysis. Most recently, this was necessary in the Persian Gulf, where the Iraqis had a complex mix of equipment, including recent U.S. HAWK air defenses. What about CBRS modifications appropriate to the mixes of equipment possessed by our allies? Are there unique host-nation or contractor-support requirements that should be planned in advance? A superb job of "catch-up" was done by U.S. Central Command in Operation Desert Shield. Fortunately, they had several months to plan and then adjust. We should be better prepared in the future. Is this a mission for CBRS, focused on allies? Perhaps this is a TRADOC mission, which needs to be acknowledged?

For example, are there due any likely U.S. doctrinal modifications caused by the capabilities or inadequacies of allies we want in the forefront for political reasons? Allied capabilities or lack thereof certainly caused modification of air-ground operations doctrine in Operation Desert Storm. Tables of equipment (TOEs) had to be modified to accommodate new or different items—allied, host-nation, or contract. Innovative training was initiated for Arab allies. How much of this could have been done in advance, were there a mechanism for full CBRS analysis with potential allies as one element of landpower (TRADOC) support to the U.S. regional CINCs and Army commanders?

No organization is currently charged with these kinds of component CBRS analyses in preparation for likely operations, yet the Army is increasingly oriented to regional contingencies. It would seem prudent to institutionalize a capability to do this. One useful by-product could be more convincing landpower force-generation rationales.

There is one other aspect of the CBRS that seems vital as the Army declines in size and there is a temporary respite from global threats. We need to retain the quality, gold-collar talent of today's Army for the inevitable buildup of the future, when nationalism, population migrations, economic

shortages, ecological disasters, or religious strife might provoke conflict re-quiring U.S. intervention, as one or more surely will. To keep these quality leaders, they must remain fully challenged. The CBRS provides a challeng-ing, intellectual, and practical war-fighting focus for the peacetime Army. Emerging technology permits distributed tie-in of practical, ongoing CBRS work to officer professional-development programs. We should encourage a test-fix-test iterative process between unit and CBRS proponent to stim-ulate the vital innovations of talented leaders.

Fortunately, the Army today is moving aggressively to exploit CBRS. There is potential to address virtually all of these issues in the Louisana Maneuvers '94. Executing the personal vision of the chief of staff, the Army is creating theater-level war exercises patterned on the Louisana maneuvers created by General Marshall before World War II. The concept was pre-sented to the House Armed Services Committee in Gen. Gordon Sullivan's statement presenting the fiscal 1993 budget:

The purpose of Louisiana Maneuvers '94 is twofold:

* First, it is a focal point for the changing Army. As we move toward the vision it gives us a common goal. It brings the institution together, forging cohesion in a reshaped Army.
* Second, it is a demonstration of progress made toward the vision. Louisiana Maneuvers '94 will be a laboratory in which to see the effects of our work on doctrine, organization, training, materiel requirements, and leader de-velopment. Starting with exercises this year, it will be a vehicle to try out new ideas, make mistakes, assess them, provide feedback, and try again.

It will involve the Total Army—active, Reserve, Guard and civilian—in a se-ries of exercises to generate forces for a warfighting CINC and to engage those forces in simulated operations. It will encompass mobilization and deploy-ment, warfighting, redeployment, and reconstitution phases in a full exercise of adaptive planning. It will include a full range of armored, light, and special operations forces and will be a strategic laboratory in which to evaluate AirLand Battle doctrine; force generation, mobilization and deployment; force pooling concepts; organizational designs; and combined arms training strategies for large-unit simulations. By means of games within games, it will operate across the full range of the continuum of military operations. It will leverage the technology inherent in existing and emerging command-and-con-trol systems, and simulations to exercise the force. It will validate or challenge emerging doctrinal concepts and lessons learned, to enable the Army to com-plete its new doctrine and organizational and equipment concepts and designs. It will draw on the great tradition of large-scale maneuvers and will lay the groundwork for a whole new generation of training and readiness concepts.

I believe that today's changing Army requires a landmark process to control, direct, and understand change; to provide leadership on the way to our vision of the future Army. Louisiana Maneuvers '94 will provide the first

step in what could become a recurring exercise that will provide the focus for the post-Cold War force. It is just one of the means the Army will use to ensure we are on track to meet the needs of the Nation the next time we are called. The future is by nature unclear. To the extent that we can test our capabilities in diverse sets of conditions and scenarios in such a manner, we will improve our preparedness for the eventualities the future holds, and *keep our eye on the ball*.[14]

The chief of staff has it exactly right. The CBRS has been extremely helpful. It is just begining to recognize its potential.

7   The Training Revolution

THE COMPETENCE OF THE FORCES DURING OPERATIONS
Just Cause and Desert Storm was clearly evident to the American people.
Nearly all in the chain of command credited improved training of U.S.
forces as a decisive factor in the successes. Perhaps in no other area was the
contrast with preceding operations, particularly the abortive hostage rescue
in Iran, more evident than in training. One particularly pleasant surprise
was the soldiers' evident familiarity with and confidence in weapons previously untested in battle. All appeared to work as designed or, in some cases,
even better than predicted. Soldiers had been obviously very well prepared
in the use of new capabilities, even though some had trained previously only
in simulation. Few tankers had ever fired the new, depleted-uranium combat
round for the Abrams. Even fewer had seen, much less fired, the newest
round deployed to the Gulf. The only training had been on gunnery simulation—the unit conduct-of-fire trainer. Soldiers commented after the war
that there was absolutely no difficulty in making the transition to combat
ammunition. The preparatory training had done its job. To the Army, this
was vindication of an intense effort, focused to revolutionize Army
training.

My purpose here is not to summarize the revolution, impressive
though it was; rather it is to analyze key components of the success and
then project them into the post-industrial Army. Where could the revolution
be in five or ten years, and what are probable implications for national
landpower policies and programs?

The single most important ingredient to improved training was the
institutionalization of the systems approach to training (SAT) combined
with a focus on learning by doing: train and evaluate, while performing

tasks against a live enemy whenever possible. Defining task, condition, and standard for individual and collective training was accomplished by an analytical process of unprecedented rigor. It was a major undertaking that consumed some fifteen years. Not only did all tasks have to be defined, but they had to be set in order of priority and incorporated into thoughtful training documentation. Individual and collective tasks were prescribed with ways suggested to train to proficiency.

Unanticipated, long-term changes developed from this exhausting analysis of battlefield tasks. As leaders thought through, then defined various functions, they focused on minute detail of battle. Who or what did which tasks, to whom, how, and why? What was acceptable performance? What were the standards for judging success or failure? What were the necessary conditions of battle performance, whether individual or collective? The rigor of the analysis focused the Army on war-fighting basics, and it brought about much finer resolution in statements of requirements for systems acquisition. In time, this stimulated detailed analysis of man-machine interfaces. It seems safe to assert that a new order of professional precision and attention to detail was introduced to the Army with the training revolution.[1]

A second profound effect was that SAT moved the Army from normative to criterion-referenced evaluation. No longer would grading be "on the curve." Soldiers were expected to train and demonstrate proficiency in task, condition, and standard—"go, or no go." They were expected to demonstrate by performance, preferably in a battle context, rather than describe "what if." Personnel actions were based increasingly on objective, measured performance in battle-related tasks. Acceptance of performance-basing was to prove critical later, when issues of equal opportunity and affirmative action arose. The soldier was promoted or dismissed, "up or out," based on demonstrated performance or lack thereof—not on race, creed, ethnic background, or gender. SAT permitted the competence-basing of the Army.

The changes, therefore, did much more than improve training. Other, sometimes unforeseen beneficial effects occurred. Most important, it reengaged senior Army leaders in the details of war fighting. Preoccupied with survival during the early seventies, in the face of drugs, race, dissent, and the Modern Volunteer Army, there simply had not been sufficient command attention paid to the basic rationale for the Army: to fight and win. Now generals refocused on the contents of the individual performance test (SQT) and the training and evaluation of small-unit battle tasks (ARTEP).[2] It was the exact focus on basic mission that a healing army needed.

There was even greater effect over time, as the engine of change, or doctrine, was formulated. After soldier tasks had been codified, attention turned to the interactions among and between doctrine, materiel, and organizations. Rigorous analysis and thoughtful judgment produced the battlefield operating systems, analytical descriptions of the capabilities

needed to fight on the modern battlefield. Consisting of maneuver, fire support, command and control, intelligence, combat-service support, air defense and mobility, countermobility, and survivability, the BOS established the essential intellectual framework for the AirLand Battle doctrine. It was then possible to conceptualize potential new interactions and synergies within or among the various BOS. Multi-BOS collateral operations, such as joint suppression of air defense (JSEAD), could be thought through by task, condition, and standard in order to define the next step of actualization: What had to be developed to make it happen? Now, that conceptual advance is in the process of being reinforced by another, virtual simulation, which creates fully interactive, three-dimensional, digital battlefields, where concepts can be fought in visual battles. More revolutionary changes in how the Army decides to fight are just around the corner. These are other by-products of the information age.

There was one other, more subtle impact as task, condition, and standard moved into collateral operations. The Soviets, as we did, recognized the changing nature of war. In some areas we even followed them, as in coalition theater war, or theater strategic operations. But, as part of their "scientific approach" to the laws of war, they put their doctrine into effect by reducing it to numbers of norms in order to govern the actions of commanders in considerable detail. Individual initiative was discouraged at lower echelons. The United States, having codified individual and collective tasks and unit missions, could leave much broader discretion to subordinate commanders. SAT gave us the best of both worlds: necessary rigor plus extraordinary decentralization to local initiative.

Another impact of the training revolution was that systemizing training provoked useful debate on how to divide responsibilities between institution and unit. For example, what was the unit commander's responsibility for leader training, as distinguished from that of the training base? Once responsibilities were explicitly defined, resources could be targeted for explicit results, measured by performance. The whole training process was moved from the sphere of subjective remembrances of the senior officer present to a defined system with known inputs and expectable outputs. This rigor was critical not only to the introduction of complex, new weapons but also to the quantification of the need for quality soldiers and to sustain the momentum of increasing excellence in the volunteer force. For example, we could prove that better soldiers were essential to better performance on the Abrams tank. Tank gunnery training matured to the point where statistically credible data could be developed to reflect poor performance from less capable gunners or crews. In time, similar analysis of various weapons became possible.

Today, the basic system is in place. The concept-based requirements system demands that essential training development occur for the constituted force. The immediate challenge now is to fine-tune the training system

for specific operational requirements. Although more is required, research is under way on the following issues:

- Impact of unit-personnel turnover on collective-training requirements.
- Decay over time of task proficiency as a function of general mental aptitude.
- Refresher training requirements for units and individuals of varying ability.

A second major achievement of the training revolution was to create a sensible, accepted, war-fighting bottom line for the peacetime Army. The skill qualification test and military qualification standard (MQS) provide for evaluating individual officer and noncommissioned officer proficiency, but not in a battle environment. The battle context is provided in the combat training centers (CTC).[3] The CTC combination is extraordinarily powerful: doctrinally correct battlefield missions; a demanding opposition force, fighting to win; and credible instrumentation, and mentors (observers-controllers), in a tough, fair training and evaluation war-fighting environment. Increasingly, senior commanders (corps and division) have been promoted to command because they have demonstrated tactical competence at a CTC. They were outstanding fighters in the most realistic battle we can create. They laid it on the line in "kill-or-be-killed" situations in front of their soldiers, where they were unable to control enemy actions. Today, we extend this opportunity to corps echelon in the Battle Command Training Program, so commanders at every tactical level have to demonstrate their proficiency in war fighting. No other army in the world approaches this demand in rigor of training, size of physical plant, or willingness to expose the chain of command to such uncontrolled risk in front of subordinates. In fact, few businesses have such a difficult, frequent, personal "bottom line."

The CTC challenge for the future is to use the technologies of the information age, particularly distributed war fighting on the virtual (SIMNET) battlefield, to immerse constituted forces and our likely allies in war fighting. We know what our doctrine requires for successful fighting by BOS. Just as telecommunications, entertainment, and education converge on distributed locations, eventually the home or workplace, we should be able to distribute the quality training and individual-performance "bottom line" of the CTC to the citizen-soldier's armory or reserve center. In time, we should be able to separate individual and small-unit task performance from larger unit war fights on the ground and in distributed simulation. Global telecommunications offer the prospect of involving likely regional allies in contingency-operations training.

Structured training has followed systemization through SAT. As rigor evolved, it became obvious that training situations could be designed (structured) to achieve very specific training results. Just as mission, enemy, ter-

rain, troops, and time-available (METT-T) dictate execution of any tactical operation, they can be tuned relatively easily in tactical engagement simulation to create effective training situations. The tactical mission prescribed in doctrinal manuals can be modified easily by the next senior commander. Enemy, represented by the OPFOR (opposing forces) can be varied in mission, composition, weapons, and even the level of proficiency (hit probabilities). Terrain can be varied by changing it or the heading of the axis of operations on fixed terrain. Composition or capability of friendly troops can be changed by modifying the task organization.

When simulation is used, commanders are provided a great deal of latitude in designing the training environment. Some forms of simulation can be "restarted" to permit very precise "replay" of specified METT-T. All of the training is reinforced by extensive after-action reviews (AARs), which encourage self-analysis of error and corrective action. Some simulation permits very detailed battle-analysis data that reinforce the AAR process. Then missions and collective task situations can be replicated or changed selectively for training purposes.

Tactical engagement simulation applies the computer to the training representation of fighting a war. Simulation capability is expanding rapidly, as is the computer itself. It now consists of three complementary, but distinctly different, applications—subsistent, virtual, or constructive. Subsistent simulation is use of the multiple, individual-laser engagement system (MILES), appended to actual equipment at the CTC and in local training areas. Virtual simulation is the creation of a virtual, seamless, three-dimensional "electronic battlefield" (SIMNET), where one can fight on digitized terrain with manned, semiautomated or automated equipment or units. Constructive simulation fights with equipment and units "made" by processors using accepted algorithms like the joint exercise simulation system (JESS) to drive command post exercises. The most common form of structured training is lane-training, using subsistent simulation, and is normally employed for small-unit armor or infantry training. More and more, distributed, virtual simulation is being used. As technology advances, the opportunities to distribute good training seem particularly favorable for constituted reserve forces.

Simulation will never fully replace the absolute necessity of training on the ground. Nothing can substitute for the training benefit of being tired, cold, wet, and miserable under live fire. But simulation will permit training on tough tasks too dangerous to execute in peacetime, such as a response to attack from 360 degrees, or tasks that are ecologically unsound, like firing depleted uranium ammunition. Also simulation is generally less expensive; it conserves fuel, spare parts, and ammunition. Simulation is here to stay.

Future structured training can provide very intense, immersion battle experiences designed to train constituted forces in a much more time-effi-

cient manner. Using a combination of the three types of tactical engagement simulation, new doctrine, equipment, or organizations can be introduced to units. Diverse units, separated by hundreds of miles, can be assembled on a common electronic battlefield by networking them on digitized terrain. Unit-training applications should, in time, be transferable to individual and leader training, either in the schoolhouse or at distributed locations. Institutional quality control can be maintained as centralized observer-controllers observe trainee activities. The possibilities seem unlimited, for the training process the Army has designed draws directly on probable advances of the information age.

The rigor of task, condition, and standard, combined with the structured training described above, provides a logical framework for improvement of the unit-readiness reporting system. An improved reporting system is especially desirable now, when a quality force faces resource anemia, with attendant dangers to the validity of the reporting system, and more critically, to the integrity of the profession. We now know enough about training to perform well in battle and about associated resource requirements to be able to correlate training to standard with the resource requirements of corresponding battle events. These could then tie directly to combat-readiness levels. Uncertainties of different METT-T factors in the situational training exercise can be eliminated by focusing on bread-and-butter tables or baseline exercises with predefined, fixed METT-T for combat-readiness reporting. Tables can be developed for both small-unit battle tasks and battle command-and-staff tasks. The chain of command will determine "how." The point is that there are now individual and collective task-readiness measurement tools that are war fighting based and accepted. Technologies are coming that support uniform, distributed execution in joint and coalition operational training. How does the Army wish to apply them?

The momentum of the information age will further refine these readiness-measurement tools. Tactical engagement simulation improves as technologies evolve. Processing capability increases and costs decrease predictably. Distribution will be amortized by the entertainment industry. On the other hand, there is well-founded concern about attempting overprecise measurement of unit-training readiness, which is more influenced by intangibles of leadership than it is by measured training exercises. Some objective measurement system seems essential not only to inform senior civilian and military leaders but also to reinforce the integrity of the readiness reporting system, particularly during a period of reduced resources.

It seems entirely possible that, in five years, precise tools for measuring individual and collective training readiness will be available at reasonable cost at distributed locations. When they are, variable readiness becomes feasible. Constituted units can be trained and sustained to prescribed readiness gates, with known training and resource requirements to bring units

of average effectiveness to deployability readiness. Since the capabilities and requirements are defined by CBRS and are amenable to global distribution, there is no technical reason why we should not be able to similarly evaluate allied proficiency. We could do this in selected battlefield operating systems, such as air-defense. Perhaps unit proficiency could be tied to regional or UN military assistance. There would seem to be wide-ranging possibilties.

It seems evident that the training revolution has just begun. Most of the tough, costly spadework has been done. We have defined individual and collective task proficiency; the CTC has all necessary facilities; and SIM-NET (combined arms tactical trainer) and hundreds of other improvements have been purchased during years of relative affluence. Most important, stemming from combat performance in Operations Just Cause and Desert Storm, the Army leadership "believes." This is a generational advantage over any other army in the world. If other military establishments "believe"—and most still do not—other nations will have difficulty affording the manpower and funding costs of creating an initially controversial, modern training system.

Now is the time to exploit and use what the Army has to improve dramatically the training readiness of citizen-soldiers and to extend quality training to likely regional allies. A shift in perspective from saving money and manpower to saving time could quickly revolutionize reserve training. Weeks of summer training could become days of weekend training. Focus of our system on intense, culturally based training in selected regionally important BOS could shift balances of regional military power. By all reports, Army special forces did a fine job in Operation Desert Storm. To what extent had the training infrastructure—the TRADOC proponents or the CTC infrastructure—been focused on the problem before the contingency? What might have been done with selected Gulf allies in CBRS, including focused combined training in preparation for likely contingencies?

The *National Military Strategy* (1992) poses a formidable continuum of potential conflict, particularly regional contingencies.[4] It would seem that the known rigor of training and evaluation institutionalized in the current system could be harnessed to accelerate adaptation to the new strategy. The training system could

- Develop structured training exercises, that would train and assess regional allies' abilities to employ selected U.S. battlefield operating systems on the ground or in simulation.
- Prepare rapid, contingency-force package training modules to execute combined, collateral operations.
- Prepare structured joint and combined command-and-staff training exercises involving likely regional contingencies and develop schooling tables as well as likely situational exercises.

- Assess readiness of various contingency packages designed to respond to specialized "niche" crises, such as strategic nuclear-warhead security in country X by no-notice "employment" in constructive simulation.

New training requirements abound, and fortunately, the training system has great potential to respond. New principles for training design may be both desirable and wholly feasible, given advances in training theory and technology.

- Create immersion-training situations in which the individual or unit is trained through full immersion in a tough, competitive, win-or-lose war.
- Distribute training to the most effective locales for training. For the reservist, it could be a network to the local armory or reserve center; for the potential regional ally, use his local exercise control center.
- Intensify the process of training to compress the time required to task-train and to rapidly bond individuals into teams.
- Prepare separate training regimes for reserves and potential coalition partners. These could consist of special reserve task lists and intensive structured programs designed to compensate for limited training opportunities and culturally oriented training support material to facilitate rapid "train-up" for likely regional allies.

The list could go on and on. The rigor of SAT is available. Demanding force-on-force training with after-action reviews has been institutionalized. There are great opportunities before the Army today. Distributed tactical engagement simulation, tied to structured training, can literally do more with less. Critical training requirements can be dissected, and training solutions can be designed and structured for broad application while retaining quality control. Then, that training can be distributed anywhere in the world to achieve measurable results. Technology can be focused to conserve funding, manpower, or time. Unit costs per megabit stored and processed or per bit transmitted decline rapidly. Semiautomation or automation can reduce dramatically the manpower cost of conducting realistic war-fighting training to precise standard. Compression permitted by immersion in training through experiential learning can reduce time requirements to a quarter of what they are now. And this entire system is possessed uniquely by the U.S. Army.

How should the revolution proceed?

8 Blue-, White-, Gold-Collar Landpower

THE CONCEPT-BASED REQUIREMENTS SYSTEM (CBRS) AND the revolution in training have clearly powered significant change in landpower. But the Army consists of people. The Army does not man equipment; it equips the man. Therefore, more than any other factor, the secret of today's excellence is quality people at all levels. That should not be a surprise. The cold war's need for near-immediate readiness of substantial forces, the "come-as-you-are" war, combined with the clear national choice to go for quality over quantity in the volunteer force, demanded a focus on personnel. In time, quality people became both prerequisite and rationale for transition to AirLand Battle doctrine. The doctrine mandated broad flexibility to subordinate commanders in executing senior commanders' concepts, to capture sudden opportunity and to minimize the unexpected peril characteristic in the rapid pace of modern war. Subordinate commanders had to be highly competent. Then, to take advantage of competent leaders, the CBRS produced complex new equipment, organizations, tactics, techniques, and procedures. The CBRS became a reinforcing cycle of increasing excellence, powered by more and more capable soldiers.

By the early eighties, some could half-joke that training the force was no longer like preparing the local high school team; we were instead preparing the Dallas Cowboys. Elsewhere, the impact of the doctrinal change has been compared to the automobile market. We were Chevrolets; but the obvious need was to get to the Cadillac level to execute the complex warfighting requirements dictated by the doctrine, at least for the constituted, rapid-reaction force.[1] To continue the commercial analogy, the United States

had moved "up market" in the search for competitive strategies against the Soviet Union. SDI was up market, a track the Soviets would find difficult to follow. AirLand Battle was the same. It was an astute strategic move to turn the Soviets' mass and momentum from assets to liabilities. In retrospect, the move up market was brilliant. We literally broke the Soviet bank. In so doing, we created a new military capability that will be difficult to match for the emerging information age.

But landpower did far more. Deliberately or unconsciously, the Army moved personnel requirements equally upscale with profound, long-term impacts. The TRADOC proponents for the various battlefield operating systems defined new levels of competence, which will be critical to successful warfare in the information age. We have not yet thought through the policy implications of this shift, which is similar in many ways to the work force's transformation now under way in modern global industry. The challenge today is how to attract, train, motivate, and sustain this force for the long term. The purpose of this chapter is to suggest new landpower personnel requirements associated with the post-industrial era and then to suggest appropriate new personnel policy issues.

Although soldiers wince when the terms are used, because they create an occupational, rather than professional, view of military service, traditional landpower leader requirements consist of blue-collar and white-collar responsibilities. Blue-collar emphasis focuses on what has to be done and how to do it. Blue-collar responsibility within the military is to execute precisely defined tasks exceedingly well despite danger, fear, and fatigue. This is sergeant's business: to prepare the organization to fight, then execute directed tasks to standard. The white-collar commissioned officer leads the fight, deciding what is to be done and when. He or she is concerned with the larger goals of the organization, determining when new circumstances dictate change, in accordance with broad, conceptual direction.

Operating weapons and equipment has been a traditional blue-collar responsibility in the U.S. Army. Increased complexity of equipment has muddied the distinction. Equipment-related training requirements for the individual soldier have varied, largely reflecting different levels of concern by developers about the complexity of individual interaction with equipment. Some new capabilities have appeared as benign to prospective users. Concealing the complexity of the average car, now possessing more processor capability than the Apollo moon shot, is a case in point.[2] Thermal-imaging on the Abrams tank is a very complex technological improvement that yet appears as a soldier-friendly addition.

Other interfaces are more difficult when the man-machine interaction is neglected. For example, the simplified test equipment (STE), designed to diagnose vehicle maintenance requirements, was not soldier-friendly. To many, the cure was worse than the original problem. Another example, the artillery tactical-fire direction system (TACFIRE) requires frequent sustain-

ment training. Increasingly assured of a quality soldier in the volunteer recruited force, the materiel developer has generally tended toward developing more capable and complex equipment. Fortunately, the Army has also paid much more attention to the perils of man-machine interface in managing the system acquisition process (MANPRINT).

In addition, some computer-directed equipment genuinely requires white-collar direction to take full advantage of its potential. Almost any computer today has enormous flexibility to respond to innovative new requirements. The ability to exploit this advantage is one discriminator between blue- and white-collar soldiers. There is constant pressure to draw greater tactical advantage from the computer. The average blue-collar, noncommissioned officer, therefore, is expected to know much, much more to do his or her job. And better people can handle more capable equipment, which requires better people, creating a closed-loop rationale that can subtly change expectations of blue-collar performance. This is exactly what has happened.

This pressure is even more evident in leader tasks. Here, requirements have become consistently more challenging, as units themselves have been provided more capability. The Bradley squad leader must master many more tasks than the M113-equipped squad leader. One could argue that, except for protection, the Bradley has more battlefield capability than the Patton-series tanks, the generation that preceded the Abrams. Add to that the complexity of leading a squad of infantry dismounted from the Bradley and out on the ground. The Abrams M1A1 is only marginally more challenging than the M1 or the M60A3, but the M1A2 is much more complex, providing the officer or noncommissioned leader new intercommunications and target-acquisition capabilities.

The escalation of capability and responsibility, mandated by evolving doctrine, was recognized in the Division '86 reorganization, when the smallest unit expected to cross-reinforce from infantry platoon to armor company, or vice versa, was elevated from platoon to company. The logic was that only the battalion commander with a staff could be expected to master the complexities of fighting Abrams and Bradley together. Clearly, this tactical challenge was expected to be too complex for the average young company commander.

In practice, the doctrine was not accepted by the force; there was little change in cross-reinforcement. Today, the professionally developed platoon sergeant of the Abrams unit is expected to be able to command the cross-reinforced tank company team on the battlefield in the event of heavy casualties. The MLRS section sergeant is expected to take action looked for previously from the chief of section or possibly the battery executive officer when battlefield circumstances dictated. His MLRS has the battle effectiveness of the old cannon battery. This is a definite departure from traditional, noncommissioned officer responsibilities. In each of these cases, the

noncommissioned officer has been moved into traditional, white-collar responsibilities.

A comparable shift has occurred in officer responsibilities at about the major level. Officers are expected to master their own battlefield operating system, and also be able to apply multiple BOS, focused in time and space, to create synergistic battle effects. Counterfire, the destruction of opposing artillery, demands quick fusion of intelligence and fire support consistent with rapidly changing maneuver. Joint air attack (JAAT) involves the co-ordination of fixed- and rotary-wing firepower, synchronized with artillery and maneuver forces, to destroy large concentrations of armor. All this was done exceedingly well in Operation Desert Storm, largely by heavy forces, although the 101st Air Assault Division, too, executed some complex, deep-air-assault operations. In fact, as a general proposition, BOS coordination must be even more rigorous in light forces than in heavy, because there simply is not combat power to dissipate in inefficient application. SOF and conventional air assaults in Operation Just Cause were multiple, simultaneous, supported night assaults. They require extremely competent coordination. Clearly, professional requirements are changing for both officer and noncommissioned officer.

The old blue-collar–white-collar distinction seems dated. I believe that this traditional distinction is inadequate today, post–AirLand Battle.[3] It is more useful to think in terms of iron-, blue-, white-, and gold-collar personnel requirements. Iron-collar requirements are robotic, computer driven.[4] Blue collar now includes disciplined execution of assigned individual and collective tasks by blue and iron collar. White collar refers to leading in the accomplishment of single BOS missions (maneuver, fire support, air defense, or combat-service support). Gold collar refers to the ability to integrate iron, blue, white, and other gold successfully, in a rapidly changing situation, under stress. More precisely, it is the ability to conceptualize and successfully execute the focusing of multiple BOS functions in time and space to achieve the intent of the higher chain of command.[5]

Think of iron collar as tasks accomplished by computers. Clearly, the number of such tasks is increasing, and each of the others—blue, white, and gold—needs to incorporate the iron collar to take advantage of information-age opportunities. In fact, a key discriminator in defining the other parts of the work force may be the potential to use iron collar. Perhaps, the Army should define positions in terms of the ability to use the computer as the dominant "machine" of the information age. Consider blue collar to be a position that can be replaced by a computer (robot) on a one-for-one basis. Replacing the soldier who loads a tank gun with an automatic loader defines the loader as a blue-collar position. Iron collar can obviously conserve blue-collar personnel or save lives by doing some high-risk, blue-collar tasks.

A white-collar position could be distinguished by the ability to achieve at least two- or three-to-one increases in effectiveness or efficiency over the status quo by incorporating the iron collar. Consider replacing the tank crewed by four with four tanks crewed each by one soldier or crewed robotically by one or two soldiers from a nearby work station. Whoever is fighting with those weapons has clearly used technology to achieve a definite increase in efficiency and effectiveness. They are occupying white-collar positions.

Gold collar could be the capability to accomplish innovative tasks that achieve tenfold to hundredfold increases in capability. They include the imaginative identification of new "solutions," exploiting existing capabilities as they have not been combined before, or conceptualizing and actualizing—by computer—new ways to fight. Such broad opportunity for tactical innovation may seem unlikely. Remember, doctrine is generally broad-brush and usually not directive. Subordinate innovation is expected within the guidance of the commander's intent, and METT-T is infinitely variable. The AirLand Operations concept imagines aggressive, highly decentralized execution within and between BOS. There would seem to be many gold-collar opportunities.[6]

Is this a useful way to define positions? Perhaps; there must be a nugget of truth here somewhere, because something very different is happening. We are talking about people. If we believe that exploiting the power of the computer is central to future military success, classification of personnel position based on this belief may be one way to consider and accelerate the assimilation of computers in information-age landpower. This view may provide valuable insights into new professional-development requirements. Current officer and noncommissioned officer development programs might look very different, were the policy and program issues stated to include a soldier's performance as blue-, white-, or gold-collar, as they have been defined above.

How did landpower get into all this? The transition to gold collar is evolutionary, as the nature of the land battle itself has changed. There has been a steady increase in the mobility and firepower available to the individual soldier since the Industrial Revolution. By every measure, war has become increasingly capital intensive, with more equipment, more mobility, longer-range weapons with greater lethality and fewer soldiers per kilometer of front. All represent the application of the assembly line of the industrial age to the nation at war. The assembly line distinguished the blue-collar line worker from the white-collar manager. Now, complexity expands in a new direction, that of the microprocessor. The chip has become ubiquitous on the modern battlefield. Capital intensiveness is measured not in horsepower or numbers of vehicles but in processor speed and storage and by the ability of the organization to convert computer potential into military capability.

Virtually every battlefield function has been changed dramatically by the computer. This was evident in Operation Desert Storm. Tanks and fighting vehicles employed thermal-imaging to "kill" Iraqi armor beyond Iraqi range. New opportunities arose in staff planning, with rapid change to complex deployment plans or development of the single air-tasking order. Very effective counterbattery fires were executed with MLRS cued by highly responsive acquisition. All of these significant battle actions were heavily processor based.

This is gold-collar business, no less complex than those integrative skills required by investment bankers to negotiate global takeovers across multiple markets. Pick your own business example; the conceptual and integrative skills are virtually the same. In the Army, however, the real bottom line is achievement or death—yours or those in your charge.

All this is profoundly different. This essence of agility, depth, initiative, and synchronization, expounded in AirLand Battle doctrine, was revealed to all in Operations Just Cause and Desert Storm. The sports analogy is no longer to football and its relatively set-piece sequencing of actions. Now, the analogy is to soccer and its rapid shifts from offense to defense to offense, as the ball moves on the field. We knew we had changed the doctrine. It works. Now to the challenging tasks of institutionalizing—of moving the noncommissioned officer corps from blue to blue-and-white collar and the officer corps from white to white-and-gold collar—across the force.

Institutionalization will not be easy. Classification as either officer or noncommissioned officer provided a convenient policy demarkation for personnel. Industrial-age enlisted personnel division (EPD)–officer personnel division (OPD) "stovepipes" are firmly established. As the Army developed professionally early in the century, accession, professional and personnel programs followed traditional blue-collar–white-collar expectations inherited from the assembly line. Now, each is complicated by subdivision: noncommissioned into blue and white, and officer into white and gold. Some of the personnel policy issues are evident in the following questions:

• Is gold collar solely combat arms related? Or is it combat support or combat-service support?

• The officer personnel management system (OPMS) and the enlisted personnel management system (EPMS) predate AirLand Battle and the advent of the information-age gold collar. Should these policies be revisited? Should gold-collar officers be generalists? Are joint staff officers gold collar by definition? Since there are specific integrating skills required for certain positions such as brigade S3 or all division staff, should these be coded positions, that is, ones restricted to those with prescribed training or experience? Is there specific position-oriented pretraining? What training should be provided the white-collar noncommissioned officer and when? If the Ser-

geants Major Academy (SMA) provides that training, what should be offered at the advance course level?[7]

• The ongoing drawdown of the Army complicates the problem. How encompassing can each officer speciality code or enlisted MOS be with a much smaller Army? Will each soldier have to be prepared to do more? Better people should be able to do more, particularly if and as tasks are redefined. Complex equipment may or may not demand increased support, depending on whether iron collar is issued to lessen complexity, as discussed above. Whatever the response for the active force, can it be sustained for reserve forces, who are frequently faced with much fewer assignment opportunities for professional development?

• Gold-collar leaders will be very competitive with industry, much like nuclear submariners and pilots in the past. Should they receive special inducements to remain in the force? Are traditional professional incentives enough in a much smaller force?

• In the past, unit personnel stability was sacrificed to permit individual development. Despite unit-cohesion programs like COHORT, there were tens of compelling personnel reasons for individuals to be removed from assignment orders.[8] Unit integrity created for unit training at the combat training centers was normally broken after the training rotation. Do AirLand operations and the clear need for integrated blue, white, and gold competence in constituted contingency forces demand a change to policies for individual personnel development?

This is a basic philosophical issue that has to be faced. With distributed information in the information age, is unit cohesion more important than individual development in active units maintained at very high proficiency levels? It may be possible to have different policies for various units. Units could be specially trained for various "niche market" situations, as discussed in chapter 2, "Coalition Conflict." Distributed information combines with new accounting capabilities such as the living TOE and the computer dog tag to permit maintenance of extensive detailed, networked, personal records. This should permit great variety in policies and personnel development programs and still keep track of individuals.[9] At the same time, we know much more today about the processes of team building, to achieve cohesion in units. So, "just-in-time" unit composition may be both desirable and feasible in certain BOS functional areas. This may be another striking landpower parallel to established manufacturing practices in the information age.

• What are the training and education requirements of gold-collar personnel? Is graduate school necessary to gain mature integration skills? Is graduate school one stepping stone from white to gold collar? What others

are there? Young, blue-to-white collar mobility has been encouraged by Officer Candidate School (OCS), ROTC, and the U.S. Military Academy. Is OCS sufficient, without an undergraduate degree, if there is to be further potential for development to gold collar?

These questions focus on the regular Army, specifically the constituted contingency force. Yet, when we fight, we acknowlege that we will fight as a Total Force in coalition operations. How does this distinction relate to reserve forces? It is difficult enough for citizen-soldiers to master traditional white-collar war-fighting skills. Results in the past have been spotty. Now we have increased the professional body of knowlege required to fight. Successful execution of integrated BOS, collateral operations, requires considerable preparation. New training technologies, distributed to local armories or reserve centers, can intensify the professional development process, but what is the professional development program? How do we achieve appropriate development for the citizen-soldier? May the "good old boy" no longer be acceptable? Of course, the requirements of increased reserve readiness and competence-basing may have already resolved this issue, for better or worse.

• The challenge becomes more acute when we consider our allies, some of whom will join our gold-collar leadership ad hoc almost as the contingency operation begins. How do we ensure that they understand our doctrine? More critically, how do we ensure that they can use the capabilities we may provide to increase their landpower? MLRS, Apaches, or sophisticated intelligence support to airpower could all be provided. The rationale for and circumstances of employment are gold collar at its best. In Operation Desert Storm, battlefield functional support was provided to increase significantly the combat effectiveness of allied units. U.S. Special Forces were invaluable "translators," with six months to interpret.[10] Such advantages may not be present in the future. How do we inculcate the skills and knowledge of gold collar under these circumstances? At a minimum, some improved professional development programs seem essential both here in the United States and probably by invitation in the regional area. Perhaps gold-collar doctrinal and execution training could occur under some multilateral form, similar to the current School of the Americas in South America. Seapower and airpower face the same problem. Perhaps the answer must be joint programs.

So, transition to gold collar is not without challenges, and some less obvious implications seem important:

• Conscription with average people may be no longer a valid accession alternative, at least for constituted forces expected to fight AirLand operations. Iron-, blue-, white-, and gold-collar operations demonstrated so effectively during the Just Cause and Desert Storm operations are not performed by average people.

• We have embarked almost irreversibly on the high-technology route. An increasing percentage of the contingency force may be dedicated to support the complex systems that create and sustain the leverage for the combat soldier, who will be more and more in the minority, at least for light and heavy forces. If we are not prepared to see disproportionately fewer uniformed warriors in our future force structure, do we need to place more of the support structure into host-nation or contract support or something comparable?[11]

• We need to think through the application of gold collar to the citizen-soldier, both for mobilization forces and in the unlikely event of a future global war. Professional development needs to be made much more friendly for the highly mobile white- and gold-collar populations. Distributed simulation has genuine promise, but significant training development is required to produce as many trained leaders as possible before the war. The development should focus on training alternatives, should personnel quality decline in total mobilization. What modifications have to be prepared to continue effective individual and unit training to performance standard as personnel quality deteriorates? This sort of preparation is essential insurance, once the nation embarks on quality-intensive policy in an area like landpower, so fundamental to abiding national security.

• The personnel-quality route of AirLand Operations places the Army in direct competition with industry for gold-collar officers and white-collar noncommissioned officers. Public support requires landpower fully representative of race, gender, religion, and ethnic background. The past record of retaining talented minority leaders has not been good. We need to prepare for the competition, but the bill may be high. Is the Army, or more properly the Department of Defense and Congress prepared to provide necessary resources for incentives to keep quality people?

These are challenges, indeed, but they are not impossible ones, provided we all recognize the path embarked upon. In the future, as the information age matures, we may be able to increase the combat power of individuals or small groups by more mechanical leverage, improved individual information displays, and access to weapon systems. The individual may possess the combat power of the company or even the battalion of today. That may be "platinum" collar, yet another challenge in assimilation.[12]

Whether gold collar is yet here or not, there are clearly new requirements for competent personnel associated with the post-industrial age. Near-term fixes seem possible. Immersion training based on experience and on distributed simulation in collateral operations can alleviate the training problem, but longer-term education and training solutions seem essential for constituted active and reserve forces, reconstitution forces, and for potential allies. A new personnel model appears necessary.[13]

9 Developing Leaders

COMPETENT, CONFIDENT LEADERS AT EVERY ECHELON ARE the essence of landpower capability. More than many armies, the U.S. Army establishes broad doctrinal guidelines and encourages each leader to exercise wide discretion in executing the guidance received from his or her next senior commander.[1] This, of course, increases the initiative desired and expected within the chain of command. It is also precisely what is required in wide-ranging, decentralized operations on a confusing, rapidly changing battlefield, where opportunities and threats can appear and vanish in seconds—Third-Wave war.

This philosophical direction demands brave leaders who know their business and "lead forward" on the battlefield. They must remember the calculus of the various battlefield operating systems that govern their effectiveness in executing war-fighting doctrine. Checklists are essential in periods of great stress or fatigue, but checklists cannot provide the expected levels of sheer personal proficiency. Performance-oriented training, preferably in a war-fighting environment pitted against a skilled, unremitting enemy, is increasingly the crucible employed to prepare our leaders. Normally expected to demonstrate personal proficiency in the pacing weapons of their organization, they lead by personal example to accomplish the mission, subordinating personal safety and comfort to that of their soldiers.

Leadership is not solely physical and tactical. The desired characteristics of the leader shift from tactical to operational and also to strategic levels. Those characteristics have been documented thoughtfully. At all grades, the Army expects leaders to have internalized the values of the organization. "Duty, Honor, Country" is not an abstract slogan. It is a guide for daily behavior. Thus, there is a broad measure of education in the prep-

aration of leaders. This applies not only to the officers but also, more and more, to the noncommissioned officers corps.

All in the constituted active forces are expected to be able to command in battle at one or two echelons higher than their current grade would indicate. This is a useful legacy from decades of preparation for the "come-as-you-are" war. Recently, this impetus toward improved professional competence has been complemented by a conscious *Reichswehr* philosophy of peacetime training for higher responsibilities in wartime; this is accomplished by increasingly capable personnel.[2] This was the successful model of professional officer development between World Wars I and II.

There is another important aspect to the preparation of leaders that is unique to the Army as the landpower guardian of the United States: the development of leaders (officers and noncommissioned officers) as models, exporting by their actions the values of landpower in a democracy. Most nations have air forces; some have navies; but all have armies, because armies (landpower) control people. People relate to people (armies). The U.S. Army, by its demonstrated competence across race, gender, religion, and origin, contributes to national military power and the general dominance of our culture.[3]

As a result of our national immigration and military accession policies, the United States can commit proud, confident, competent young Americans anywhere in the world and, should we desire, match local role models with soldiers of the same general characteristics. This is a national strategic advantage of incalculable value in the information age, which places a premium on personal leadership, particularly by gold-collar leaders. Active forces represent what professional forces should be in a democracy; reservists are equally credible as citizen-soldiers. They can demonstrate clear competence in their military skills, as well as in civilian occupational experiences, comparable to those in other nations. This can give reservists great credibility.

Of course, such models may not always be welcome in traditional societies. For example, competent, confident women, clearly in command of male and female soldiers, can be threatening in traditional Islamic cultures. Our culture, however, is pervasive and is widely admired and emulated. The ability to project practical role models, appropriate to local situations, gives a nation power. We need to ensure that leader development prepares people for these kinds of roles, integral to peacetime military activities in the future.

The "bottom line" of leader development, however, remains preparation for successful fighting. As war-fighting doctrine evolves, officers find themselves expected to master complex tasks, involving rapid assimilation of new information, as well as to determine critical events in swirling, changing situations. Next, they must focus resources in space and time to achieve decisive results. Agility, initiative, synchronization, and depth called

for in AirLand Battle doctrine are not mere words; they define a new capability and complexity in integrating battlefield resources. Successful, cross-BOS collateral operations such as counterfire, joint suppression of air defense (J-SEAD), and joint air attack (JAAT) require exceptional skill in visualization and split-second coordination in execution. These are demanding tasks, well beyond white collar and into the new, gold-collar tasks of the information age. In addition to new responsibilities for officers, senior noncommissioned officers are expected to plan and execute, much as junior commanders were in the past. The senior NCOs are, in fact, in transition from traditional blue-collar tasks to the white-collar management and execution tasks, formerly reserved for officers. This is an important change, requiring new initiatives in leader development.[4]

The kinds of competence described above are not a stylized, romantic wish list. They are the lifeblood of the current Army, revealed frequently at the combat training centers and, occasionally, to the public in combat operations like Operations Just Cause and Desert Storm. These characteristics are vital to the execution of AirLand Battle. They will be even more necessary as the doctrine evolves into the post-industrial age. Therefore, review of the new challenges and opportunities of leader development is particularly important in assessing the change to the post-industrial Army.

Current leader preparation is finely honed to develop the war-fighting skills of the constituted active force. Responsibility for training and educating leaders has been carefully divided among the individual, the training institution, and the leader's chain of command. The requirements have been established, and the performance evaluations embedded. Skill-qualification testing has evolved into self-development testing for the noncommissioned officers, and military qualification standards for the officers are coming on line. Institutional courses have been refined. In general, they are excellent, at least for active forces. They offer the individual basic "school learning," the professional knowledge that is the threshold to war-fighting competence. But they are, fundamentally, passive learning experiences. They do not reflect the speed, the fine edge of risk, nor the rapid pace of change that are hallmarks of battle, particularly of Third-Wave war. "Active" learning comes from another quarter: the combat training centers that both educate and train the unit.

Probably the most crucial element in professional leader development for Third-Wave war, the combat training centers have created demanding war-fighting experiences for units, so the focus and stimulus for intense leader training has shifted. The competitive and stress-filled nature of the CTC provides precisely the proper sorts of diverse, unanticipated situations that stimulate intense practical learning. They create a unique and exceptionally powerful "school." The after-action reviews, professionally conducted by seasoned observer-controllers (O/Cs), not only reinforce learning at the CTC but also establish combat-related professional standards for con-

tinuing and, in fact, expanding professional development back at the home station. Numerous "combat" examples are readily available for continuing leader training within the unit.[5]

So, it would appear that sensible training innovation almost two decades ago—that inaugurated realistic, simulation-based, force-on-force unit training with an elaborate training-and evaluation-infrastructure (CTC with AAR and O/Cs)—did more than improve unit training, important as that is. These innovations also solved the gold-collar-leader training requirement; that is, they created a replicative professional development model, appropriate for development of gold-collar competencies.[6] White-collar training for noncommissioned officers is not a problem, for that has already been tested in officer development. Blue-collar training has already been improved, as was obvious in the Persian Gulf War. The challenge will be in distributing these gold-collar, structured training situations to dispersed, constituted active and reserve units and leader-training facilities and maintaining quality control.

While there are problems evident in continuing modernization, little appears "broken" for the constituted active force. The challenges will be to take advantage of new training technologies of the information age and to sustain the intensity of the leader-training effort, despite greatly reduced resources. Fortunately, new technologies should assist. An emerging insight concerning the information age is that the telecommunications, education, and entertainment industries are converging. Sooner, rather than later, interactive communications will show up in the average American home. From three-dimensional interaction with "Sesame Street" situations for preschool to interactive participation with characters on Agatha Christie stories on home TV and to video-fax interaction on your "telephone," distributed virtual simulation is years, not decades, away. If this can come into the home, it should certainly be available in the company area at Fort —— or the Guard armory or the Army Reserve center. Current training developments are creating the techniques to use these emerging technologies for personal immersion in virtual realities and in structured learning situations. There would appear to be a significant opportunity here for distributed leader development and potential unit war-fighting training—blue, white and gold collar.

Evaluation has begun. In early 1990, as an Army-DARPA experiment, a brigade of the 1st Infantry Division fought at Fort Knox, Kentucky, against an interactive, thinking enemy on a virtual SIMNET battlefield. Tank and infantry were represented by certain companies with all crews in Abrams and Bradley simulators. Others had only the company commanders and platoon leaders in fighting-vehicle simulators. The rest were represented by semiautomated forces. Helicopters flying on the battlefield were manned simulators, and semiautomated forces flown at Fort Rucker, Alabama, and netted to the common battlefield at Fort Knox and Fort Rucker. Division

was tied to the virtual battlefield from a command post at Fort Leavenworth. Full artillery and fixed-wing, close air support was present. This was a positive training experience for the troops. After they returned from Operation Desert Storm, the leadership of the 1st Infantry Division praised the practical readiness benefits of their SIMNET training experience.

A challenge now is to channel this development to better support leader training. The training—perhaps expressed better as leader-development experiences—needs to be distributed to the officer or noncommissioned officer to be trained. Equally important, the distributed training environment should duplicate as closely as possible the intense, stress-filled learning atmosphere of the CTC. In essence, in order to develop the leader competence necessary to fight and win in Third-Wave war, that war needs to be brought to the individual. The leader needs to learn by "sink-or-swim" immersion in confusing, rapidly changing battle situations. Coincidentally, immersion intensifies the training process: More can be learned faster in structured, interactive situations. Immersion may permit more people to be trained in a school or unit in the same amount of time or the same training in much less time. Leader training now reserved to the school can be sent to the unit chain of command or to distributed unit-analog situations for individuals—active and reserve—not assigned to units. Significant change in the techniques of leader training appears in the offing.

Unfortunately, the quality of leader training currently available to the professional force does not extend to other leader-training challenges; this will prove increasingly important as the active force becomes smaller. Today, the constituted reserve force—the Total Force, including the Guard and reserves—and our potential allies have insufficient leader-development opportunities for proficiency needed to fight together successfully, under modern doctrine. In no case has the professional force fully addressed the leader-development challenge.

The problems with leader development for reserve forces are twofold. First, *active forces have assumed that reserve proficiency should mirror that of the active force. Thus, citizen soldiers are encouraged to attend active Army courses by both active and reserve leadership. Failing that, they attend reserve courses, conducted primarily by reservists.*

There are several questionable policies here. It is not necessarily true that the body of knowledge required of the active Army be required of citizen-soldiers. Peacetime Army administration really does not apply to a regionally distributed reserve force subject to reserve jurisdiction. Reservists mature in their civilian occupations, but their essential, active-duty learning objectives relate solely to fighting at their grade. There is not much *Reichswehr* affordable here. Also, the least effective instructors for those with limited military experience would be others with equally limited experience. But that is the current policy, which charges reservists, often with little combat-unit experience, with the responsibility to train their reserve peers in

Third-Wave war. Precisely the reverse should prevail. Seasoned, highly knowledgeable active soldiers, who can distinguish what is important, should conduct the training; otherwise it becomes the "blind leading the blind."

Second, *reserve courses consist of a lesser number of active-Army courses.* Army courses are designed to conserve dollars and manpower. Reserve courses should be designed to conserve time. Direct translation of regular-Army courses to reserve programs of instruction (POI) without tailoring to the reserve environment makes poor use of reservist's time. To date, time-saving training technologies and techniques are seldom applied to reserve courses. It would be preferable to start from scratch with a task list and design the course specifically for distributed execution with predictable quality control.[7]

There is a clear need to restructure many of the reserve forces' leader-training policies and programs consistent with the increased role of reserves in constituted forces. Several broad guidelines might be useful in designing new programs:

• Treat the reserve leader-training requirement as the baseline Army leader-training requirement; that is, design the training and training support to ensure the reserves' competence to fight, using current doctrine, with issue equipment. Institutional training will remain important, particularly for inculcating soldierly values, but severe time limitations will increasingly drive leader development in the reserves to the chain of command and individual preparation. Both will be increased by the reserves' use of CTC (such as reserve battalion training centers) and the presence of distributed, structured training to standard (the telecommunications, entertainment, education revolution). As already discussed, immersion in structured learning situations is both more effective and more efficient in developing leaders for AirLand Battle.

• Design courses to train to war-fighting proficiency in current grade, not one or two levels up. As the baseline leader-development requirement, the institutional part of peacetime Total Force leader training should be conducted by the active Army. It should also assume a more forceful role in support of leader training within the reserve chain of command and in design and quality control of self-development programs for reserve leaders. In other words, reserve leader development is too important to leave solely to the reserves.[8]

• Active-Army leader development could be added to the baseline described. Regular Army soldiers should probably attend the baseline courses, regionally distributed, followed by necessary and well-documented active, professional development. Areas of specific development include the *Reichswehr* train-up and landpower management issues—structuring, equipping,

training, manning, sustaining, mobilizing, and deploying the force. Such a policy would address several problems. It would bring active and reserve gold- and white-collar leaders together in a learning environment, so each more appreciates the other. Also, it would ensure that the active professional knows, and has experienced, what leader development the citizen-soldiers, who join for contingency deployments, have received.

The problem is not that the U.S. Army has a poor leader-development program. It is among the best in the world.[9] In fact, deliberately or inadvertently, it has solved the gold-collar leader-development problem in centralized locales such as the combat training centers. The challenge is that leader development is becoming dated: it has not yet responded to new requirements outlined in the revised *National Military Strategy*. It emphasizes neither the much greater importance of reserves nor the impact of a new continuum of potential employment, particularly in regional contingencies and forward-presence operations.

Training of allies is not bad; it just fails to acknowledge the dominant role that allies, including regional ad hoc "friends," will have in our future landpower operations. Working with allied leaders is no longer "nice to do." In the emerging world environment, it is critical to success.[10] For a combination of political and economic reasons, the American public simply will not go it alone on the ground. Operation Desert Storm proved the point. Without host-nation support or the financial and equipment support of key allies, CENTCOM, VII Corps notwithstanding, simply could not have pulled off the land campaign so rapidly and with so few casualties.

Training of allied military leaders has not changed much since World War II. U.S. training courses are made available to foreign military of all grades. The training opportunities vary from vehicle-familiarization and mechanics courses to attendance at the Command and General Staff College or the Army War College. The broad assumption is that training suitable for U.S. soldiers is proper for allies. For many foreign leaders, the training is excellent. Over the years, NATO allies have made fine use of Army officer and selected noncommissioned officers' courses, and we of theirs. There has been useful learning of our doctrine. The U.S. Army has had the opportunity to exchange professional experiences in an academic environment and many long-term friendships have been made. This has been a win-win for all concerned, with a notable payoff in supporting coalition operations in Operation Desert Storm.

On the other hand, many officers from other regions, generally the Third World—with no expectation that their Army will ever have the resources to fight as current doctrine demands—learn "how to" against an unlikely enemy, on different terrain, and with equipment they cannot afford. To an army with no noncommissioned officer corps, the U.S. division of material between officer and noncommissioned-officer curricula is baffling.

Traditionally, it has been their problem to adjust to us, not us to them. Frequent language difficulties impede training. However, useful personal relationships can be created by classroom association with U.S. officers and noncommissioned officers. And as these people are encouraged to travel in the United States, they have an opportunity to learn our culture.

All Third World leadership training is certainly not negative. Over the years, extremely valuable political, as well as military, networking has occurred. The highlight of allied support has been the outstanding work done globally by Special Forces. Probably the best regional programs exist with the Latin and South American nations. The InterAmerican Defense College, School of the Americas, and extraordinarily capable SOF have made major contributions.

Institutionalized training for allied leaders has been a well-intentioned and worthwhile addition to normal U.S. professional development. It has been an important secondary effort. The challenge now is to intensify leader preparation among longstanding and ad hoc allies around the world. As the information age matures, the Army can be perceived as a global corporation, with new patterns of relationships. With this view, training of allies is no longer secondary; it becomes a major Army program. Leader training is an imperative of "market" development. Several new requirements arise:

There will be new, international peacekeeping doctrine as well as warfighting doctrine. NATO standardization agreements (STANAGS) will become global, with clear modifications for Russian "good ideas." STANAGS provide a solid base. But, given the utility of BOS as an analytical concept, there appears a clear need for regional analysis to develop BOS requirements for various combinations of allies.

Then, institutionalizing leader development, appropriate to these new requirements, could take several forms:

- Regional institutes could be established at Fort Leavenworth to analyze and conduct leader development for both U.S. and allied officers. Allies aside, there is a very substantial U.S. leader-training requirement for the Army to retain regional proficiency. Both joint and combined leader-training opportunities need to be developed for use in likely contingencies.
- Regional orientation courses for unit leaders could be offered in U.S. employment of BOS, when the United States would be likely to provide regional functional support. The training could be conducted by cadre from the regional institute or area Special Forces personnel.
- Courses in international (UN) staff procedures could be established, through which combined staff officers could be trained, as they are in joint training now conducted in the United States.

Allied leader-development requirements arise as one aspect of new patterns of relationships in the information age. There are other new pat-

terns related to Army tie-ins to the national civilian labor pool. Two are the social productivity of the Army and the impact of new requirements on the training of both officer and noncommissioned officers. If the Army is seen to have explicit responsibilities to bring in the less qualified and build them into productive soldiers or to provide leader training to very competent volunteers and then release them, leader development will have to be modified accordingly. The former could disrupt significantly the current readiness if less capable soldiers, like we had in the seventies, return to mire the chain of command in correcting the bad, rather than rewarding the good. The latter would not have as great a negative impact; it could speed promotion flow for those who remain. Leader development would have to address transition preparation, but any skill training could be conducted by the gaining civilian organization. There may also be other opportunities for contracting leader training in civilian-related skills.

The overall issue of contract training is certain to become more important as the Army becomes smaller. Socialization training clearly needs to be conducted in a demanding military environment. Direct, war-related individual training should be conducted in a combat environment. Some of it seems amenable to execution by employing former military. Unit warfighting training should be on the ground or in sophisticated simulation. If used, observer-controllers should be highly competent, serving leaders. Opposing forces might be contracted. Most other training in civilian-related skills could be contracted to civilian industry. The rigor of current training to task, condition, and standard is such that quality control can be maintained, despite considerable decentralization. This might permit economies in leader training: scarce resources could be focused on combat training, beneficial to the unit and white- and gold-collar leader alike.

In sum, the status quo is good, but essentially, it is an extension, albeit a substantial improvement, on Second-Wave training of the industrial age. New requirements and new training technologies are now appearing. Substantial change to current leader-preparation policies and programs appears necessary to sustain the Third-Wave preeminence that U.S. landpower achieved in Panama and the Persian Gulf.

10   The Army of Excellence: A Competence-Based Force

THE COMPETENCE OF THE U.S. ARMY OF THE EARLY NINE-ties, the Army of Excellence, is no longer hypothetical. It has been proved in combat. Logistics achievements during Operation Desert Shield, the combat record of Operation Desert Storm for heavy and light forces, and that of Operation Just Cause for light forces are credible proof of excellence. Desert Shield was a major, national, strategic deployment, much larger than any during comparable duration buildups in the Korean or Vietnam wars. During the six months, 9,000 aircraft and 500 ships were received. They discharged 350,000 personnel, 12,400 tracked and 117,000 wheeled vehicles, 1,800 helicopters, and 2.2 million short-tons of cargo. The armored corps, VII Corps, consumed 9,000 short-tons of ammunition and 2.4 million gallons of fuel per day of operations.[1] Such are the costs of overwhelming superiority in modern Third-Wave war.

New doctrine, organizations, and equipment performed beyond expectation. Some organizations possessed greater combat power than units one or two echelons higher in the last global, industrial-age war, World War II. Equipment exceeded predicted performance. The readiness rates of the Abrams and Bradley were phenomenal. Divisions moved several hundred miles without breakdown. Long-range, precision tank fires of remarkable accuracy occurred night and day. Detailed review of one action revealed that in ground-maneuver direct fire, Abrams and Bradley hit probabilities were above 95 percent, with virtually 100 percent kills against modern Soviet equipment.[2] While it was clearly a joint and allied victory, critically dependent on devastating airpower applied at every level, the final killing blow was delivered by landpower.

The American soldier exuded competence and pride, particularly the young soldiers. This was probably the most competent, large fighting force ever fielded by the U.S. Army and perhaps in the world. By every measure, landpower—the Army and the Marines supported by allies—displayed a new order of military capability, particularly at the small-unit level. It established a new world class of one. This force of excellence is a far step from the post–Vietnam War Army of the seventies. How did this competence-based force come about? As the Army draws down; how can the United States retain this dominant edge in the future? What can the Army question, reduce, or eliminate to generate the resources necessary for excellence in the force that remains?

The current Army of Excellence is a direct product of several key factors:

- better soldiers acquired with the volunteer force, then subjected to rigorous professional development, with continuing authority to dismiss given to local chains of command;[3]
- explicit definition of training requirements by task, condition, and standard available to and understood by all and backed up with sufficient resources for vital training;
- the absolute support of the personnel system that accepted individual or collective task performances as major criteria for favorable personnel actions, such as promotion and retention; and
- consensus among the officer and NCO leadership as to what needed to be done.

These factors were critical to success in the buildup. They appear to be equally essential in keeping up quality in building down. But what parts of these clearly successful policies must be retained? Are there new requirements for competence emerging that are critical for mastering the military challenges of the information age?

Continued accession and retention of quality personnel is, of course, critical. Equal opportunity is fact. It must always be subject to continuous command attention in a diverse army, but the major battles have been won.[4] If you are competent by performance evaluation, you are rewarded, regardless of race, gender, or national origin. If found wanting, you are not rewarded. In fact, you may be asked not to remain in the force. At virtually every level, there are positive models of your race, gender, or national origin prepared to reinforce the reality of competence-basing. You, the individual soldier, are fully responsible for your competence or incompetence.

The need today is not solely one of quality in support of affirmative action. There is a requirement to seek deliberately for quality officers and enlisted personnel representative of those in potential contingency areas. To influence people in the information age, U.S. landpower should be able to put in units absolutely "tuned" to the prospective region of conflict. Tuning

includes manning contingency forces with gold- and white-collar role models, who clearly relate to the regional culture. As the force's numbers are reduced, rising standards, permitted by smaller requirements, should sustain these officer and NCO models across race, religion, gender, and ethnic origin. National immigration policy ensures the proper international representation.

Rigorous, defined standards of performance are understood and accepted as valid measures of individual and unit excellence. These were embedded in difficult training programs, requiring demonstrated performance to standard at every grade. From individual proficiency test to combat training center, individual and collective proficiency is evaluated fairly to standard. These evaluations must continue, as should rigorous training for remaining units.

Now, the challenge is to apply necessary parts of this training system to potential regional allies. Evolving doctrine must first include appropriate tasks, conditions, and standards and then be validated as training suited not only to U.S. forces but also to selected regional allies. As functional capabilities, such as fire support or intelligence, are deployed from the United States, they should be able to merge rapidly with allied BOS capabilities for effective coalition warfare. As an example, a command-and-staff training program in coordination procedures could be prepackaged for UN forces who need to employ U.S. air defense to support ground-maneuver units in UN peacemaking operations on the periphery of the former Soviet Union. Another example could be applying techniques and procedures to coordinate U.S. engineer, medical, and military police units deployed to South America as part of an OAS force to restore order and public health after a nuclear meltdown.

During the rebuilding after Vietnam, important favorable actions, such as promotion, retention, and assignment, were related to performing successfully to standard. The training and personnel systems were tied together under the positive recruiting themes of "Be All You Can Be" and the Army of Excellence. Recruiting promise became service reality. Difficult personnel decisions were taken. Personnel were conditioned to "up or out"; that is, be promoted in a prescribed period of time, or be released from the Army. As the Army modernized, career change was forced from overstrength to understrength career management fields. All of these policies are now valuable precedents in a smaller Army. All are volunteers. Who goes, who stays, and why?

Personnel actions for many will have a negative effect. Volunteers who expected a career of service will be dismissed. Fair, accepted selection processes for retention must be kept. It is required to continue, if not expand, demanding performance evaluations. Large personnel-action "boards" should be kept, not only to ensure awareness of all the affected career fields but also to have witnesses who can attest to the fairness of the process

throughout the Army. This is expensive in the midst of major changes, but it is essential to the morale of the future force and to the public attitudes of those released.

Last, and perhaps most important, the measures above were understood and implemented eagerly by senior officer and NCO leaders. They were, in turn, supported by the policies and programs of the civilian leadership, particularly during the Reagan years, when relative resource affluence was backed by key leaders in Congress. Philosophical, if not financial, support from civilian leadership has every promise of continuing, since policies supporting excellence have so clearly worked.

Competence has evoked almost effusive praise from responsible media. Respect for the professional military has increased for all the services, but perhaps most for the Army, since it always has the farthest to go in the popular image. David Gergen expressed this observation well in an editorial in *U.S. News & World Report* during Operation Desert Storm, relating obvious military success to resolution of other national problems:

> There are lessons here for all of us. If our military is successful because it provides equal opportunity and achieves personal loyalty within the ranks, why can't our major companies? If military officers learn how to compete by re-educating themselves, why can't our CEOs? Training, good management, discipline, community: These are values that should take root across the nation.[5]

There is strong civilian support, intensified by the numbers of citizen-soldiers who served and who offer believable local testimony.

Unified support from within the military is less certain. Institutional change of the magnitude required to adjust to the post-industrial age is accepted only gradually. The unity of support of uniformed leaders during the seventies and eighties, born in the miasma of Vietnam, will not be present automatically during the transition to the new national military strategy in the information age. Support will have to be cultivated carefully, starting at the Army War College and at the Command and General Staff College.

All this said about the "rebirth" of the Army is the grist of national legend. Doctrine has been developed to exploit fully individual and unit excellence. Operations Just Cause and Desert Storm demonstrated exceptional professional competence in achieving national military objectives against major military threats. That was the perception of the Iraqis before the modern, processor-based blitzkrieg hit them. Now, because of success over the past decade, the honeymoon is about over. Although dangers abound in the international community, credible force-generating threats to the security of the United States are disappearing. The Army faces substantial drawdown. Under these circumstances, some strengths of the competence-based Army of Excellence become potential liabilities in drawdown.

Young soldiers know exactly what they need for training to remain combat-ready. No army has defined training requirements in the detail currently available to the U.S. Army. Through performance evaluation, soldiers know what they know and do not know. If funding is reduced, the rank and file of the Army will note in alarm the reduction in readiness. There will be a serious lessening of professional satisfaction; because of absent fuel, spare parts, and training ammunition, the amount of on-equipment field training will decline. Soldiers who fought in the Persian Gulf, with full manning and showcase equipment, will find resource anemia characteristic of democratic armies at peace. This is particularly disturbing when added to the uncertainty of retention within the service.

It involves a deeper issue than just the decline of readiness, important as that is. It becomes also an issue of organizational integrity, if readiness requirements and standards do not lessen as the resources required for proficiency decline. The "hollow Army" of the seventies is simply not consistent with the reality or rhetoric of the Army of Excellence. Without resources, the esprit and confidence of the Army of Excellence will decline, as surely as did those of the Army in Europe during Vietnam. Better to have a few fully supported units than shadow flags, harboring a severely compromised professional army.

The threat to unit and individual soldier competence and morale is real, and it will increase in the future. It is really difficult to retrench significantly and retain excellence. It may be time now to begin thinking of alternative ways to reduce operating costs, thereby conserving resources to sustain individual and unit excellence. Some paths will be very tough to contemplate, much less bring to responsible policy and program. The good faith of past commitments may appear breached, just at a time when the self-confidence of the force is undermined by decline.

One of the most slippery slopes is the manpower end strength of the active force. Rigorous planning is impossible, if the lifeblood of the Army, people, is vitiated in every appropriations cycle. Most of the rebuilding of the Army after Vietnam occurred under a manpower floor negotiated by Gen. Creighton Abrams, as Army chief of staff in the early seventies, with an understanding that savings could be reapplied within the Army. Economies effected by quality accessions, stemming from national support for the volunteer force and sizable increases in the reserves, made for a remarkable record of accomplishment within that active end strength level. Largely under the analytical eye of TRADOC, more combat capability was generated, technological changes were assimilated, and the highly professional Army of Excellence was born. Is a similar "pact" appropriate now for the years after the current glide path down? Is it reasonable to bet on further economies in the active element of the constituted Total Force and further amortization of the processor revolution? The proved rigor of the concept-based

requirements system (CBRS) may allow forced assimilation of changes to meet significantly lower active manning levels while maintaining the Army of Excellence.

A second support in the face of decline may be more explicit acknowledgment of the special role landpower plays in our democracy. For years, the national ecology was placed essentially in the hands of the Corps of Engineers. Charged with regulating the flow of water, the corps undertook truly massive facility engineering projects. These have been budget programs, separate and distinct from conventional landpower programs. Because river and harbor civil engineering was a clear national requirement, needing consistent support despite international commitments or lack thereof, Army civil engineering has been sustained as a major national program distinct from the normal landpower budget.

Today, the Army supports the Total Force, configured not necessarily for optimum readiness but rather in response to the political imperatives of the United States—a democracy, a nation, state, and people. Citizen-soldiers are provided an opportunity to serve individually or as members of units distributed nationally. As discussed above in "Reserve Force Challenges," there is a broad range of socially useful tasks being accomplished by the National Guard and Army Reserve. They go from drug suppression to support of the upgrade of local infrastructure, so long as the support is not competitive to local business. Gold-collar officers and white-collar noncommissioned officers not in units could provide valuable backup to local government in education, protection, and coordination of services—all improvements advocated for the inner city. How many of these tasks could be regarded as modern equivalents of the river and harbor works of the Corps of Engineers and, thus, subject to separate appropriations?

Similar savings could accrue if active-Army support to reserve forces were to be charged to reserve appropriations with full accounting of the overhead costs.[6] For example, should the active-Army budget bear the personnel costs of supporting reserve combat readiness, such as the readiness groups, or the costs of developing particular courses of reserve instruction, or specialized training support, not required by the active force, but necessary because reserve units are dispersed? Who should pay for maintaining major facilities, like Fort McCoy, Wisconsin, used primarily for summer training of reserves?

There are other worthy activities that are supported but do not directly contribute to mission readiness, such as the Junior ROTC program in high schools or the national rifle marksmanship program. Are there other, similar programs that are complementary to general manpower readiness in the information age? What about national computer familiarity at the high-school level or teaching English as a second language? Landpower in a democracy bears special "quasimilitary" national obligations and responsi-

bilities, separate and distinct from airpower and seapower. Should these general obligations be discharged off the DoD budget?

Traditionally, the Army has been a fully constituted force of uniformed "fighters," organized and trained to execute the full range of combat, combat-support, and combat-service-support tasks to fight and win. The size of the support force compared to the fighting force is consistently controversial. The relative size of the support force has grown as war has become increasingly technology based. The individual fighter has seen his battlefield range of influence expand geometrically, at a cost of increasing backup support. This is certain to continue in the information age. Already, there are concepts that give the individual infantryman firepower ability previously available to platoons or even companies. At what point does the fighter's service support no longer need to be uniformed? In Desert Storm, bountiful host-nation support was required and provided as part and parcel of the allied contribution. Full allied financial support was sought and received. Contract maintenance support was provided for critical weapon systems of all services. Clearly, a fully composed, internationally credible contingency army needs expertise across the range of combat-service support. But must it be uniformed?

Perhaps, there is a case to focus the uniformed force on the cutting edge of combat and combat-support forces. Clearly, all AirLand operations empowering important BOS capabilities should be under the umbrella of the highly competent and professional constituted force. What about the rest, the civilian-related sinews of war, otherwise known as the logistical tail, which grows consistently?[7] Why could not that be in a "support army," provided as needed by contract, host-nation support in coalition warfare, or Department of the Army civilians? There are some precedents. German Army logisitical support, other than that forward in tactical units, has been civilian rather than uniformed military, ever since creation of the *Bundeswehr* in the fifties. The U.S. Air Force and the civilian air carriers understand this well in creating the CRAF.

Are there Army applications that might permit the focusing of Army end strength more on combat than support capabilities? Perhaps the uniformed force could fight the deep, close, and near-rear battle, but support behind the division could be primarily from allied uniformed units, and support behind the corps could be from contract civilians or the host-nation. Yet, rear battle is important, and in very fluid, fast-paced, Third-Wave war, where is the close battle? These are very tough issues. Landpower simply cannot endanger its ability to achieve quick, decisive victory. Still, the Army will need more "bang for the buck" out of reduced soldier end strength. Were not some precedents established in Desert Storm?

There is a deeper issue here. With the advent of the global economy, and potential global, common equipment platforms as national defense in-

dustries wither, what must be the unique, national uniformed capability? The *National Military Strategy* (1992) envisages fighting coalition warfare, with allies in regional contingencies. What common combat-service support should accompany U.S. commitment? What should we require from the regional organization in whose name we intervene, or from the United Nations, if that organization is the patron? There is no intent here to erode the absolute U.S. requirement of a robust contingency corps, fully manned with combat, combat-support, and combat-service-support landpower units, to fight unilaterally a major regional contingency. That is the irreducible minimum to remain the global superpower. But beyond that, what capabilities must be maintained in the uniformed military?

Another major overhead issue is the social infrastructure required to support an army composed of soldiers, spouses, and children. There is no question of the absolute desirability of supporting the Army family; the Army is a family army. There are important societal expectations that simply must be satisfied if we are to attract and retain quality people. The issue is, what can the Army afford?

There were broad discrepancies in the family support provided during Operation Desert Shield. Constituted units from Europe needed every bit of institutionalized family support, Army Community Services (ACS) and the Family Liaison Organization (FLO). Wartime Europe was a potentially hostile environment, with a terrorist threat. European languages and mores can be intimidating and even more so under stress of impending combat. The inherent casualty risks of Desert Storm all added to family fears. The magnificent leadership achievement of U.S. Army, Europe, can be best appreciated when one thinks of all the potential "disasters" that did not occur. Clearly, for the deployed force and service families overseas, full family support is essential.[8]

Desert Shield was supported from the United States with comparable infrastructure. Is the same level of support necessary for service families at home in the United States? Philosophically, should service families routinely have more support than that available to other Americans? Should it be available day in and out or just during periods of crisis? What about reservists who deployed for Desert Shield from hundreds of locations without any comparable safety nets other than locally available social services? If they were not supported adequately, what more is required? If they were, why should the active part of the Army have more?

The point is not to deny the need for support, but to suggest that other, fair, compassionate ground rules be established to assure some minimum, common level of support for families. Perhaps, support could be provided by local civilians, on a reimbursable basis, for U.S.-based, deploying units, both active and reserve. Both requirement and solution seem similar to what is involved in providing education to soldiers' children: Subsidize the local

economy to provide comparable services to the Army family and local citizens. Overseas, continue the programs honed during the eighties.

There are also opportunities to force processor-based management innovations on the traditional bureaucracy. This seems applicable to the support (TDA) Army and perhaps, in selected cases, to the (TOE-based) combat force. Most global corporations are flattening their organizations to take advantage of the amount of information processors generate. There may be applications to the Army well beyond the reforms of ongoing defense management reviews. The National Guard Bureau is a flat organization, with no intervening headquarters between national leaders and each of the states or territories. The Army Reserve Command seems about to do the same for the Army Reserve.

Perhaps intermediate headquarters could be eliminated between Army major command and the field locations for the support (TDA) Army? I do not suggest summary surgery, although that is often the way to achieve difficult change in large bureaucracies. Rather, there needs to be a painstaking review of the value added by each succeeding headquarters. There are clearly different issues for TOE units because of the need for substantially deep leadership, due to casualties and the normal friction of war. After all, the enemy is trying his best to disrupt the effective exercise of command, by any means available. We do not want to help him through misconceived economies.

There is also a need to look at the functional added value of BOS. For example, how many echelons of military police are really necessary to accomplish the mission? This is an issue different from the perceived needs for MP Colonel positions to ensure promotion flow with qualified competition. Existing structure—MP commands and brigades—may be essential to prepare the regional contingency-force packages envisaged in coalition operations. That needs to be proved. The same case could be made in numerous other functional areas. Current proponent structure, however, makes it exceedingly difficult to get objective answers. Tough, probing, Department of the Army assessments by functional area may be necessary to straighten out post-industrial-age force requirements.

Another major philosophical area is the structure required in the Army to polish essentially civilian-related skills. If accredited, civilian vocational training or training by other services is available, why maintain duplicate capability in the Army? As long as the requisite tasks can be taught to standard with Army quality control, why must the Army teach it? There is a clear need to continue amortization of the new support capabilities "bought" in the training revolution. Training that remains within the Army should be as time- and resource-efficient as possible. Amortization may consist of achieving unique, distributed training of citizen-soldiers before and after mobilization, rather than in duplicating civil capability.

Leadership training is another issue; this must be done by each uniformed service. Both active and reserve schools already have the facilities to train leaders for the Army. Current, compressed reserve skill-training is judged sufficient for the majority of the Total Force. Are there, perhaps, opportunities for the regular Army to expand applications of improved reserve training, if the active training capability is severely reduced?

Other examples abound. The problem is to reduce or shift many policies and programs, instituted for good reason in the eighties but no longer necessary or affordable in the constrained nineties. Quality in a competence-based force demands substantial operating costs; a rich training diet is essential. What can be eliminated to afford it?

PART IV

SEIZING THE FUTURE

11   Exploiting the Computer

LANDPOWER REALLY IS NOT TAKING SUFFICIENT ADVANtage of the potential of the computer. Solid use in an enormous, globally distributed organization, yes; aggressive use to retain world landpower supremacy, no. Measured on the "potentials" scale, I doubt the return today is above the midpoint of the curve; it is probably closer to one-third. Although U.S. usage is higher than any other military force's, it is, nevertheless, well below what it might be—and should be—to sustain landpower preeminence in the face of tight defense budgets. The challenges in making greater use of computers are not primarily those of technology or even funding; rather, they are problems of vision, understanding, and assimilation.

Despite notable progress in many areas of military competence, when we look back, we may see the eighties as a period of unrealized potential, roughly comparable to that of the twenties and thirties, when foot and hoof steadfastly resisted application of the internal combustion engine for mounted warfare. After the fall of France in 1940, it would seem incredible that serious professionals could still advocate horse-mobile cavalry and artillery. Yet, today, too many resist the computer, although it clearly replaces the internal combustion engine as the arbiter of land war. For example, as conventional wisdom strives to upgrade gun and armor protection, there is a tendency to look back and to advocate more and better of the same, rather than look forward to the emergent leverages of the computer. Computer-generated capabilities might be retrofitted to improve current weapons or to provide new capabilities. Similarly, when the Army applies computers to training, many see ways to execute current training practices better, rather than opportunity to effect basic changes. In fairness, while there have been good opportunities lost, there has also been some genuine, solid progress. The record is mixed.

Operations Just Cause and Desert Storm have revealed not only the excellence of doctrine but also the wealth of capabilities generated by the concept-based requirement system. Much of this superiority comes from judicious use of computers. For the Army alone, Patriot, Army tactical missile system (ATACMS), the global positioning system (GPS), and, in fact, the superior fire control of the Abrams M1A1 tank are all computer-based. More indirectly, processors increased the strategic flexibility of Desert Shield and, in operations, the single-tasking order for concentrating airpower. Many would say that Operations Just Cause and Desert Storm were "proofs" of processor dominance, skillfully exploited. They were really the first wars of the information age—Third-Wave war.[1] So, is it fair to assert such spotty utilization to date? I believe so.

The Army could have done, and can do, much more than it has to harness the computer to national military advantage. To date, computers have been used to improve the capabilities of selected systems with the technology applied to do an existing function better, not to lever decisively new functions or new ways of fighting or training. Several examples follow, suggesting new, as yet unrealized, opportunities:

- The potential is present to "fight" new doctrine, organizations, or equipment, in virtual simulation before critical decisions for implementation have to be taken. This could be a new way of doing business for CBRS.
- There are new vistas in readiness and arms control, since major weapons producers can conceal technological change within replaceable microchips or build a "destruct" virus into military hardware for export on the global market.
- A one-megabyte readable memory could be included on each soldier's dog tag to reflect both personnel data and detailed training received. This would create new decentralized personnel and training management opportunities

These examples barely scratch the surface of potential applications about to change the battlefield. The really major national landpower payoffs are yet to come. We should not permit post–Desert Storm euphoria to slow our exploitation of the computer's current capability and future potential.

Skillful maneuvering of U.S. investments could allow most development and applications for landpower to be done by national and international industry. For example, it is evident that many industries are on converging paths to provide distributed home products. Costly innovations will be paid for by Sony-Columbia or Time Warner or Disney, for they are the future of entertainment. How should the Army attempt to shape that development to help military readiness? When entertainment in the form of three-dimensional, interactive images can be brought into the home, at commercially low costs by locally maintained cable, what should have been the

pacing applications for Guard, joint, or combined-forces training or operational command and control?

Just the ability to interact locally with one's unit, however widely distributed, would seem to "break the code" on reserve training. Imagine the training proficiency impact of the following hypothetical National Guard small-unit training situation—which should be absolutely feasible in several years; although the example describes armored forces, there is comparable application to light forces. *Virtual* simulation is simulation networking (SIMNET), in the future, a combined-arms tactical trainer (CATT). *Constructive* simulation is the joint-exercise simulation system (JESS) or corps battle simulation (CBS) and, in the future, CBS 2 or war simulation 2000 (WARSIM 2000). *Subsistent* simulation is the multiple, integrated-laser engagement system (MILES). These are three different but complementary forms of tactical engagement simulation now coming into use, which can be combined for near-revolutionary effects. Note that the concept described is not an extension of current policies and procedures. It draws on new training development and new training technologies to create a new way of training by immersion in a realistic training environment.

A National Guard Armor Company Commander has decided to train the Platoon Attack mission this weekend, in preparation for platoon lane training to be conducted during Annual Training. He moved his Abrams Trainers (simulators) to the WET (Weekend Training) site Friday. The MUTA 4 (Saturday-Sunday drill) has been divided up into several major events for each platoon.

The first platoon comes in Friday evening and crews 4 actual tanks. They will be on equipment "fighting" in a succession of structured lanes as late as possible on Sunday. Their tanks have been instrumented so the fire control and vision blocs can view into the virtual (SIMNET) battlefield the rest of the company is fighting on or use the actual WET site terrain. Their entire weekend consists of tactical tables (tactical exercises) on terrain including precombat checks, operational and organizational maintenance drills including recovery situations, and tactical resupply. The local Active Component Readiness Group provided an experienced senior noncommissioned officer to assist the platoon leader in conducting After-Action Reviews (AARs) on the tables although the platoon leader had trained on these same tables when he attended the Tank Commander Course and feels well-prepared to train and evaluate the tables. The platoon executes platoon drills and tactical tables on the ground day and night. When one or more of the other platoons or the company trains attack tables in virtual simulation, the platoon can observe and participate interactively from a stationary position. The remainder of the time they maneuver their tanks, changing off crew positions to hone on-equipment skills. They lagger (assemble) tactically both Friday and Saturday nights.

The second and third platoons will have their on-tank training on coming weekends. This weekend, they are training both gunnery and maneuver tables. Saturday morning, all the drivers and loaders gather on 4 Abrams

Trainers for driver matrix training with the Company Executive Officer. At the same time, the tank commanders (TCs) and gunners train gunnery table VIII (Tank), then gunnery table XII (Platoon gunnery) working with the company master gunner. The company commander is using the two Headquarters Tanks to coach two new TCs personally using the tank commander training matrix of the Abrams Trainer. That afternoon, the platoon leaders take over the Trainers for their platoons and conduct the coordination level tactical tables on hasty attack. They make three runs each, including AARs.

That night, the tone of training turns to competitive proficiency training. The company commander will continue the table VIII competition that had started the previous weekend. The gunnery matrix in the Abrams Trainer has a competition class set of very difficult, multiple simultaneous engagements. Battalion has authorized a $1000 cash award and special patch for the Top gun crew in each company. There is a similar competition open to platoon leaders who have to fight common platoon reaction tables across the battalion. That competition won't start until next month and the chain of command encourages platoon-leader practice during the week using one of the Abrams Trainers left in each armory and the semi-automated force (constructive simulation) which has been set up to support the table. Nevertheless, two of the platoon leaders want to try it in advance so they can talk the table over with their TCs. The AAR will automatically assess their performance, and each platoon leader feels that talking this over with his young leaders will be a good way to develop platoon spirit and teamwork. The platoon leaders had been exposed to this type competition in the Armor Officer Basic Course at Ft Knox and felt quite confident they would demonstrate competence, not incompetence, to their TCs. Anyway, both had practiced once already off-line, just themselves with everybody else automated at the armory one afternoon after work.

Sunday morning, the company commander turned up the heat. Each platoon was given three platoon tables—two tactical action and one platoon reaction table in succession–movement to contact, hasty defense then retrograde. The company commander alternates between platoons in conducting the AAR. Finally the leaders turn over their units to the first sergeant and the platoon sergeants and the weekend training is completed with a Fire Coordination Exercise conducted by the company commander, the Fire Support Team (FIST), and the platoon leaders. They fight from their Abrams Trainers with all other friendly and enemy forces represented by semi-automated forces (SAFOR-constructive simulation). The Battalion Operations Officer and Fire Support Officer monitor and conduct the AAR netted to the virtual battlefield from the battalion headquarters armory located about 150 miles away.[2]

All of this, of course, is speculative, although everything proposed has been done manually, recently in parts. Parallel effort is under way to improve battalion and brigade staff training. Some of the training and technology development to permit distribution to standard will materialize; some will not. But the magnitude of the potential change in training programs, through extensive use of the processor, is evident. In one weekend,

this tank company could have had more, better combat training than the average Guard unit now experiences in a week of two-week annual training. A similar example could be presented for active contingency forces, fighting on objective-area terrain, while their equipment is at sea.

The weekend described is a huge shift in current ways of doing business. New training development, combined with new processor-based training support, offers dramatic potential: improved reserve training, distributed to the local armory or the home. This is really different training, made possible by the processor. No existent Army training "futures" envisage such a big shift. In fact, in the initial buy, the planning for the future "SIMNET," the combined-arms tactical trainer (CATT), excludes long-haul networking of distributed training. It is a bit like replacing the engine of a new BMW 750il with two horses or a VW "Beetle" engine. It may not even appear to be an opportunity missed, if you have spent your life in Beetles, and you distrust new-fangled gadgets anyway.

Unfortunately, there is similar room for misunderstanding or underestimating computer potential in other important programs. For example, combined-arms heavy force is shaped about the Abrams and Bradley. Today, a vital issue is continued development of the Abrams. The program currently calls for eventual production of a new M1A2 tank, perhaps followed by an M1A3 tank or, in time, by development of a family of vehicles—armored systems modernization (ASM). Budget constraints will probably preclude any new platforms, but planning continues. Most design discussion centers about the defensive-offensive (armor-gun) equation, although mobility, weight, and sustainment costs are also considered. Processor improvements arise as useful additions, not major increments to tank-fighting potential. The traditional dialogue of industrial-age action and reaction continues much as it has for decades, while the revolutionary battle-command data systems of the information age languish for lack of user attention.

I suggest a rather different way of looking at future combined-arms, heavy capability to bring out the potential of the computer. Rather than a tank, consider the Abrams platform as mobile, protected space that can be filled with different capabilities. Aside from the proved modularity of traditional gun (105mm to 120mm) and armor (special armor to special armor plus depleted uranium), both of which have already been changed, think of other capabilities that the processor could permit once a power bus is provided to the vehicle. Adding a power bus is "wiring" the tank for data passage, similar to what has been done on the Apache attack helicopter. If it goes into production, the M1A2 tank will have this bus. In addition, the M1A2 should have an embryonic capability to pass tactical data to other tanks, as well as a turret drop-in commander's independent thermal viewer (CITV), which provides a highly effective night-vision, hunter-killer acquisition means for the vehicle commander. Tactical information can be passed

rapidly within the combined-arms team and permit very fast concentration of firepower.

Imagine other drop-in capabilities in lieu of the CITV: a millimeter wave-imaging system (M1A2a), perhaps a tunable laser (M1A2b), a high-powered microwave (M1A2c), or specialized command communications for rapid passing of data to other vehicles or aircraft (M1A2d). Imagine that each of these capabilities has been configured as a look-alike CITV and that the interior of the tank has been designed so the electrical power, air conditioning, cubic space, and weight allowance on each tank will accommodate various drop-ins. Now, add this capability to the Bradley. Further, imagine that the field commander (division?) can vary the differential loading, including the drop-in of very high-value, "black" capabilities, just before combat. The enemy would not know what mix of which capabilities was where on the battlefield. If the enemy is unable to locate the high-value systems, perhaps three per company, we have just provided a "stealth" capability of sorts. The processor-based combinations suggested could have a profound effect, particularly when data-linked with other AFV, and attack aviation with equally mobile and protected command and control. And the improvements do not necessarily require production of new platforms. Some could be added to the existing Abrams M1A1 tanks.

Now, this is all a concept drawn to demonstrate really new, perhaps unconventional, potentials permitted by processors. These might be applied to the "vanilla" M1A2 or perhaps an improved M1, and, in time, perhaps armored systems modernization (ASM), if ASM development progresses in the next several decades. Note, this is not extending or improving existing capabilities. Rather, it is introducing different, new capabilities, through use of the processor, to existing platforms. A new way of fighting is suggested based upon new capabilities not feasible before the computer. Returning to the Beetle engine in the BMW, recall that the "vision" for the combined-arms tactical trainer lost the "whole," powerful distributed simulation, to incremental gains in individual "parts," such as improved terrain and out-of-hatch vision. To date, there has been little vision to force integrated development. To bring out processing potential, it would have been necessary to sketch out a different future, one that would stretch the profound capabilities of the processor. That was done above in the "mark-on-the-wall" description of a possible National Guard weekend training session. More such marks on the wall are necessary.

Conceptual work on the M1A2, leading to ASM, may not be sufficiently bold to cause the major force improvements allowed by the processor. Many soldiers see individually good, conceptual parts, such as different armored fighting vehicles, each AFV with a common configuration. They may not see the much larger potential of mobile, protected space, and differential loading done by processor. It may take creating and fighting these

conceptual vehicles in unit warfare before many realize that a bold departure in war fighting is sought and workable. "Fight before you buy" is now feasible in virtual simulation.

In any event, no serious study of the impact of differential loading has occurred for improved Abrams platforms, despite the power bus, and no similar bus is currently programmed for the infantry Bradley. So much for really new, different, and imaginative applications of the computer to heavy-force improvements, at least for the near term. ASM evidences more of the same, not insignificantly, as demonstrated to the world in Desert Storm. But it is justified by improvements in general operating costs, not as a new way of fighting based on the national exploitation of new capabilities virtually unique to the "arcade" upbringing and sheer quality of the American soldier.

Underexploitation of the computer "revolution" is truly an unfortunate situation, particularly since resources are drying up. Starved in R&D and procurement, landpower should be capitalizing on the developments of others, whenever possible. The Army should be driving to take advantage of Air Force and Navy developments and to capitalize on civilian industry. Encourage Time Warner to solve the distributed training problem while it strives to revolutionize entertainment. The computer is perfectly suited to give significant added value to existing capability. It is an area of national advantage. Why does the Army seem to be failing to exploit fully this extraordinary potential?

Much of the difficulty stems from the great potential of the computer itself. Computers do not provide just an easier way to accomplish old tasks; their greater capability is to execute new ones. The computer can undertake actions never possible before. To exploit the processor, one must think of the future. Think of breakthroughs, of bold departures never before possible. This is not as difficult as it may seem, but it does require a new way of thinking. Consider the following example from small-unit training:

How much is the traditional training analysis of small-unit, live-fire training conditioned not by what one sees happening on the battlefield of the future but by what the individual has been able to experience on today's ranges? All present-day ranges are severely constrained by safety, cost, and local ecology. What if they were unlimited—multiple targets appearing over the Abrams or Bradley back deck, or attack by multiple-attack helicopters, or . . . ? The processor (SIMNET-CATT) can create the complete battlefield that should constitute the front-end analysis for combined-arms, direct-fire training. Once that is done, tasks can be assigned for execution in live fire, or in simulation. *The answer is not using simulation to substitute for "safe" live-fire tasks, already so constrained as to be unrealistic.* Think how few tasks there are involving Abrams, Bradley, and Apache fighting together, because there are so few places in the world where they can actually do this

often enough to develop a combined-arms task list. The processor permits the Army to correct this lack and to undertake actions never before possible outside actual combat.

The real challenge is to use the computer to think, and to train, as no Army has so far. Has the Army forgotten to consider processor-based breakthroughs, or has it perhaps focused its talent in other areas? If so, it seems time to reconsider, despite significant budget reductions, if U.S. landpower intends to retain tactical and operational advantage in the information age.

Another aspect of the problem is generational change. Many senior leaders are not yet really comfortable with the computer. Some discomfort reflects the parochialism of the traditional management-information specialist, who has been jealously guarding the expertise and the positions. Try as I might, I detested computers when forced to use the DOS system. It was like a daily initiation rite, with a usual call for help from the "expert" when I inevitably missed cues. When I retired, I bought a Macintosh. It is almost fun. More to the point, it is so easy to use that normal curiosity draws one deeper and deeper into understanding the power of the computer. This is the more fundamental issue: It is very difficult to understand computers or simulations by listening to a briefing. Total participation in accomplishing demanding tasks is essential to understand the profound power available. A briefing on SIMNET will never convey the excitement and learning potential of immersion for training in simulations. To understand, you have to fight, and become emotionally involved in the fight. Briefings will not convey the power of the processing capability on the M1A2. You have to "do it."

The bottom line remains that the Army is not getting the mileage required out of the processor. It is not wholly a problem of technology or of money. It is a challenge of vision, understanding, and assimilation. Young officers and sergeants understand, and are comfortable with the processor's power, but they do not have the experience to propose or to judge landmark changes. Senior leaders need these insights. In sum, Sergeant Brown and Captain Smith are comfortable relying on a processed image in combat. In fact, to many, the thermal sight is the AFV sight of choice. Colonel Jones and General Green are less comfortable and much less certain. Perhaps it is time for senior leaders to "pull up their socks" on computers. We really cannot afford to repeat the saga of horse cavalry, which not only delayed mechanization but also retarded tank development so U.S. soldiers in World War II had to fight valiantly on inferior equipment. Never again should there be disasters like Task Force Smith.

12   The Army: A Vehicle of Social Change

SOCIAL RESPONSIBILITIES OF THE ARMY WERE TOPICS OF general discussion in the sixties and seventies. Some were stimulated by the concerns of the Johnson administration that the Department of Defense was not doing enough in the war on poverty. This resulted in Project 100,000—essentially, an unwelcome experiment in charging the services with Job Corps responsibilities to train the marginally trainable. At the other end of service, Project Transition was established to support the development of salable civilian skills for those in combat arms to ensure that their service would increase their potential value in the civilian workplace.

As the Army groped for its soul after Vietnam, the issue of social roles also arose. The lack of self-confidence, which stimulated "The Army Wants to Join You" as its initial recruiting theme for the Volunteer Force, infected service and other informed views of roles for the post–Vietnam War Army. Implicit in the discussion was the assumption that combat readiness alone was not enough to justify the Army. Something else, some broader social contribution, was required to reestablish credibility to the American people.

What was not appreciated at the time was that the Army, in rebuilding itself, would become immersed in the absolute front edge of social change in the United States. Re-creating the skilled, tough, disciplined, "ready" Army envisoned in the early seventies—the Army of Excellence in the nineties—required the institutionalizing of massive social change: equal opportunity, a drug-free environment, and even reduction of smoking. In any event, by the mid-seventies, the Yom Kippur War had refocused the naysayers on the clear need to rebuild and modernize the Army. The Soviets had

145

moved a generation ahead of us, while we were engrossed in Vietnam. Combat readiness for "come-as-you-are" modern war was a necessary and sufficient objective for sustaining the Army. Meanwhile, however, the necessary social changes were taking place within the organization. Proactive leaders, quality volunteers, and a competence-based approach joined to create a quiet, but nonetheless effective, revolution.

The rebuilding effort was successful. During Operations Just Cause and Desert Storm, the American people discovered that all the services, and particularly the Army, had achieved beneficial change. Corrective programs had actually occurred to include self-improvement of the individual soldier and his or her maturation to a positive, motivated leader sought after in the civilian labor market. And most impressive, the change did not appear to be limited to the regular force. The reserves seemed to be equally thorough in their execution of these social programs. The praise was effusive and sometimes almost embarrassing, as columnists "discovered" the new military. Suddenly, the services became the hallmark of disciplined excellence. They became the embodiment of the American dream of individual improvement and one for other organizations to emulate. Now, various interests look to the military example for a solution to their problems. This is a refreshing change for the military after post-Vietnam vilification.

The story of this sea change is remarkable but not surprising. A competent organization, focused on common goals for a long-term development effort, was provided funding resources—particularly by the Reagan Administration—as well as necessary backing by Department of Defense and Congress, to eliminate soldiers who did not want to "be all they could be." Service values were rehoned, standards were reestablished and reinforced by competence testing, and an outstanding noncommissioned officer corps was re-created. Most of the social programs became "sergeants business," administered fairly across race, gender, religion, or ethnic background by tough sergeants absolutely representative of their soldiers. It was hard to complain if you failed the same performance evaluation passed by others who trained with you, particularly when the sergeant bearing down on you was of your race, gender, religion or ethnic background.[1]

Against this backdrop, issues of social roles arise again. Now, they are fed by national military success and the extraordinary difficulty with a national budget deficit, of generating funds for new programs, social or otherwise. Since national program funding has been made a zero-sum game—something must be canceled to generate funds for a new effort—remarkable pressure will be put on the defense budget to support domestic social programs. This should prevail, at least until some new executive-legislative budget compromise. It is likely to persist well beyond any compromises, given the systemic nature of domestic economic and social programs. The case for increased Army involvement in pressing domestic social programs might be thus stated:

As threats appear to recede around the world, the acknowledged talents of the Army can be turned to pressing social problems which continue, in fact seem to grow worse, each year. If the Army cannot or should not help, withdraw the funding, and apply it directly to needed social programs. The defense "insurance policy" can be maintained by a much smaller active force (300,000–400,000) in the Army, backed up by the reserves, who, all agree, are much improved. The Air Force and Navy can defend our remaining foreign commitments.

There is a deeper issue here that seems certain to propel the Army into domestic programs. The last time the nation faced major economic dislocation—the Great Depression of the thirties—the management talents of the Army were called upon to administer the successful jobs program of the Civilian Conservation Corps (CCC). The nation is now in a parallel period, although the issues are social and cultural as much as economic. Now, however, the Army has not only the management skills, but it is also a respected national role model for rebuilding individual and group competence and confidence. The combination of declining external threat, the Army's past record in the thirties, and its current reputation for excellence mandate substantial involvement in addressing what might be called the economic and social "Depression of the nineties."

As of mid-1992, neither case has yet been made, although it seems to be simply a matter of time. For now there are increasing calls to national public service or perhaps support of a modern CCC as a part of a larger national jobs program.[2] These are not because the volunteer force has failed but rather because there are too few job opportunities and other incentives for youth today to grow while performing clearly needed public service.[3] The next calls will assault the Army end strength much more directly. What should be the responses?

Answers also lie in the changed nature of world security and the Army's potential role in continued development. They may also rest in extending the social revolution the Army has already achieved. The challenge is definition, communication, and imaginative extension of the known and accepted achievements of the Army for the past two decades. It appears to be possible for the Army to demonstrate by example the desirability of the objective as well as the acts taken to achieve it. This would seem to be applicable both nationally and internationally.

First, consider the new overall environment. Modern doctrine and technologies mandate highly competent soldiers in constituted forces. This appears to be accepted, at least within the United States. We now lead the world in transition to the new military emerging in the information age. It is a highly proficient, intensely capitalized, volunteer force. In our search for the most capable people, irrespective of race, gender, religion, and origin, we have embedded significant positive social change in the force itself. In turn, these social changes have contributed to the general competence of

the force at war, as demonstrated in the performance and attitudes of our soldiers in combat.

This is one very positive message of Operation Desert Storm: the importance of discipline, of respect for the rights and responsibilities of all soldiers, of absolute equal opportunity, and of rigorous training. Embedded social change is no longer optional; it is a key ingredient to military success in the new atmosphere of world security. It not only provides access to all the talent nationally available when gold-collar skills are needed, but it also creates a socially cohesive force during a time of increasing international racial, ethnic, and religious tension. *Full social cohesion is absolute combat power.* Understanding this concept, then explaining it to the military establishments of other nations, is an important security and social responsibility for the Army. This can be done at home and abroad, within the institutional training structure. Suitably tailored for the various recipients, this message can be incorporated in Special Forces' training opportunities abroad.[4]

We traditionally think of support to other national military establishments as military training teams of experts, describing how to use and maintain weapon systems. Often, in low-intensity conflict, we have considered staff support to improve the effectiveness and efficiency of the military as a positive contributor to local nation-building. Other tasks come to mind such as training engineers to support public needs, improving medical support, and so forth. These are not the kinds of support suggested here for military establishments in the post industrial period. The critical path for the armies of our allies, long-term and ad hoc, is to convert to competence-based forces that support the political, economic, and social development of their nations and assure requisite military security. This is absolutely consistent with the *National Military Strategy,* (1992), which sees peacetime activities as providing global strength ". . . to encourage continued democratic and economic progress and respect for human rights in an atmosphere of enhanced stability."[5]

U.S. Army support could consist of the following information, tuned for intended domestic and international "markets," to develop understanding of competence-basing and its practical applications:

- Accession measurement tools, so quality across race, gender, religion, and ethnic background can be identified.
- Techniques for introducing the systems approach to training, so individual and collective performance can be trained and evaluated to task, condition, and standard in task-based job descriptions applicable to both military and general public service.
- Application of performance evaluation to personnel selection, advancement, and elimination.
- Recommendations for assimilation of the computer, given the particular local culture.

- Recommendations for specific institutional or unit training to develop blue-, white-, and gold-collar military skills in selected battlefield operating systems.

These could be supplemented by structured case studies in the following areas, tailored for local presentation in various regional cultures:

- Merits of competence-basing
- Utility of frequent performance evaluations
- Applications of broad guidance and flexibility in execution to standard
- Translation of personnel-development responsibilities for armies without a noncommissioned officer corps, usually traditional cultures, with armies composed of officers and "peasants"

These comments are certainly not intended to be all-inclusive; they represent the breadth of support that could be necessary. Traditional training teams (MTTs) will still be appropriate, particularly to develop local understanding of the various battlefield operating systems expected to be used in contingency operations. Nor will these measures ensure a fully representative force, unless the leadership in a country wants to make it happen. The point is, there is a new range of policies and programs required to encourage credible, competence-based, socially representative armies around the world. Influencing this evolution, probably integral to the information age, seems an important part of the broad social responsibilities of landpower in the United States.

The same support opportunities apply domestically. The methodology is not complex. The secret of Army success is task definition, followed by performance training and evaluation. They, in turn, are followed by performance test (based on "go–no go," not on norms) and selection, where performance—not race, gender, religion, or origin—is the criterion. It is not an issue of quotas but of being sensitive to social representation, then of training and retraining to competence on a cold, impersonal, specific performance test. Over time, as noncommissioned officers become fully representative, the training and retraining can be conducted by someone with the individual soldier's characteristics.[6] The policies above, relating to competence-basing, could apply to a state or local transit agency, department of recreation, police force, fire department, or other initiatives that may arise as a result of the urban unrest of spring 1992. The training could be given as a public service through the local National Guard or Army Reserve, both of which absolutely understand competence-basing or by recently separated Army personnel. While training of individuals is important, the expert could also guide the institutionalizing of the competence-basing process.

Other, more direct support could be offered if desired, without impairing the readiness of the force. The hallmark of today's Total Army is the individual young officer or sergeant accustomed to a socially responsive organization and who has been provided superb leader training. That young leader could be "seed corn" for state and local government in the practical, competent execution of important programs. He or she knows what competence-basing can do. They can become the stimuli for its introduction in key state or local organizations for economic, social, and educational development.

The role of the Army here is not to repeat Project 100,000, providing survival skills to the marginally trainable who can handle today's weapons only with difficulty. That is an absolute nonstarter proved by rigorous evaluation.[7] Rather, the Army's role can be to recruit quality young people, turn them into white-collar noncommissioned officers or gold-collar officers, then turn them over to public service as accomplished leaders. There will have to be some vesting for military service as well as incentives from public service to sustain the flow of competence. To be sure, the Army will lose competent leaders, but it is to a necessary cause. Forced throughput is not bad in terms of maintaining a flow of young Army unit leaders, fully in tune with our nation. And those who leave the Army can be powerful spokespeople for landpower.

Other support could consist of training "camps" or structured, positive job experiences for youth in the CCC model. They could be designed to develop individual discipline, performance to standard, challenge, self-confidence, and pride in nation and self. The Army knows how to do this well. The ROTC basic camp, designed to challenge and attract uncommitted young college students to ROTC, is an excellent example. However, such a national mission is simply beyond the capability of the constituted active force, which already nearly "stands down" every summer to support ROTC and the training of the reserves. In the future, this promises to be an even greater drain. If capability were to be empowered by separate statute, funding, and personnel, and not charged to Army combat-readiness accounts, it could be feasible to sustain landpower readiness while addressing the "Depression of the nineties."

For the long term, *if* this task must be performed by the military, it would seem best to do it with the constituted reserve force, which does not have to be in as rapid a response-readiness posture. That is, draw on units that have available more than 180 days of post-mobilization training before deploying on contingency operations. This is tough for the reserves, who are already stretched to sustain unit readiness with citizen-soldiers faced with occupational civilian and military development problems. So, this seems to be a job for full-time regulars, supporting the constituted reserve force, and maintained by separate statute similar to that affecting engineers

on civil works. This would preclude erosive competition with the manpower needs of the contingency force.

This is a really difficult challenge for landpower. The Army has demonstrated convincingly the ability to institutionalize competence and equal opportunity. The nation faces a tough challenge in these areas. Landpower should help as a national force. Yet, the basic mission and rationale for Army resources is to provide the military landpower component to serve national security. The magnitude of national social and economic problems is such that the Army could easily become submerged, losing its basic and unique capability. Therefore, separate statute and funding seem preconditions to any substantial involvement.

This is an issue that simply cannot be avoided, even though it may complicate landpower readiness. Service to nation is an important and abiding element of landpower's professional ethos. It is to that aspect that we now turn.

13   Vital Intangibles of the Profession

THE INFORMATION AGE APPEARS CERTAIN TO INFLUENCE the ideals and practices of the military profession, as have preceding major developments in technology. It may be too early to attempt to redefine professionalism in the U.S. Army, but we do need to be sensitive to new domestic and international pressures. They will have a major impact on current formulations of the professional ethos, which will, in turn, directly or indirectly, influence important policy and program decisions. For example, equal opportunity is now an integral element of military life, making possible new sources of talent required for modern battle and the cohesion essential to sustaining capable units. Accordingly, the professional ethos has had to change: from passive tolerance to proactive endorsement of equal opportunity. Women at West Point is one example. Now rationalized in the professional ethos, the Army found in the Persian Gulf that institutionalized equal opportunity provided a new and very useful addition to combat effectiveness.

Several caveats are in order. First, I am discussing the U.S. Army, not any other. The analysis may apply, but I suspect that, for other than perhaps the Israeli Defense Force, what I describe is ten or more years away—the incubation period for assimilating the information revolution. Nor am I considering the Navy or Air Force of the United States. As others have said, they are already more equipment-oriented. They "man equipment," not "equip the man," as does the Army. The influence on the individual of a deluge of technology is not so novel to them; thus, the professional impacts should be less.[1]

Second, I am not going to go into the often involved arguments whether the Army is a profession or an occupation. Whatever a volunteer's

152

initial motive for enlistment, I believe the overall effects of the rebirth of the Army after Vietnam have generally made moot for him the question of eroding professionalism in the All-Volunteer Force. Events have passed by such debate. There is no discussion today of military unions. A body of professional knowledge has been rigorously defined and enforced through competence-basing. Concern for personal progress has been institutionalized in officer and noncommissioned-officer development programs. Values have been reembedded in the professional development model and are reinforced regularly. The Army's self-image has been restored, most recently by public acclaim after Operation Desert Storm. This does not mean that challenge to the professional ethos is gone. On the contrary, new, far different, yet equally risky problems prevail today. It is these challenges and their potential impacts I shall address.

Third, truly major forces for change are now in the wind. The processor is as revolutionary an instrument of war as were the atom bomb or the internal-combustion engine. We have just won the first war of the information age. The military implications are still unfolding. Add to all this the breakup of the post–World War II world and the demise of the Soviet Union and the traditional Russian empires. Remarkably fast—characteristic of the information age—and with minimum use of military force, a superpower has waned, creating wide-ranging instability. For the U.S. Army, the rationale eroded for the deterrence-based force of forty years' duration. A superb Army, flushed with victory, finds itself facing a greatly diminished role, for all the right national reasons. More big surprises are inevitable as the world order shifts. Too many changes continue to arrive to attempt predicting elaborate, detailed outcomes.

Nevertheless, some important road signs are already posted to point the general azimuth of the evolving professional ethos. The first immediate direction is highlighted by the competence of the force that fought Operations Just Cause and Desert Storm. It was exceptional, led well at all echelons by Gen. Maxwell R. Thurman and General Schwarzkopf. The biggest and most pleasant surprise was the ability of the young leaders, the sergeants and captains. They were not just good, they were outstanding. As one division commander, Maj. Gen. Barry R. McCaffrey, commented, our soldiers were so good that we could have switched equipment with the Iraqis and still won.[2]

Detailed analysis of some of the battles has now been accomplished. It is apparent that genuine attempts to fight by the Iraqi Republican Guard were consistently preempted by aggressive U.S. counters. The initiative was seized and exploited again and again as the brief ground campaign proceeded. Perhaps most impressive were the frequent, documented cases of U.S. soldiers' fighting without quarter, until the Iraqis surrendered; at such times, U.S. soldiers not only immediately ceased fire but also left cover sometimes at personal risk, to tend Iraqi wounded.

It seems clear that, by most standards, the U.S. Army, ably supported by the other services and allies, established a new "world class" in Operation Desert Storm and in Operation Just Cause. Doctrine, organization, equipment, training, and, most important, competent people were combined in a whole much greater than the sum of the parts. The Army generally knows which policies and programs are required to sustain the best army in the world and stands insulated by justifiable pride in its significant accomplishments. The psychic effect of the coming decline, therefore, will be initially moderated. Longer-term effects, however, may be negative: Competent professionals, who know what is required to win quickly and decisively, realize that vital Army ability often seems no longer available in many units or activities. This is a tough pill to swallow, just as the next wave of change rolls in and requires major adaptations. In some ways, it may prove to have been easier to assimilate major change after Vietnam, because we all knew things were "broken" then.

In sum, the Army has set an important, quite expensive, perhaps unsustainable standard of excellence for itself that, now embedded in myth, will be very difficult to alter. Professional anguish and withdrawal may be in the offing, just as landpower should be breaking out into a new, positive cycle of change.[3]

A second road sign of change in the professional ethos is the recent shift of traditional responsibilities between the officer and noncommissioned officer corps. After the decline of the noncommissioned officer corps in Vietnam, the Army had to recreate "sergeant's business"—the position and authorities of the noncommissioned officer. Because there were not enough competent noncommissioned officers in the seventies, officers became enmeshed in "sergeant's business," to the detriment of both. This was corrected by the eighties, when the noncommissioned officer corps was reconstituted. Sergeants expanded into traditional "officer's business," while officers addressed the emerging challenges of AirLand Battle. Traditional blue-collar–white-collar distinctions became blurred. Increasingly, senior NCOs are expected to execute traditional company officer tasks, such as command in high attrition battle—the *Reichswehr* model. Simultaneously, the officer corps moves into the high-tecnology, integrative, gold-collar skills, of AirLand Operations. These are the same skills—"Have computer, will travel"—as those required by industry now transitioning into the global economy. These changes promise to become more pronounced in the future, as the Army seeks iron collars (robots), blue collars (young NCOs), white collars, (senior NCOs and young officers), and gold collars (field-grade officers) to execute the war-fighting doctrine. These are not mere semantic changes. New models of professional responsibilities for officers and noncommissioned officers seem in order, as the Army makes the transition to a post-industrial force.[4]

The third road sign really proceeds from the second, the changed nature of leader responsibilities in the information age. While *war* can be described persuasively as *First Wave,* or the product of the agricultural revolution, *Second Wave,* or that formed in the Industrial Revolution, and *Third Wave,* or that characteristic of the emerging information age, future battles will be a combination of the three.[5] Traditional formulations of the professional ethos normally include some body of unique skills, a sense of calling to a higher cause, and unlimited liability, or service to and including death.[6] In Third Wave, or gold-collar war, requisite war-fighting skills seem increasingly to be not unique to professionals. Doctrine, tactics, techniques, and procedures are expected to be fought by the Total Force of active and reserve soldiers. Both must master the same tasks, conditions, and standards. Combat training center experiences are uniform. Decline of the defense industry may erode the distinctly military nature of materiel. Distinctions between military grade and responsibility seem more and more related to ability to take advantage of the power of computers—and that is a civilian skill.[7] What, therefore, sets the "professional" apart? Why are "professionals" needed?

A contemporary answer rests in the complexity of Third Wave war, fought at operational and strategic levels. A lifetime of study produced highly competent strategic leadership in the Persian Gulf—Gen. Colin L. Powell, Gen. Carl E. Vuono, and General Schwarzkopf, just to mention the most senior leaders. Extremely sophisticated joint operations were conducted with other services and our allies in combined operations well within the tactical echelon of war. Success was also a product of exceptional "managership": an army built by the meshing of complex, effective systems that ensured the structuring, equipping, training, manning, sustaining, mobilizing, and deploying of landpower. War fighting at the strategic and operational echelons, joint and combined operations, and management of landpower seem to be the unique body of knowledge that sets the professional apart. They are the skills of the landpower professional; development of the active force should focus on these skills.

All the other skills and values associated with the tactical echelon of war, particularly at battalion-command level, are vitally important, but they do not set aside the professional. This, of course, does not mean that performance at platoon, company, or battalion is not decisive in battle outcomes. It is critical to success. It does suggest, however, that active and reserve development should converge as fully as possible at the lower tactical echelons.[8]

A fourth road sign of change is a much broader conception of the military professional's commitment to a lifetime of service to nation. The traditional model had extolled purely military service. Now, broader nonmilitary avenues, such as public service and leadership in other professions,

are recognized as useful contributions to nation by former professional military officers. The mission of the U.S. Military Academy was recently broadened to reinforce this shift in emphasis. The mission statement now includes ". . . to inspire each (graduate) to a lifetime of service to the nation."[9] Practically, this may be belated acknowledgment of the increasing national attitudinal shift to personal expectations of multiple careers. Conceptually, a broader view of service to nation encourages individual and perhaps even institutional, involvement in nontraditional, nonwar-fighting areas. This alone does not necessarily imply change to the institution (a calling of unlimited commitment) versus occupation (nine-to-five like any other job) models of military service described by respected sociologists. Rather, it suggests that the basic concept of nature and duration of individual service is changing. This broadening seems wholly consistent with evolving employment expectations of the information-age work force.[10]

Reviewing the health of the profession in the U.S. Army in the early nineties, the prognosis is mixed. Clearly, great good has been done to reestablish traditional, proved values across the force. Capability has not eroded in an occupational mind-set by adopting a fixed idea of occupation. However, the purposes of service are changing, and traditional responsibilities need review. Yet, flushed with decades of relative affluence and recent success, the Army is not disposed to break something clearly "not broke."

Several lurking issues challenge the professional ethos:

The first and arguably most important to the professional ethos is the mixed blessing of the systems approach to training—the task, condition, and standard. *The Soldiers Manual* and ARTEP mission training plan codify in exquisite detail what is required to be trained. They have been the engine of the competence-based force. It is fair to assert that no other army in history has known in such detail what is required to be "ready."

That is the danger as the Army contemplates decline.[11] It is the Army of Excellence; all believe it; the world believes. Each can read exactly what he or she needs to be able to do by task, condition, and standard. As resources decline, it will be difficult to sustain the operational training intensities to which the Army has become accustomed. As training pressures decline, so must readiness decline—or an integrity crisis will occur among talented young leaders, who know precisely what they should be doing to be "ready" and what they are unable to do. You cannot tell them they are ready when, by internal or external evaluation, they are not. The resource rape of U.S. Army, Europe, during Vietnam created an integrity gap when readiness expectations were not lowered. This was an egregious failure of Army leadership at the strategic level, which required a decade of patient leadership and abundant resources to correct. So, we must be honest with ourselves. This, too, poses challenges. The Army will lose some who are exhilarated by the excellence but who do not want to serve in a severely resource-constrained force. Probably, the "summer soldiers and sunshine

patriots" are better gone. The same thing happened after Vietnam and the Army certainly survived.

It is difficult to be honest in decline. The Army develops aggressive, "can-do" people unaccustomed to failure. Nor do we want them to fail in combat. But the peacetime Army, during a cycle of decline, is another matter. Leaders must be prepared to relate doable task, condition, and standard to honest readiness reporting, even if the picture produced under their watch is one of declining training readiness. Smart leaders can anticipate and act before the crisis develops. For example, the danger here may be so acute that it could stimulate subordinate input to efficiency reports as a preventive. Obviously, there is a serious danger to integrity associated with the drawdown.

Another challenge relates to the Army's compassion as an organization. The humanity shown the enemy in Operation Desert Storm was notable, evoking an image of chivalry. It underscored respect of the individual, which goes to the inner core of the military as a calling as well as the American self-image. These were not the actions of nine-to-five soldiers, regular or reserve. They were a by-product of extraordinary excellence and self-confidence, an expression of *noblesse oblige*. Where is that compassion now as the service dismisses many who contributed to the excellence of Operations Just Cause and Desert Storm? This is as much an issue for Department of Defense and Congress as it is for professional military. But the importance of this element of the professional ethos is such that it needs to be stated again and again.

The issue goes deeper than compassion toward the dismissed. It also applies to continuation of the broad range of beneficial "people programs" established during the years of affluence. Measured in day-to-day productivity, the Army probably cannot afford them. In fact, they can be an absolute drain on unit stability: the many reasons for removing someone from assignment orders make the regular replacement flow difficult. Many can think of other hallmarks of the organization that "cared." The Army discontinues them at professional peril. To be sure, many people programs will go. The challenge is to maintain those supporting soldiers serving overseas and to replace the critical programs for those assigned in the United States with services comparable to those for other Americans living in the same area. After all, this is what Guardsmen, Army reservists, and their families expect and receive. They are integral parts of the Total Force on the battlefield. Should they not be beneficiaries of the same professional compassion?

This raises another, more fundamental issue. What is the professional ethos as it relates to the citizen-soldier? He or she may be "nine to five" when training during the weekend or summer, but the citizen-soldier is an essential partner in battle. Some serve solely for pay and social contacts as do some full-time soldiers. Are they thereby less professional than the full-

time soldier? Is long-term professional status measured in hours-per-month or by motives for enlistment? Many reservists, in fact, devote sixty to eighty or more days a year to reimbursed and unreimbursed service. Unreimbursed time, often described as "God-and-country time," has been a characteristic of selfless reserve service. This attitude requires devotion to duty, reflecting, certainly, "the intrinsic motivation of an institution," not "the extrinsic motivation of an occupation," as expressed by Charles Moskos.[12] The body of expertise that sets the military apart from civilians is mandated for the reserves, at least in wartime, in detailed task, condition, and standard. Unless mobilized, Guardsmen are loyal to the state governor, but that should not preclude their acceptance as professionals. All resonate to the values of duty, honor, and country. On the other hand, a depth of understanding of military issues, implicit in prolonged service in various positions sets apart the military competence of the full-time officer or noncommissioned officer. Should that be the criterion?

This returns us to the original question: What is the professional ethos of the citizen-soldier, soon to become the major element of our landpower capability? I suggest that, at the tactical echelon of war, it is the same as that for the active-duty soldier. It behooves the regular force to accept this, in fact, to reinforce it.

Approach the question a bit differently. Assume that the base values of the military profession in the U.S. Army are those of the reserves. What, if anything, needs to be done to reinforce their values and attributes? Then, what should be added for the active force at the tactical level? What should be added at the strategic and operational levels? What about war fighting at the operational and strategic echelons, joint and combined operations, and management requirements for the Army, discussed as guideposts above? Is that sufficient for more senior professional officers?

One could also approach from another direction the nature of service in determining professional status. Extraordinary mobility in the labor force seems to be a characteristic of the information age. Two or three careers may become the norm. A difficult issue in the ongoing drawdown has been the release of the mid-termer—a person with more than eight to ten years' service but not vested for retirement. As organizations become flatter, with fewer echelons, and as the individual soldier becomes more capable of levering action through processors, there will probably be smaller units with fewer soldiers. Perhaps, the optimum period of blue-collar service will include intensive training and use for ten years before another job in industry or public service. White-collar and gold-collar skill development and service could be on another cycle. Who are the "professionals"? How can the Army bond them into cohesive, skilled, tough, proud, ready units? How long does one serve to become "professional"? The Army needs to start developing the professional ethos now to cope with the service patterns that seem to be coming.

The Army may not even have the clear-cut advantage of fighting under the U.S. flag in some future contingencies. Posted to a regional area with an air-defense, or intelligence, or fire-support unit to reinforce a new ad hoc ally, Army units may be subordinate to a UN or regional organization. Alternately, Army people might be committed, individually or in small units, as equal-opportunity models, to inculcate "modern" values in the military of new democracies. These may seem unlikely examples. If so, select your own, based on the swirl of change about us. The moral is that quite different missions appear likely in the near future. The Army should be molding the professional ethos and personnel development to accommodate them.

14   Capturing Accelerating Change

It HAS ALWAYS BEEN FASHIONABLE TO DESPAIR ABOUT change and to reflect back on the "good old days." They usually seem better and always less complicated than the present. In the Army, the golden days tend to be one major event ago, a war, if there has been one in the recent past. Otherwise, the watershed is an event like transition to the All-Volunteer Army. I reflect back on at least five "armies" in which I served: the "brown-shoe" Army in the late fifties before Vietnam (very good); the early days in Vietnam (good); the late days in Vietnam (poor); the fifteen rebuilding years (fair to good); and now the Army of Excellence (excellent). Others more senior than I could do the same, centered on World War II. When were the "good old days"?

Each of "my" five armies was complete unto itself. All were bound by the common professional ethos of "Duty, Honor, Country"; however, day-to-day governing policies and programs varied enormously. In retrospect, they differed for good reason. The national military strategy shifted from mobilization to deterrence, then tentatively back to mobilization. The quality of both officer and noncommissioned officer corps changed dramatically. Resource availability went from famine to feast, to famine, and to feast. Technology changed from metal bending to chip dominance. Last, but perhaps most important for landpower in a democracy, national attitudes concerning the military went from apathy to disdain and later to support. With the exception of the steadying influence of the Soviet threat that served as a magnet for readiness, about everything else changed, often several times. Now, we have lost that steadying influence of the unequivocal, accepted threat.

So, when people wring their hands about change, I reflect back and think, so what's new? The Army has handled all that, mostly quite well. But that is not really true. Each major change, at the time, seemed to roll in unexpectedly. We scrambled, and because we were competent, genuinely devoted to our nation, and occasionally quite lucky, we adjusted. There was too much to discover, learn almost after the fact. Were there any general policies we could have pursued that might have positioned us better to handle the challenge of the "five armies"?

Today, we peer into a future that promises increasing rates of change in all aspects of human endeavor. Knowing that, is it not prudent to plan and even to organize specifically to master change? The Army seems well-positioned to do just this. The salient leverage of the information age appears to be innovation and initiative in acquiring and using information (knowledge). We, as a nation, are adapting to the processor. We take pride in our stereotype of the "shrewd Yankee trader," using our heads to solve problems. Moreover, the Army has demonstrated both competence and even a flair for shaping change, in formulating and executing AirLand Battle. What may the Army do to maintain the momentum? How could the Army institutionalize rapid adaptation to accelerating change in order to sustain its current competitive advantage in landpower?

• One of the most important actions is to continue the priority for quality over quantity, particularly in personnel. Better people of all grades (high mental category in blue, white, and gold collar) not only perform better under stress, employing novel capabilities, but they also adjust more easily to new situations. Competence and the self-confidence derived from competence are essential to strike out in new and uncharted directions.

To draw the best performance from these capable soldiers, they need both increased responsibilities and accompanying authorities to act. Fewer links in the chain of command seem clearly desirable, although the redundancy essential to robustness on the battlefield needs to be sustained. In fact, it should be reinforced where it was cut too severely in the Army of Excellence. A useful decision rule for AirLand Operations might be the elimination of every other headquarters in the current chain of command. This could be a design premise for the support (TDA) Army and a design possibility for the fighting (TOE) Army.

A second aspect of drawing out the potential of quality personnel is developing policies to "power down." The concept is to push more decisions lower in the chain of command. Without circumscribing the flexibility the Army wants to accommodate varying command styles, there needs to be a clear and persistent push to decentralize decisions as low as possible. Current programs that develop noncommissioned officers capable of command on the battlefield support and, in fact, encourage "power down" in peace-

time. The white-collar noncommissioned officer and gold-collar officer shift mandated in the information age necessitate "power down" to more competent subordinates.

• All organizations must have frequent "show and tell." For military organizations, frequent battles are obviously out of the question. The combat training centers (CTC) provide the next best thing—a bottom line involving battle performance on a realistic battlefield. This experience is as important for the constituted reserves as for the active force. Attendance should be required routinely for early-deploying reserve units. The CTC provide much more than training. They are battlefields that can also be designed to assimilate change in doctrine, organization, equipment, or training. Acceptance of the new by sergeants and captains in the crucible of CTC battle enables change to be accepted more quickly from the bottom up.

The CTC capability should be maintained, despite increasing absolute and relative dollar or manpower costs, because it keeps the focus of a peacetime army on war-fighting performance. There may be useful ways to amortize the considerable cost. Future distributed war-fighting technologies may permit inexpensive representation of costly battlefield operating systems in scmiautomated or automated simulations. To underwrite operating costs, the facilities could be made available for systems-acquisition use. The reserves and perhaps selected regional allies could use the facilities on a reimbursable basis. Better answers will arise. The issue is preservation, indeed expansion, of the CTC as the appropriate unit bottom line and as a critical element of capturing change, by forcing its assimilation in a war-fighting environment.

• Landpower in any democracy should be fully representative of the people it exists to defend. This is particularly important in our democracy as a state, a continent, and a nation of diverse peoples. At all levels, we should seek national representation. Equal opportunity is embedded; it needs to be stressed continually. The officer corps should continue to draw from the U.S. Military Academy, nationally distributed ROTC, and OCS, with due allowance for gold-collar potential. Service should be an avenue for citizenship to encourage immigrant representation. While the Army must retain rigorous socialization to military values and English as the only language, diverse racial, ethnic, and religious pride in service should be encouraged. Where the smaller active force cannot maintain a presence, the National Guard or Army Reserve should. All of this is not new; much is being done today. The point is that close ties with, and representation by, the diverse peoples in our nation's landpower is essential as change sweeps across the continent. The Army learns from its soldiers; they, in turn, inform far better than the media the people whom the Army defends.

• Educated and trained personnel can respond to change. The Army needs more blue-, white-, and gold-collar innovators—disciplined military professionals, who not only sense what is coming but also have the drive and organizational skills to determine what needs to be done and how to make it happen. They have to be encouraged to risk and to experiment.

All of this is very hard to accomplish in a bureaucracy. Too many innovators, each marching to his own drum, produce chaos. One answer rests in extensive professional-development programs. They should provide diverse leader-development patterns to attract and retain promising individuals, provide the basic professional tools, and offer unique development experiences like the foreign "sabbaticals" permitted in the past to officers. The Army has excellent means to do this now with various scholarships. But more than programs are required. The anti-intellectual bias has to be repressed. Standard injunctions against creative thought—"too many good ideas" or "don't fix it; it's not broke"—should be discouraged. Sustained landpower preeminence in the information age requires enlightened, innovative leaders—the gold-collar officer and the white-collar noncommissioned officer—who quest for opportunity and challenge at every echelon.

• The importance of competence-basing has been one of the real lessons of the past two decades. It ensured that the Army developed and retained the most capable personnel during a period of great personnel turnover. There was a generally unanticipated benefit, too. Fairly administrated, with accepted performance evaluations, competence-basing provided the engine for guaranteeing equal opportunity. Competence was the clear and unequivocal reason for personnel actions. If you were not competitive, the Army saw a responsibility to support you in your self-development. The ball, however, was in your court. If you performed to standard, you were in and promoted. If not, you were out. It was your decision. "Up or out" forced competent performance at every level in the organization. Now, as the Army declines, competence-basing provides the objective fairness essential to acceptance of the shrinking process. There will be inevitable assertions of bias, some undoubtedly true, but the existing system should serve well.

The Army clearly wants to retain competence-basing in the future. It is a contemporary "mandarin" system founded on professional ability and verified by validated performance test. It is to be hoped that, in the future, the Army will be able to base the assessment system more on personal performance in war fighting. The major measure should be how one performs in the heat of battle, regularly, in simulation if not in contingencies. Future training technology should augment this system across the force, as it has improved senior commander validation at the CTC. In general, the rigor of continuing education and the evaluation process should increase with se-

niority of position. Willingness to innovate and receptiveness to change could be two of the criteria. In sum, the tools for continued competence-basing are there. Their validity is increasingly accepted. The Army should expand the system in the future.

• Change can also be encouraged by structuring organizations so that there is a built-in creative tension. The drafters of the Constitution understood this when they separated powers among the executive, legislative, and judicial branches of government. Landpower has this tension in the felicitous division of responsibilities among regular forces (national and federal), National Guard (state and regional), and Army Reserve (federal and regional). The creative tension is obvious; all are better for it. Over the years, the Ballistic Research Laboratory achieved remarkable results, because armor (defense) and projectile (offense) were pitted against each other competitively in the same organization. It may be facetious to say, "Never organize so that the rabbit can carry the lettuce"; but as the Army builds down, it should strive to create creative tensions within the subordinate bureaucracies.

• The most important thought may be unnecessary to mention, because the basic decision was taken in the seventies. To lead in change, the Army needs to institutionalize a bureaucracy of change. An organization is needed with the breadth of mission and perspective to move into the future, define changes to achieve the objectives, then look back, and make necessary adjustments in today's Army. The charter must be all-inclusive, extending from doctrine to material, to organizations, and to the development of soldiers. Fortunately, the Army has that now in TRADOC, employing the concept-based requirements system. The challenge is to use it.

This engine of change could be fine tuned to converge authority and responsibility better and to "enable the future" for all, including joint and combined contingencies sized by unit and function. The physical infrastructure exists at the Army's war-fighting intellectual center at Fort Leavenworth. The gold-collar potential already there is immense. How can we take advantage of this capability?

The accelerated development process stands ready. The doctrine can be written at the college, then put to use at the National Simulation Center, with organizations and equipment in virtual and constructive simulation. People from Combined Arms Command, including the Command and General Staff College, can join the operation. Then the doctrine can be fought to contingency—mission, enemy, troops, terrain, time available (METT-T)—in simulation "on the ground," at the Combined Arms Center. Next, promising developments—doctrine, organization, equipment—can be "fought" by combat units actually at the appropriate CTC. After "battle" validation, the doctrine can go back to the proponents for refinement and

then be returned to reenter the crucible at Fort Leavenworth. This iterative process will accelerate the further assimilation of AirLand Battle, within the Army and its various constituencies. Further, the process can ensure that neither the reserves nor potential allies are forgotten in the quest for increasing landpower excellence. Today, CTC rotations demand that heavy and light forces work together. Reserves and allies should be included in all CTC rotations, so we "train as we will fight" in the information age. No other army even approaches this capability in concept, much less as it is institutionalized today. In fact, this capability has the Third-Wave war potential of a fielded corps, because, used imaginatively, it will preserve landpower initiative for the United States.[1]

Change is by definition uncertain. "Armies" change to meet new circumstances, or they perish. The several thoughts above are more systemic than specific. I believe, however, that together they ensure the necessary sensitivity, responsibility, and accountability for the U.S. Army to sustain a competitive edge in assimilating change in the information age.

15   The Challenge

THAT IS IT. A DIFFERENT LANDPOWER FOR THE UNITED States? No, there is no change in the basics of landpower. Nor is there any erosion of the enduring values of the military profession—"Duty, Honor, Country." Nor is there any change to the lasting "constants" of the U.S. Army, as postulated in chapter 1, in "New Challenges to Landpower."

The Army must retain the ability to dominate land, resources, and people consistent with the National Military Strategy of the United States.

The primary focus of the Army is, and must remain, on application of the enduring Principles of War to joint and combined war fighting to win.

The Army management objective must be competent stewardship for the Total Force, for joint obligations and for regional operations with allies.

But under the umbrella of lasting purposes, there are new challenges and opportunities that simply cannot be ignored. The international security environment has clearly changed dramatically in recent years with the end of the cold war. Now, the president's *National Security Strategy of the United States* prescribes new responsibilities for landpower, and a fundamental restructuring of American military capability is under way. The issues involve not whether there is to be change, but how to change. How will U.S. landpower be modified to respond to imposed external change?

This work responds to this issue. It does not presume to prescribe or even to describe, "the way" to bring about change. It does propose "a way," a comprehensive, integrated vision to stimulate reflection and possible action from the professional military leader and concerned layman.

There are several insights that drive the observations and recommendations made and are absolutely central to the work. These insights should

166

be either confirmed, and their implications converted to policy and program, or rejected and replaced by other perspectives.

• Landpower must adjust to an ongoing global shift from the industrial to the post-industrial, or information, age. This age is still undefined, although its salient characteristics are becoming evident: a greater, almost obsessive, use of the computer, increased need for and the power of knowledge; and a significant rise in the tempo of change. The military instrument of national policy should look to the economic instrument, specifically the global market, for insights as to necessary change. Most contemporary landpower is a product of the industrial age. Military preeminence will reside with those nations that adjust most rapidly to winning Third-Wave war of the information age. But increased reliance on capturing accelerating change in science and technology cannot distract from the basic truth that landpower is fundamentally individual soldiers. Competent and confident young men and women, proud to serve our great nation, are and will remain the basic strength of the American Army.

• Landpower has traditionally been committed by unit. Today, the unit is normally a corps or division, or occasionally a brigade task force, composed of balanced, all-purpose combat, combat-support, and combat-service-support units. For contingencies, the combined-arms unit is structured to respond to almost any expected or unexpected challenge. The appropriate "counter" had already been included in the balanced force; but by being ready for anything, the force could not use to its best advantage the national military strengths. In the future, the decisive capability may not be the balanced unit. More likely, it will be the appropriate battlefield operating systems, packaged as the crisis develops, to respond to specific, regional-contingency, military needs. The force package will exploit the military assets of the United States. Responsive strategic transport will provide the reinforcing hedge in the event that the initial estimate of requirements was faulty.

• The current Total Force, composed of active Army (federal and national), National Guard (state and regional), and Army Reserve (federal and regional), is well suited for landpower in the United States—a nation, people, state, and democracy on a continent. If we did not have the Total Force, we would probably have had to invent it to sustain national support in the future. The active force is immediately ready; it establishes the standards. The National Guard is units. The Army Reserve is people. Each element should be designed to make best use of these strengths and then be supported aggressively by the other to provide both constituted capability and reconstitution potential.

• The traditional blue-collar–white-collar distinctions of the industrial age are no longer descriptive of landpower personnel needs in the computer-driven information age. Today, better categories are iron, blue, white,

and gold collar. Future war-fighting success will be based on competence-based development of white-collar noncommissioned officers, and gold-collar officers able to focus battlefield operating systems in time and space on the battlefield, consistent with evolving AirLand Battle doctrine. Personnel and training policies should change accordingly.

• The essence of landpower is competent, confident soldiers. Now, skilled white- and gold-collar leaders, not discriminated against for race, religion, gender, or ethnic origin, have become a strategic national asset. They should be deployed as combat power, demonstrating national preeminence in the knowledge-based information age. New organizational and employment concepts are required as U.S. landpower responds to new domestic and foreign challenges.

• The United States is on the verge of distributing individual and unit training, both joint and combined, to a quality standard to the home or work place. This action, integrated with the rigor of the concept-based requirements system and TRADOC to focus development of doctrine, organization, equipment, training, and personnel, allows a revolutionary assimilation of change by U.S. landpower. The capability is present today in TRADOC, and the vision exists in Louisiana Maneuvers '94. Only the will is required to create the next breakthroughs; the application of landpower must be tested in the crucible of the CTC, from individual soldier to the strategic echelon of war.

These are genuinely challenging times. But the future is bright, for Army leaders seem to understand the challenge. The chief of staff of the Army said it well, in an address to the Association of the United States Army:

> . . . the dawning of the post-industrial period means it is possible for America's Army to be smaller and equally effective. This is our vision of the future Army: we are not just a smaller version of the Cold War Army of the industrial period. We are changing fundamentally to take advantage of post-industrial technology.[1]

The ingredients for continuing preeminence are present. Sam Huntington wrote *The Soldier and the State,* a reflective book on the profession of arms in the fifties, as the Army "settled in" for the long haul of the cold war. After musing on civil-military relations in the United States and overseas, he concluded:

> Upon the soldiers, the defenders of order, rests a heavy responsibility. The greatest service they can render is to remain true to themselves, to serve with silence and courage in the military way. If they abjure the military spirit, they destroy themselves first and their nation ultimately.[2]

Is there now a new military way?

NOTES

Preface

1.   It is exceedingly difficult for busy leaders to stand back and contemplate strategic policy alternatives. Nor is there much informed professional discussion of "futures" available for the inquiring military student or the concerned informed citizen. This effort is intended to stimulate responsible thought at a watershed moment in the history of the U.S. Army. It could be considered a companion piece to a similar personal effort at the last watershed in the immediate aftermath of Vietnam: Zeb B. Bradford and Frederic J. Brown, *The United States Army in Transition* (Beverly Hills, CA: Sage Publications for the InterUniversity Seminar on Armed Forces and Society), 1973.

1. New Challenges to Landpower

1.   Graham Allison and Gregory Treverton, "Rethinking America's Security," in Council on Foreign Relations and the American Assembly, eds., *U.S. Interests in the 1990s* (New York: Columbia University, 1991), p. 10.

2.   There is extensive literature on economic and social aspects of the information age. Alvin Toffler, *Power Shift* (New York: Bantam, 1990), chap. 34, "The Global Gladiators," pp. 456–466; Robert B. Reich, *The Work of Nations* (New York: Knopf, 1991), pt. 3, "The Rise of the Symbolic Analyst," pp. 171–234; Peter F. Drucker, *The Frontiers of Management* (New York: Harper & Row, 1986), chap. 1, "Changed World Economy," pp. 21–49; Kenichi Ohmae, *The Borderless World* (New York: Harper Perennial, 1991), chap. 6, pp. 82–100. For U.S. attitudes, see Ben Wattenberg, *The First Universal Nation* (New York: The Free Press, 1991), particularly chap. 1, "Thesis: America at the Beginning of the Middle," pp. 7–24.

3.   Alvin Toffler and Heidi Toffler, "War, Wealth, and a New Era in History," *World Monitor* (May 1991), p. 52. For examples of Third-Wave war, see chap. 2.

4.   The concept of modern conflict as a combination of all three waves is central to this work. Modern U.S. landpower is leading the world's military in understand-

ing and enabling Third-Wave war. It must, however, retain the capability to fight all three—a central challenge.

5.   Representative Les Aspin and Representative William Dickinson, "Defense for a New Era: Lessons of the Persian Gulf War," U.S. House of Representatives. House Armed Services Committee. Washington, D.C.: Government Printing Office, 30 March 1992, p. viii.

6.   Competence is, of course, not unique to landpower, U.S. air- and seapower radiate competence, but it is machine-oriented. Whether professional or citizen-soldier, landpower brings humans to influence other humans—a uniquely powerful role and responsibility.

7.   David S. Broder, "The Military Model," *Washington Post*, 13 May 1992, p. A 23.

8.   Jeffrey Frank, "Are There New Rules of History?" *Washington Post*, 3 May 1992, p. C 3. Just as repetitive images of the war in Vietnam influenced public attitudes in the United States, images of war in Croatia and Bosnia have conditioned the European response to Serbian aggression.

9.   William A. Henry III, "History As It Happens," *Time*, 6 Jan. 1992, p. 24.

10.   For excellent examples of changing U.S. public attitudes on defense issues, see John E. Reilly, ed., *American Public Opinion and U.S. Foreign Policy 1991* (Chicago: The Chicago Council on Foreign Relations, 1991), chap. 5 "Military Relationships," pp. 31–36.

11.   U.S. Department of the Army, *Field Manual 100–1, The Army*. 14 August 1981, p. 8.

12.   Fred C. Weyand and Harry G. Summers, Jr., "Vietnam Myths and American Realities: Commanders Call," Department of the Army pamphlet 360–828, July–August, 1976, p. 7.

13.   Cited in M.P.W. Stone and Gordon R. Sullivan, "Trained and Ready," *Executive Summary, U.S. Army Posture Statement FY93*, 26 February 1992, p. 3.

14.   Operation Desert Storm reestablished the enduring truth that modern military campaigns are won by skillful combinations of land-, sea-, and airpower. The need for increasing service interreliance intensifies in the information age. The challenge is to accomplish this during heightened competition for fewer resources and to take advantage of the unique perspectives and personalities of each service. These differences are discussed in Carl H. Builder, "The Army in the Strategic Planning Process," in Rand Report R–3513–A, April 1987. See sect. 4, "Interservice Comparisons," pp. 22–49.

15.   U.S. Department of the Army, *Field Manual 100–5, Operations*, May 1986. app. A, pp. 173–177.

16.   U.S. Army War College, *Army Command and Management: Theory and Practice*, 1988–1989, August 1988, pp. 3–15.

2. Coalition Conflict

1.   Chairman, Joint Chiefs of Staff, *National Military Strategy, 1992*, 28 January 1992, pp. 6–10.

2.   Ibid., pp. 8, 9. Emphasis mine.

3.   Ibid., p. 7. Emphasis mine.

4.   U.S. Department of Defense, *Conduct of the Persian Gulf War* (Washington, D.C.: Government Printing Office, April 1992), pp. I 49, 50.

5.   *National Military Strategy, 1992*, p. 10. Emphasis mine.

6.   DoD, *Conduct of the Persian Gulf War*, pp. 315–316.

7.   Col. Harry G. Summers, Jr., discusses the sources and impacts of limited war-fare in *On Strategy II: A Critical Analysis of the Gulf War*, chap. 3, "The Vietnam Syndrome and the Military," pp. 44–62.

8.   JCS Pub 1, *Joint Warfare of the U.S. Armed Forces*, 11 November 1991, p. 22.

9.   Caspar Weinberger, "The Uses of Military Power," *New York Times*, 29 November 1984, p. A-5. It is reasonable to assume a certain element of continuity between the Weinberger address and the current *National Military Strategy* in the person of Gen. Colin L. Powell—then military assistant to the secretary of defense and now chairman of the Joint Chiefs of Staff. Emphasis mine.

10.   Nuclear weapons have had a pervasive influence on the Army for several decades. For analysis of the impact, see Colonel Summers, *On Strategy II*, chap. 7, pp. 117–128.

11.   As the preeminent Third-Wave military power, the United States seems certain to seek Third-Wave answers to military challenges. There is scant enthusiasm in the United States, or Western Europe for that matter, to become involved in the brutal Second-, if not First-, Wave conflict in Yugoslavia. New forms of deterrence emerge as "quick, clean, decisive, low casualty" Third-Wave avoids near-medieval, First-Wave conflict across nationalities or religious beliefs. Who is to intervene to make or keep the peace in these kinds of conflicts?

12.   *National Military Strategy, 1992*, p. 15.

13.   Ibid., pp. 12, 13

14.   New interpretations of national sovereignty are emerging. What are the international interests that transcend traditional, national prerogatives such as intervention to ensure that weapons of mass destruction are not being produced in violation of international agreements? Or should protection of "peoples sovereignty" override "the sovereign's sovereignty"? John Chipman, "The Future of Strategic Studies: Beyond Even Grand Strategy," *Survival* (Spring 1992), p. 117.

15.   U.S. House of Representatives. House Armed Services Committee. "Combat Power from the Reserve Component." Washington, D.C.: Government Printing Office, 7 May 1992, p. 3.

16.   This is not as certain as it may seem. The World War II generation abhors appeasement. Nazi Germany's occupation of the Sudetenland and then the Anschluss in Austria are presented as cases when early intervention could have stopped Hitler. In fact, in his National Press Club address, Weinberger invoked memories of the reoccupation of the Rhineland to justify the need to possess credible, usable military capability. Intervention to stop an emerging Fascist regime may become more credible in the future as Eurasia fragments, nationalities clash, and inflation grows—fertile soil for dictators. The test case appears to emerge with Serbian aggression as a potential stimulant to European regional intervention. For a useful discussion of presidential action to mold support for military operations (Desert Shield), see David Gergen, "America's Missed Opportunities," *Foreign Affairs: America and the World, 1991–92* (Spring, 1992): 1–19.

17.   The adaptive planning process described in the *National Military Strategy, 1992* is grounded in planning scenarios. One set of "classified" scenarios described as the "1994–99 Defense Planning Guidance Scenario Set" appeared in the press.

Seven situations were presented, each with two troop lists, one for "adequate" and one for "overwhelming" U.S. forces. The situations were Russia invades Lithuania, Iraq invades Kuwait and Saudi Arabia, North Korea attacks South Korea, Iraq and North Korea invade at once, coup in Panama, coup in Philippines, and a hostile superpower remerges (reconstitution). Barton Gellman, "Pentagon War Scenario Spotlights Russia," *Washington Post,* 20 February 1992, p. A21. The final version of the "Defense Planning Guidance" for fiscal years 1994–99 signed in May 1992 was asserted to emphasize "the preservation and expansion of the system of alliances that has built 'sustained cooperation among major democratic powers' since World War II." Barton Gellman, "Pentagon Abandons Goal of Thwarting U.S. Rivals," *Washington Post,* 24 May 1992, p. A 1.

18.   U.S. Department of the Army, *Field Manual 100–1, The Army,* October 1991, p. 8.

19.   U.S. Department of the Army, *Field Manual 100–5, Operations,* May 1986, p. 14.

20.   Ibid., pp. 16–17.

21.   Lt. Col. Douglas A. Macgregor, "Doctrinal Concepts for Future War," unpublished manuscript, April 1992, pp. 14, 15.

22.   U.S. TRADOC, *AirLand Operations,* "A Concept for the Evolution of Air-Land Battle for the Strategic Army of the 1990s and Beyond," TRADOC *Pam 525–5,* 1 August 1991. The name will probably change several times as the future doctrine evolves, but the principles appear set. Translation to reserves and allies who will join to execute the doctrine will be challenging.

23.   Maj. Gen. Stephen Silvasy, "AirLand Battle Future: The Tactical Battlefield," *Military Review* 71, no. 2 (February 1991):3. Emphasis mine.

24.   In the evolving global market, it is a serious oversimplification of the challenge and potential of the world economy to dwell for too long on characteristics of national industries. For example, purely American or Japanese automobiles are hard to find. The Mazda Navaho is a Ford Explorer made in Kentucky; the Plymouth Laser is a Mitsubishi Eclipse; Chevrolet's Geo Prizm is a Toyota Corolla made by a GM/Toyota joint venture in California. "What Is an American Auto?" *Washington Post,* 31 January 1992, p. C1.

25.   The "1994–99 Defense Planning Guidance Scenario Set" appears to be entirely Second Wave in nature. Third-Wave additions might enhance the credibility. Gellman, "Pentagon War Scenario Spotlights Russia," p. A21.

26.   TRADOC *Pam 525–5, AirLand Operations,* p. 10.

27.   Tom Donnelly, "From the Top: How Commanders Planned Operation Desert Shield," *Army Times,* 24 February 1992, pp. 20, 24. Emphasis mine.

28.   *Ibid.,* p. 24. Judgment is still out on the effectiveness and efficiency of coalition operations. Anecdotal criticisms should not impugn good coordination in fire support and combat-service support; maritime intercept operations and the focused employment of airpower-the single air tasking order-created a "militarily effective coalition." See DoD, *Conduct of the Persian Gulf War,* p. 414, Appendix 1: "Coalition Operations."

29.   U.S. Department of the Army, *Field Manual 25–100, Training the Force,* November 1988, pp. 2–4.

30.   The competition between traditional unit-oriented and BOS-oriented functional capabilities (the all-purpose division with balanced support versus attack he-

licopter battalions with logistic support) was evident early in Operation Desert Shield. "Friction quickly developed between XVIII Corps and others as units fought over scarce resources. The corps, with standard operating procedures for its many deployment scenarios, wanted to balance the flow of combat units with supporting units. Schwarzkopf wanted to get as many tank-killing systems to the theater as fast as possible, along with Patriots. Also in demand were Apache helicopters. . . ." The four-star general "wound up directing all airplanes from CENTOM." Donnelly, "From The Top," p. 20.

The "Monday morning quarterback" tends to overlook the serious concern of the first several days of the Desert Shield buildup. The airborne infantry was highly vulnerable as would have been any land force initially. Yet, this was when joint capability was decisive. Immediately available seapower backed by deploying airpower, with precision weapons including nuclear, actually placed a firm protective umbrella over deploying landpower. It deterred the Iraqi attack into Saudi Arabia quite effectively.

31. This analogy, expressed eloquently by Maj. Gen. Don Morelli (deceased), goes directly to the heart of AirLand Battle—Third-Wave war.

32. Theory converts to practice with difficulty. UN peacekeeping in Yugoslavia borders on peacemaking to the discomfit of all. Yet the need for such international capability is reinforced almost daily.

3. A Total Force

1.   The aberration in this was the combat unit roundout brigades posted to active divisions. It was anticipated that they would deploy earlier and would, therefore, have to sustain a higher level of overall peacetime readiness. Their performance during Desert Shield, albeit controversial, is generally considered successful validation of the overall Total Force policy. For an excellent study of this, see Robert Goldich, *The Army's Roundout Concept After the Persian Gulf War,* Congressional Research Service, Library of Congress 91–763 F, 22 October 1991. While there has been considerable focus on these brigades, they are a small percentage of Guard capability. The larger issues addressed here concern the vast majority of the capabilities—the six or more Guard divisions and separate brigades of the 1995 Force, and the numerous combat-support and combat-service-support units of the Guard and the Army Reserve. They seem certain to provide most of our national landpower capability in the future. See DoD, *Conduct of the Persian Gulf War,* Appendix H for the administration's position.

2.   *National Security Strategy,* p. 29. This executive position has been sharply assailed by Congress. See House Armed Services Committee, "Combat Power from the Reserve Component." Representative Aspin proposes a slight Guard increase (six divisions), despite a major active-force reduction from twelve to nine divisions (Option C). The National Guard Association proposes a significant increase to the Guard to twelve divisions. Maj. Gen. Robert F. Ensslin, *Public Policy Dimensions of Base Force and Reconstitution Strategy for the National Guard,* National Guard Association of the United States (NGAUS), 1 February 1992; NGAUS, *An Alternative Force Structure Proposal,* February 1992, p. 4.

3.   *National Military Strategy, 1992,* p. 19.

4.   Association of the United States Army, *Operations Desert Shield and Desert Storm: The Logistics Perspective,* September 1991, pp. 3, 9, 27.

5.   *National Military Strategy 1992*, pp. 7, 8, 25.
6.   See chap. 4, "Reserve Force Challenges," and chap. 5, "Reconstitution: Revisiting Global War."
7.   These attitudes, stimulated by Desert Shield experience, confirm the wisdom of the Total Force molded by Gen. Creighton Abrams. Lewis Sorley, "Creighton Abrams and Active-Reserve Integration in Wartime," *Parameters: US Army War College Quarterly*, 21, no. 2 (Summer 1991): 35–50.
8.   *National Military Strategy, 1992*, p. 10.
9.   Today, this hardly seems routine. To many units the process is overwhelming, but to be responsive to likely force projection requirements, the processor and other management aids must be harnessed to make this "routine."
10.   Examples are discussed in chap. 2. The "air-defense division" and the "engineer division (nuclear accident)" could be rapidly formed and deployed from the Total Force.
11.   Personnel are identified as blue, white, or gold collar in chap. 8. Gold-collar expertise should "flow to the crisis." This was done in Operation Desert Shield. The theater was given broad support. Quality personnel were made available from the worldwide Army. AirLand Battle planners, *aka* "the Jedi Knights," were assembled to support General Schwarzkopf. This was an important precedent but wholly consistent with Third-Wave war.
12.   The issue is not precisely 720 days, rather, it is support of a level of readiness representing latent, not actual, military capability. Capability expected to deploy to war more than two years after initiation of hostilities would not be constituted in peacetime.
13.   See "Reserve Force Challenges," chap. 4.
14.   U.S. Department of Defense, *Total Force Policy Report to the Congress* (December 1990), p. 41.
15.   There were useful examples of this in the Persian Gulf War. Very specialized skills were necessary to handle the oil fires in Kuwait. Fortunately, highly competent "gold-collar" people—leaders in metropolitan fire departments—were available in the Army Reserves for individual call-up.
16.   This service model is explained in more detail in chap. 4.
17.   *National Military Strategy, 1992*, p. 23.
18.   This could be alleviated by reverting to a combat Army and support Army structure. See chap. 10 on competence-basing. Similar to past practices in NATO nations, TRADOC personnel also could be dual-hatted in cadre contingency units. For example, the chief of armor/CG, Fort Knox, Kentucky, could also command a cadre armored division.

4. Reserve Force Challenges

1.   This work draws heavily on Frederic J. Brown "Reserve Forces: Army Challenges of the 1990s," *Military Review*, 71, no. 8 (August 1991): 2–19.
2.   As might be expected during a period of reduction, alternative proposals surface for landpower force structure and tension builds between active and reserve soldiers. This seems certain to last until the executive and legislative branches compromise, probably well after the 1992 election. For a good summary of differences, see Wallace Earl Walker, "Comparing Army Reserve Forces: A Tale of Multiple

Images, Conflicting Realities, and More Certain Prospects," *Armed Forces & Society* 18, no. 3 (Spring 1992): 303–322.

3.   Vitally important decisions will be made in the months ahead about future landpower and the role of reserve forces. The real issues should be out on the table. The points raised here are not speculation; they are the result of personal observation and command experience in a succession of command and staff positions directly relating to the reserves over some thirteen years, including readiness group and Continental United States Army command.

4.   Unfortunately, similar rigor does not yet exist for many important staff tasks such as coordinating fire support and intelligence in support of the commander's intent—battle command and staff training—but it will come.

5.   This is an insidious process. As a colonel commander, I was directly involved with improving the readiness of two National Guard combat battalions for over six years—as the branch mentor at a home-state, major training site (an active Army divisional post). The battalions were roundout to the brigade I commanded, and then they were under my jurisdiction as a readiness group commander. The end result of a great deal of personal effort was a major recruiting problem. Too much had been asked for too many years. Fortunately, but unfortunately for the units, I was there long enough to realize the damage inflicted on the units by the intensity of my unmoderated professional requirements and to act accordingly in other positions.

6.   In all fairness, this is as much an active Army problem as it is for reserves. All too often, hard-charging active senior commanders, absolutely unfamiliar with the total reserve training environment, descend on reserve units during annual training armed with the latest Army doctrine and determined to implement, without deviation, all that "works" in their regular Army units. This is particularly galling when these commanders have a charter to evaluate the reserve unit in a way the Army would strongly resist in the active chain of command.

7.   The active Army "has been there" on this in attempting to maintain high, unresourced standards in Europe during Vietnam. It was terribly corrosive. It took almost ten years, firm leadership, and very well-resourced units to reestablish integrity.

8.   Representative Aspin acknowledges this competence issue in reviewing lessons learned from the Persian Gulf War. He proposes that a "significant percentage"— 65 percent officer, 50 percent noncommissioned officer—of accessions have prior active-duty service by fiscal year 1997. House Armed Services Committee, "Combat Power from the Reserve Component," p. 5. In addition, a substantial increase in active-Army training support is being provided in the form of resident training detachments to reserve units.

9.   As the regular Army draws down, there are certain to be competent people eager to join the reserves as full-time manning. This could alleviate the quality problem temporarily but not the more important systemic issue.

10.   Over the years, I probably worked reserve issues with thirty or forty generals or lieutenant generals. I can recall only two or three who genuinely understood and felt comfortable dealing with these problems. This is regrettable but not surprising in an Army deployed for forty years, required to develop officer nonline specialty proficiency, and become joint.

11. These opportunities are discussed in chap. 2.
12. This is discussed well in the current *National Military Strategy, 1992*, pp. 41–50.
13. Various combinations of active Army and reserve deployment capability are also discussed in "The Uncertain Path," *Military Review* (June 1990), and "AirLand Battle Future: The Other Side of the Coin," *Military Review* (February 1991).
14. This would appear to be self-evident. It has not been. Frequently, units are constituted seemingly with absolute disregard for peacetime location. I commanded one transportation battalion composed for war with five companies—active Army, Army Reserve, and National Guard—located in five states. It was virtually impossible to train together in peacetime.

5. Reconstitution: Revisiting Global War
1. *National Security Strategy*, August 1991, pp. 29–30.
2. Earlier in chap. 3, an arbitrary benchmark of 720 days' lead time for reconstituting units was postulated to permit discussion of varying levels of Total Force constituted unit readiness. This seems useful as a general planning figure for "mass production" of units; "niche production" lead time to gear up for information-age war will have to be much more precise. By when may that particular capability be required?
3. For an excellent summary of industrial-base issues, see Jacques S. Gansler, *Affording Defense* (Cambridge: The MIT Press, 1991), pp. 325–345.
4. TRADOC *Pam 525–5, AirLand Operations*, 1 August 1991, pp. 15–17.
5. Combinations discussed in chap. 2, "Coalition Conflict."
6. This is an important assumption that may appear to be a blinding flash of the obvious. Doctrinally educated to AirLand Operations, the professional force will fight as they have been taught, sensibly drawing on areas of national military advantage. Then, due to high-tech exhaustion, they regress to the information-age equivalent of the postnuclear, "broken-backed" war. The probable rate of consumption of Third-Wave capability seems certain to be a major consideration in regional contingency operations.
7. Another manifestation of the ground rules proposed in chap. 2. The Army will not be capable of engaging in substantial contingency operations without drawing upon individual soldiers or units from the reserves. Partial mobilization is a "given." The restraint will be whether or not requisite reserve unit capability is constituted and trained.
8. DoD, *Report to Congress on the Defense Industrial Base*, November 1991, p. ES–7.
9. Office of Technology Assessment (OTA Report Brief), *Redesigning Defense: Planning the Transition to the Future U.S. Defense Industrial Base*, July 1991, p. 2. The case for better defense/commercial integration is summarized in "Task Force on Defense Spending: The Economy & The Nation's Security." Statement, "Preserving The Defense Industrial Base," 17 September 1991, p. 3.
10. DoD. *Report to Congress on the Defense Industrial Base*, p. ES–2.
11. This pessimistic assessment is reinforced in a recent Association of the United States Army (AUSA) study of the defense production base. AUSA advocates increased efficiency from that base that remains, limited R&D and production to pro-

tect at least one contractor in each sector, and subsidization of defense trade. Gen. Jack Merritt, "Statement Before the Panel on Structure of the U.S. Defense Industrial Base," AUSA, Arlington, VA, 19 February 1992, p. 9.

12. A distinction must be made between a Second-Wave and a Third-Wave industrial base. The former, a product of the industrial age and represented by General Motors, is in clear decline. Third-Wave capacity represented by aggressive firms like Motorola should survive and, in fact, prosper. But platform manufacture is still mostly threatened Second Wave.

13. Foreign military sales are a major unknown. More could be provoked by increasing global instability or less as the International Monetary Fund and other international institutions become more unwilling to subsidize Third World weapon acquisitions.

14. Battlefield operating systems with clear joint commonality should fare better. Intelligence, fire support, command and control, and strategic air defense should prosper with U.S. Air Force and U.S. Navy commonality. Combat-service support could be aided by national or international industry. Maneuver, mobility-countermobility, and tactical air defense offer the least opportunities for joint support.

15. DoD, *Report to Congress on the Defense Industrial Base*, p. ES–6.

16. Seven governments, G-7: the United States, Japan, Germany, United Kingdom, France, Italy, and Canada.

17. Steven Pearlstein, "Pentagon Cites Security Issue in Sale of LTV to Thomson," *Washington Post*, 1 May 1992, pp. B 1, 2.

18. This last ground rule would not be helpful to international arms control. Increased Third-Wave component flexibility for the ground commander magnifies challenges of verification.

19. National service and CCC reemerge as policy alternatives after the 1992 Los Angeles riots. Arthur Ashe, "Can a New 'Army' Save Our Cities?" *Washington Post*, 10 May 1992, p. C 2. See also, Broder, "The Military Model," p. A 23, and, in this volume, chap. 12, "The Army: A Vehicle of Social Change."

20. Retention of the volunteer force is assumed, as is the necessity for traditional blue- and white-collar skills during reconstitution. Gold-collar officers and white-collar noncommissioned officers are essential for Third-Wave war. The need for quality never lessens because quality assures military success with the least cost in lives; however, in global war general leader quality falls as the quantity of soldiers under arms increases.

6. The Concept-Based Requirements System

1. For a civilian parallel, see Alvin Toffler, *Power Shift*, (New York: Bantam, 1990), pp. 80–82, for a discussion of new concepts in value added through change.

2. The beginnings of this process are described in Maj. Paul H. Herbert, *Deciding What Has to Be Done: General William E. DePuy and the 1976 Edition of FM 100–5, Operations*, Leavenworth Papers, No. 16, 1988.

3. For additional discussion of likely future equipment acquisition, see chap. 5, "Reconstitution: Revisiting Global War."

4. At one time, the overall process of change was described, not entirely facetiously, as comparable to a unit marching at quick time, changing to double time, with a new band, and while changing uniform.

5.   In the afterglow of Operations Just Cause and Desert Storm, we tend to forget the lasting cost and benefit of the cold war, particularly in Europe. Over three million soldiers have served in Europe since the end of World War II.
6.   Other nations, particularly our NATO allies, have been remarkably slow in understanding and using the CBRS. Now they may realize the potential, particularly after side-by-side comparisons on Desert Storm, but they no longer have the quantity of resources necessary to stimulate such substantive change. This is just another reason why the United States should remain dominant for decades in land-power.
7.   See chap. 5.
8.   The battlefield operating systems are maneuver, fire support, command and control, intelligence, combat-service support, air defense and mobility, counter-mobility, and survivability. They provide an analytical description of the capabilities needed to fight on the battlefield. Redefined as BFMA (battlefield functional mission area) in the most recent doctrinal statement, they ". . . provide the focus and the foundation for development of respective doctrine, training, leader development, organization, and materiel." TRADOC *Pam 525–5, AirLand Operations,* 1 August 1991, p. 46.
9.   The Air Force appears to be deeply committed to eliminating stovepipes in its striving to create composite attack organizations from TAC and SAC. Use of the computer to data-link the Abrams, Bradley, and Apache on the battlefield (battle-field management) may achieve similar results for the maneuver battlefield. See chap. 11, "Exploiting the Computer."
10.   Some reasons for underlying differences between active and reserve forces are discussed in chap. 4, "Reserve Force Challenges."
11.   See chap. 5.
12.   See chap. 2.
13.   Alternative Patriot deployment packages are discussed further in chap. 2 to demonstrate differences between industrial and information-age air defense.
14.   Gen. Gordon R. Sullivan, *Statement on the Fiscal Year 1993 Department of the Army Budget.* Committee on Armed Services, United States House of Representatives, 26 February 1992, pp. 26–27.

7. The Training Revolution

1.   The eyes of senior officers from other nations tend to glaze over when this is discussed. They simply do not understand what the U.S. Army has done, nor that this rigor is a precondition to excellence in the information age. Before you master the computer, you must know precisely what you want it to do or not to do.
2.   The skill qualification test (SQT) is being replaced by a self-development test (SDT). Rigorous evaluation of individual competence continues.
3.   The combat training centers are the National Training Center in California; the Joint Readiness Training Center, moving from Arkansas to Louisana; and the Combat Maneuver Training Center in Germany. They stress intense, heavy and light forces' live-fire training and force-on-force maneuver, using tactical engagement simulation, with extensive after-action reviews and seasoned Observer-Controllers. They focus at brigade echelon and below. They are complemented by the Battle Command Training Program in Kansas, which focuses on equally stressful computer-driven corps and division war-fighting exercises. Most recently, the Army has

begun a major effort to develop interactive, theater-level campaigns in simulation. The object is to recreate the joint- and combined-training challenges of theater regional-contingency operations such as Desert Shield and Provide Comfort. This effort, described as Louisana Maneuvers '94, is led personally by Gen. Gordon R. Sullivan, the Army chief of staff. It should accelerate the Army's adjustment to the new training requirements of the information age. It is discussed further in chap. 6, "The Concept-Based Requirements System."

4.   These situations are discussed in detail in chap. 2, "Coalition Conflict."

8. Blue-, White-, Gold-Collar Landpower

1.   This requirement was and is particularly challenging for reserves and potential allies. It is discussed in greater detail in Frederic J. Brown, "AirLand Battle Future: The Other Side of the Coin," *Military Review* 71, no. 2 (February 1991): 13–24.

2.   Stan Davis and Bill Davidson, *2020 Vision* (New York: Simon & Schuster, 1991), p. 56.

3.   This change extends well beyond the military. One could argue that white collar of the industrial age has become the blue collar, i.e., the rank-and-file work force, of the information age. Among other things, this would explain the surprisingly high number of white-collar layoffs during the recession of the early nineties.

4.   There would be equal validity if the term were to be "silicon collar," reflecting use of the computer chip; however, in recognition of the continuing residue of the industrial age, iron collar seems appropriate to most members of the current Army.

5.   Robert B. Reich in *The Work of Nations* (New York: Alfred A. Knopf, 1991), pp. 183–184, discusses a new requirement for "symbolic analysts" whose ". . . competitive advantage lies in skill in solving, identifying, and brokering new problems"—gold collar.

6.   A recent West Point study on future officers' leadership characteristics reinforces this fact: "The leaders' principal weapons will be their minds. In peace or war, they must be sophisticated users of technology. . . . They will require the mental agility to grasp a unique battlefield situation under conditions of uncertainty and chaos, the creative ability to devise a practical solution, and the strength of purpose to execute their plans." U.S.M.A., *Preparing for West Point's Third Century* (West Point, June 1991), p. 92.

7.   These are truly challenging issues. Debate is necessary on the "breakpoints" between gold, white, and blue collar. True command responsibility to focus in time and space may start at the colonel, brigade commander, where tangible assets begin to be traded for intangible reward. Or it may be the battalion commander, the most junior commander with task complexity warranting a staff. Similarly, the NCO blue-white collar "breakpoint" may differ from staff to line—first sergeant versus master sergeant—or from fighting (TOE) unit to support army (TDA) position. More work is needed. I am indebted in this discussion to the experts of Army Research Institute, particularly Dr. Owen Jacobs and Dr. Zita Simutis.

8.   COHORT (cohesion, operational readiness, and training) was an extended test program to evaluate the readiness impacts of unit-replacement policies for small-unit cohesion.

9.   The Living TOE was an innovative and effective program to automate authorization documentation during a period of massive change in the organization, manning, and equipping of units in the eighties.

10.   Some of the challenges of operations with allies in Operation Desert Shield are discussed by Tom Donnelly in "From the Top: How Commanders Planned Desert Shield," *Army Times,* 24 February 1992, p. 24. See also, DoD, "Conduct of the Persian Gulf War," Appendix I: "Coalition Operations."

11.   The support tail for Desert Storm appears to have been reduced. A ratio of 1 to 1 supporter-per-fighter has been advanced, but this apparently does not include contract-civilian or host-nation support. And Saudi Arabia was not bare-base, with its extensive port infrastructure. AUSA, *Operations Desert Shield and Desert Storm: The Logistics Perspective,* September 1991, p. 30.

12.   Very innovative work has been done in this area by Gen. Paul F. Gorman, USA (Ret.), in envisaging the "super trooper."

13.   For another perspective on personnel policy change—reform of the military career system—see William L. Hauser, "Career Management: Time for a Bold Adjustment," *Parameters: The Journal of the U.S. Army War College* 22, no. 1 (Spring 1992): 50–59.

9. Developing Leaders

1.   For an excellent discussion of current Army policies and programs for leader development, see Department of the Army, *Pam 600–32, Leader Development for the Total Army: The Enduring Legacy,* 31 May 1991, pp. 51.

2.   The *Reichswehr* model is that followed by Germany after World War I. Limited to an army of 100,000 by the Treaty of Versailles, the Germans opted for quality, training the core of their future expansion army. Sergeants were trained to become officers when expansion occurred; officers were trained for positions of much greater seniority.

3.   Clearly, landpower has no monopoly on influence. Navies and air forces are focused at air bases and seaports. Armies, by their nature, disperse throughout the state and thus influence the population more broadly.

4.   These new requirements are discussed in greater detail in chap. 8, "Blue-, White-, Gold-Collar Landpower."

5.   This reinforcement of focus on the basic mission of landpower—war fighting—will be absolutely central not only to combat readiness but also to sustainment of the warrior ethos in a time of severely reduced resources.

6.   Another reason to exploit Third-Wave war: only the United States has the necessary complex training support. For additional discussion of white and gold collar, see pp. 110–112.

7.   Structural deficiencies such as these are discussed in greater detail in chap. 4, "Reserve Force Challenges."

8.   This does not mean that reserve units charged with leader training should be disbanded. Rather, there must be more extensive active-force professional involvement in conducting certain functional BOS training and in designing structured leader training for distributed execution with quality control.

9.   Other nations do not have the rigor of the systems approach to training tied to a concept-based requirements system, all put into being during a decade of relative affluence. The only major shortfall is leader selection. Some armies (Israeli Defense Force) select the best privates to be sergeants, the best sergeants to be officers. That is not feasible in the United States for social reasons—a desire to have nationally distributed college graduates as officers.

10.   The variety of potential missions is discussed in chap. 2.

10. The Army of Excellence: A Competence-Based Force

1.   AUSA, *Operations Desert Shield and Desert Storm: The Logistics Perspective,* September 1991, pp. 15–16.

2.   DARPA—Center of Military History Project; "The Battle of 73 Easting, G Troop, 2nd Armored Cavalry Regiment," 26 February 1991.

3.   Nearly 40 percent of the first all-volunteer cohort separated from the Army before completing their term of service. Throughout this period, civilian authority consistently backed the Army chain of command in eliminating unworthy soldiers. Increasingly, senior NCO leaders today entered in the seventies as the first group of volunteers. They are the product of constant winnowing, with demanding NCO development programs training those who remained at each grade level. This is continuing today with quality begetting quality. By 1991, "98 percent of the Army accessions were high school diploma graduates, with thousands of those having some college." Maj. Gen. Jack C. Wheeler, "In Recruiting, Quality is All," *Army* (September 1991): 36. College-experienced enlisted soldiers sustain the momentum of white-collar NCOs for the future.

4.   New strains are coming as minorities feel "squeezed" by drawdown. "Letters to the Editor" of the *Army Times* reflect allegations of prejudice in selection for retention. A cover story in *Army Times* concerned racism in the building-down Army. "State of Race: Is Opportunity Really Equal in the Army?" *Army Times,* 23 December 1991, p. 56.

5.   David Gergen, "America's New Heroes," *U.S. News & World Report* (11 February 1991): 76.

6.   This could be very similar to costing procedures used for foreign military sales, which normally try to include all true direct and indirect costs of goods or services.

7.   Forces on the ground in Operation Desert Storm would appear to have changed this progression since there were about 1.1 sustainers for each fighter. But this does not account for the unique nature of the theater with the extensive Saudi infrastructure and widespread use of contract personnel behind the divisions.

8.   Another difficult issue is the delineation of responsibilities for execution of unit support of families. Traditionally, this has rested with the commander's spouse, supported by professionals. There is decreasing credibility in imposing on commanders' spouses, not selected necessarily for their leadership skills and who have competing economic demands on their own time. Volunteers backed by professionals worked well on Desert Shield.

11. Exploiting the Computer

1.   Discussed in chap. 1, "New Challenges to Landpower."

2.   Frederic J. Brown, "A Simulation-Based Intensified Training Readiness Strategy for the Reserve Component," Institute for Defense Analyses, IDA Paper P–2611, December 1991, pp. C–13 to C–15.

12. The Army: A Vehicle of Social Change

1.   This is well summarized in Charles C. Moskos, "How Do They Do It?" *The New Republic* (August 5, 1991): 16–20.

2.   William Kaufman gets close in a recent defense study which projects a 2001 low-option DoD budget of $169.2 billion contrasted with 1996 DoD projection of $243.7 billion. The low option projects seven active-Army and four reserve divisions. William W. Kaufmann and John D. Steinbruner, *Decisions for Defense: Pros-*

pects for a New Order (Washington, D.C.: The Brookings Institution, 1991), pp. 65, 71. It seems probable that when a new budget compromise is negotiated, landpower may be a notable loser. Representative Aspin has proposed a defense option that reduces the active Army to nine divisions and expands the Guard (Option C). House Armed Services Committee, "Combat Power from the Reserve Component," pp. 9–11. For suggestions as to programs that could be undertaken directly by landpower or by those separated involuntarily, see David Gergen, "Heroes for Hire," *U.S. News & World Report* (27 January 1992): 17; Broder, "The Military Model," p. A 23; and David Boren and Harris Wofford, "Lessons of the '30s: Not the Dole, Not Welfare, But Work," *Washington Post,* 21 May 1992, p. A 25.

3.   Charles C. Moskos, *A Call to Civic Service* (New York: The Free Press, 1988).

4.   This potential is discussed in greater detail in chap. 3, "A Total Force."

5.   *National Military Strategy, 1992,* p. 17.

6.   It is better routinely to mix race, origin, and gender for a socially integrated, responsive force, but there is a clear need to establish and reinforce discipline in an objective environment. It is easier when the "enforcer" is of the same sex, race, and origin.

7.   A 1986 ARI study found ". . . a statistically significant and positive relationship exists between AFQT scores and performance measures . . . across a wide range of military occupational specialities." Cited by Maj. Gen. Jack C. Wheeler, "In Recruiting, Quality is All," *Army* (September 1991): 35. For a useful discussion of quality personnel requirements, see Gen. Maxwell R. Thurman, "Sustaining the All-Volunteer Force, 1983–1992: The Second Decade," in William Bowman, Roger Little, and G. Thomas Sicilia, eds., *The All-Volunteer Force After a Decade* (McLean, VA: Pergamon–Brassey's, 1986), pp. 266–285.

13. Vital Intangibles of the Profession

1.   Each military service has a unique perspective of technology and virtually every other aspect of professional identity. See Franklin D. Margiotta and Michael Maccoby, "Future Challenges to Military Leadership: Adjusting to the Human Implications of Advanced Technology," in Franklin D. Margiotta and Ralph Sanders, eds., *Technology, Strategy and National Security* (Washington, D.C.: NDU Press, 1985), pp. 90–103. Also Carl H. Builder, *The Army in the Strategic Planning Process: Who Shall Bell the Cat?* Rand Report R 3513–A, April 1987, sect. IV, "Interservice Comparisons," pp. 22–49.

2.   Professional expertise and enthusiasm of a very competent combat leader notwithstanding, few U.S. tankers would trade an Abrams (M1 or M1A1) for a T72. Another issue is the extraordinary, almost incredible, competence of the force in the Persian Gulf. Units were provided full manning of trained leaders—generally in the proper grades—issued new equipment, stabilized for the duration of the war, and focused for months with limited distractions on field training against an explicit enemy.

3.   Army leadership seems fully sensitive to this problem. The costs of precipitous decline immediately after World War II were evident in the travail of Task Force Smith in Korea. Unpreparedness resulted in defeat. This example is being used skillfully to sensitize civilian leadership to the perils of too-rapid reductions.

4.   This transformation is discussed in greater detail in chap. 8, "Blue-, White-, Gold-Collar Landpower

5.   This formulation, conceptualized by the Tofflers, is described in chap. 1, "New Challenges to Landpower."

6.   See *Field Manual 100-1, The Army*, October 1991, pp. 15–18, for an excellent discussion of the Army ethic: duty, integrity, loyalty, and selfless service, as well as the soldier values of commitment, competence, candor, and courage. These are enduring values that will remain essential in future war.

7.   See chap. 8.

8.   There is a useful and necessary distinction between the readiness expected of active and reserve units. Active units are expected to be ready to deploy, globally, with very short response times. Reserve units are expected to require some period of training after mobilization and before deployment. Ability to fight virtually any enemy, on any terrain, in any weather, "tomorrow" demands exceptionally competent soldiers and units in the active force. The impacts of "variable readiness" are discussed in chap. 3, "A Total Force."

9.   U.S.M.A., "Preparing for West Point's Third Century," p. 91. In explaining the mission statement, the report comments: "Their (graduates') dedication to selfless service, even beyond the time in uniform, is both a national need and an historical expectation. They are to be leaders for a lifetime."

10.   A distinction elaborated by Charles Moskos in postulating armed forces' membership identification as evolving from institutional or occupational in the cold war to civic today. "Armed Forces and Society After the Cold War," a paper prepared for presentation at the Woodrow Wilson International Center for Scholars, 12 June 1991, p. 1a.

11.   This aspect of drawdown is also discussed as a reason for reducing force structure in chap. 10, "The Army of Excellence: A Competence-Based Force."

12.   This is a difficult issue. Traditionally, reserves have been considered the epitome of occupational service. Increased readiness requirements have blurred the model. See "Introduction" in Charles C. Moskos and Frank R. Wood, eds., *The Military: More Than Just a Job?* (McLean, VA: Pergamon–Brassey's, 1988), p. 5.

14. Capturing Accelerating Change

1.   This would appear to be the vision of the Army leadership. See chap. 6, "The Concept-Based Requirements System," for discussion of Louisiana Maneuvers '94.

15. The Challenge

1.   Gen. Gordon R. Sullivan, "The Army in the Post-Industrial World," prepared address for AUSA Land Warfare Forum, 9 January 1992, p. 8. Emphasis mine.

2.   Samuel P. Huntington, *The Soldier and the State* (Cambridge, MA: The Belknap Press, 1959), p. 466.

BIBLIOGRAPHY

Allison, Graham, and Gregory Treverton. 1991. "Rethinking America's Security." *U.S. Interests in the 1990s.* Seventy-ninth American Assembly, 30 May–2 June. New York: The American Assembly.

Ashe, Arthur. 1992. "Can a 'New Army' Save Our Cities?" *Washington Post,* 10 May, p. C2.

Bradford, Zeb B., and Frederic J. Brown. 1973. *The United States Army in Transition.* Beverly Hills, CA: Sage Publications.

Broder, David S. 1992. "The Military Model." *Washington Post,* 13 May, p. A23.

Boren, David and Harris Wofford. 1992. "Lessons of the '30's: Not the Dole, Not Welfare, But Work." *Washington Post,* 21 May, p. A25.

Brown, Frederic J. 1991. *A Simulation-Based Intensified Training Readiness Strategy for the Reserve Components.* IDA Paper P–2611. Arlington, VA: The Institute for Defense Analyses.

Builder, Carl H. 1987. *The Army in the Strategic Planning Process.* Rand-Arroyo Center R 3513-A. Santa Monica, CA: The Rand Corporation.

Chipman, John. 1992. "The Future of Strategic Studies: Beyond Even Grand Strategy." *Survival* (Spring): 109–131.

Davis, Stan, and Bill Davidson. 1991. *2020 Vision: Transform Your Business Today to Succeed in Tomorrow's Economy.* New York: Simon & Schuster.

Donnally, Tom. 1992. "From the Top." *Army Times.* 24 February, pp. 8–24.

Drucker, Peter F. 1986. *The Frontiers of Management: Where Tomorrow's Decisions Are Being Shaped Today.* New York: Harper & Row.

———. 1989. *The New Realities.* New York: Harper & Row.

Ensslin, Maj. Gen. Robert F. 1992. "Public Policy Dimensions of Base Force and Reconstitution Strategy for the National Guard." NGAUS, 1 February, p. 13.

Fehrenbach, T. R. 1963. *This Kind of War: A Study in Unpreparedness.* New York: The Macmillan Company.

Frank, Jeffrey. 1992. "Are There New Rules of History?" *Washington Post,* 3 May, p. C3.

Gansler, Jacques S. 1991. *Affording Defense.* Cambridge, MA: MIT Press.

Gellman, Barton. 1992. "Pentagon War Scenario Spotlights Russia." *Washington Post,* 20 February, pp. A1, A21.

———. 1992. "Pentagon Abandons Goal of Thwarting U. S. Rivals." *Washington Post,* 24 May, A 1, A 23.

Gergen, David. 1992. "Heroes for Hire." *U.S. News & World Report* 112, no. 3 (27 January): 71.

———. 1992. "America's Missed Opportunities." *Foreign Affairs* (Spring): 1–19.

Goldich, Robert L. 1991. *The Army's Roundout Concept After the Persian Gulf War.* Congressional Research Service, Library of Congress, 91-763 F.

Hauser, William L. 1992. "Career Management: Time for a Bold Adjustment," *Parameters: U.S. Army War College Quarterly* (Spring): 50–59.

Heller, Charles E., and William A. Stofft, eds. 1986. *America's First Battles: 1776–1965.* Modern War Studies. Lawrence, KS: University Press of Kansas.

Henry, William A. III. 1992. "History As It Happens." *Time,* 6 January, pp. 24–27.

Herbert, Maj. Paul H. 1988. *Deciding What Has to Be Done: General William E. DePuy and the 1976 Edition of FM 100–5, Operations.* Leavenworth Papers no. 16. Fort Leavenworth, KS: Combat Studies Institute.

Huntington, Samuel. 1959. *The Soldier and the State.* Cambridge, MA: The Belknap Press.

Kaufman, William W., and John D. Steinbruner. 1991. *Decisions for Defense: Prospects for a New Order.* Studies in Defense Policy. Washington, D.C.: The Brookings Institution.

Macgregor, Lt. Col. Douglas A. 1992. "Doctrinal Concepts for Future War." Unpublished manuscript, April, p. 24.

Margiotta, Franklin D., and Ralph Sanders, eds. 1985. *Technology, Strategy and National Security.* Washington, D.C.: National Defense University Press.

Merritt, Gen. Jack. 1992. "Statement Before the Panel on Structure of the U.S. Defense Industrial Base." Association of the United States Army. 19 February, p. 13.

Moskos, Charles, 1991. *The Military: More Than Just a Job?* McLean, VA: Pergamon–Brassey's

Moskos, Charles and Frank R. Woods, eds. 1988. "Armed Forces and Society After the Cold War," In Woodrow Wilson International Center for Scholars, Washington. D.C. unpublished, 12 June.

Naisbitt John. 1982. *Megatrends.* New York: Warner Books.

Naisbitt, John and Patricia Aburdene. 1985. *Re-inventing the Corporation.* New York: Warner Books.

Naisbitt, John and Patricia Aburdene. 1990. *Megatrends 2000.* New York: William Morrow.

National Guard Association of the United States. 1992. "An Alternative Force Structure Proposal." February, p. 6.

Nunn, Sam. 1990. "A New Military Strategy." Chairman, Senate Armed Services Committee. Unpublished remarks prepared for delivery, 19 April.

Ohmae, Kenichi. 1990. *The Borderless World: Power and Strategy in the Interlinked Economy.* 1st Harper Perennial ed. New York: Harper.

Pearlstein, Steven. 1992. "Pentagon Cites Security Issue in Sale of LTV to Thomson." *Washington Post,* 1 May, pp. B 1, B 2.

Peters, Tom. 1987. *Thriving on Chaos.* New York: Alfred A. Knopf.

Reich, Robert B. 1991. *The Work of Nations: Preparing Ourselves for 21st-Century Capitalism.* New York: Alfred A. Knopf.

Rielly, John E. 1991. *American Public Opinion and U.S. Foreign Policy 1991.* The Chicago Council on Foreign Relations.

Sorley, Lewis. 1991. "Creighton Abrams and the Active-Reserve Integration in Wartime." *Parameters: U.S. Army War College Quarterly* (Summer): 35–50.

Stone, M. P. R., and Gen. Gordon R. Sullivan. 1992. "America's Army Trained and Ready." *Executive Summary United States Army Posture Statement FY 93.*

Sullivan, Gen. Gordon R. 1992. *Statement on the FY 1993 Department of the Army Budget.* House Armed Services Committee, 26 February.

Summers, Col. Harry G. 1992. *On Strategy II: A Critical Analysis of the Gulf War.* New York: Bantam Doubleday Dell Publishing Group.

Task Force on Defense Spending, the Economy & the Nation's Security. 1991. *Preserving the Defense Industrial Base.* Statement, the Defense Budget Project.

Toffler, Alvin. 1990. *PowerShift: Knowledge, Wealth, and Violence at the Edge of the 21st Century.* New York: Bantom Books.

Toffler, Alvin, and Heidi Toffler. 1991. "War, Wealth, and a New Era in History." *World Monitor,* May, pp. 46–52.

U.S. Army War College. 1988. *Army Command and Management: Theory and Practice.* Washington, D.C.: Government Printing Office.

U.S. Chairman Joint Chiefs of Staff. *National Military Strategy 1992.* Washington D.C.: U.S. Government Printing Office. 28 January.

U.S. Department of the Army. 1966. *FM 100–5, Operations.* Washington, D.C.: U.S. Government Printing Office.

U.S. Department of the Army. 1988. *FM 25–100, Training the Force.* Washington, D.C.: U.S. Government Printing Office.

U.S. Department of the Army. 1990. *A Strategic Force for the 1990s and Beyond.* White Paper. Washington, D.C.: U.S. Government Printing Office.

U.S. Department of the Army. 1991. *AirLand Operations: A Concept for the Evolution of AirLand Battle for the Strategic Army of the 1990s and Beyond.* TRADOC *Pam 525-5,* U.S. Army.

U.S. Department of the Army. 1991. *FM 100–1, The Army.* Washington, D.C.: U.S. Government Printing Office.

U.S. Department of the Army. 1991. *Leader Development for the Total Army: The Enduring Legacy. Pam 600-32,* Washington D.C.: U.S. Government Printing Office.

U.S. Department of Defense. 1990. *Total Force Policy Report to the Congress.* Assistant Secrectary of Defense for Force Management & Personnel, Assistant Secretary of Defense for Reserve Affairs.

U.S. Department of Defense. 1991. *Report to Congress on the Defense Industrial Base.* Under Secretary of Defense (Acquisition), Assistant Secretary of Defense (Production and Logistics).

U.S. Department of Defense. 1992. *Conduct of the Persian Gulf War.* Final Report to Congress, April, p. 418.

U.S. House of Representatives, House Armed Services Committee. 1992. *Defense for a New Era: Lessons of the Persian Gulf War.* 30 March, p. 89.

U.S. House of Representatives, House Armed Services Committee. 1992. *Combat Power From the Reserve Component.* 7 May, p. 11.

U.S. Joint Chiefs of Staff. 1991. *Joint Warfare of the U.S. Armed Forces.* Joint Pub. 1. Washington, D.C.: U.S. Government Printing Office.

U.S. Military Academy. 1991. *Preparing for West Point's Third Century: A Summary of the Years of Affirmation and Change 1986–1991.* Office of the Superintendent.

U.S. The White House. 1991. *National Security Strategy of the United States.* Washington, D.C.: U.S. Government Printing Office.

Walker, Wallace Earl. 1992. "Comparing Army Reserve Forces: A Tale of Multiple Ironies, Conflicting Realities, and More Certain Prospects." *Armed Forces and Society.* 18, no. 3 (Spring): 303–322.

Wattenberg, Ben J. 1991. *The First Universal Nation.* New York: Free Press.

Weigley, Russell F. 1973. *The American Way of War: A History of United States Military Strategy and Policy.* The Wars of the United States. Louis Morton, ed. New York: The Macmillan Company.

———, 1984. *History of the United States Army.* First Midland Book ed. Bloomington: Indiana University Press.

INDEX

ABOUT THE AUTHOR

Frederic J. Brown, Ph.D., retired from the U.S. Army in 1989 as a lieutenant general and commander of the Fourth Army. He commanded armor units in the United States, West Germany, and Vietnam and served as the chief of armor and cavalry from 1983 to 1986. He also taught international relations at West Point and was a staff officer at every level, including the White House Office of the President. General Brown's previous books include *The United States Army in Transition*, which proposed an action plan for rebuilding the Army after Vietnam.